SOCIAL JUSTICE IN ISLAM

SOCIAL JUSTICE IN ISLAM

by
Sayyid Qutb

Translated from the Arabic
by John B. Hardie

Translation Revised and Introduction
by Hamid Algar

ISLAMIC PUBLICATIONS INTERNATIONAL
P.O. Box 705
Oneonta, New York 13820
U.S.A.

This work is a complete translation of *Al-'Adalah al-ijtima'iyah fi 'l-Islam* by Sayyid Qutb, published by Maktabat Misr, Cairo, n.d.

Published and distributed by
Islamic Publications International
P.O Box 705, Oneonta, NY 13820. USA
Telephone: 800-568-9814   Fax: 800-466-8111
Email: Islampub@Islampub.com

Printed in the United States of America

Qutb, Sayyid, 1903–1966.
    [Adalah al-ijtima iyah fi al-Islam. English]
    Social Justice in Islam by Sayyid Qutb;
    translated from the Arabic by John B. Hardie;
    translation revised and introduction by Hamid
    Algar. — Rev. ed.
      p. cm.
    Translation of al-Adalah al-ijtima iyah fi
    al-Islam.
    Includes bibliographical references and index.
    LCCN 99-76692
    ISBN: 1-889999-12-1 (hc.)
    ISBN: 1-889999-11-3 (pbk.)

    1. Sociology, Islamic 2. Social justice—
Islamic countries.   I. Hardie, John B. II.
Algar, Hamid.   III. Title

    HN40.M6Q683 2000   305.6'2971
                        QB199-1884

Director of Publications: Moin Shaikh
Cover and Book Design: Chris Alaf
Cover layout: Kathy Yang Chen
Book Composition: Archetype Typography, Berkeley, California
Indexer: Jane Merryman

CONTENTS

INTRODUCTION

Sayyid Qutb, who some twenty-eight years after his death is still the most influential ideologue of the Islamic movement in the contemporary Arab world, began life in the obscurity of the village of Musha (or Qaha) near Asyut in Upper Egypt. He was born there in 1906 to a father who was well regarded in the village for piety and learning, despite the hard times on which he had fallen. Sayyid Qutb was the eldest of five children. He was followed by a brother, Muhammad Qutb, also destined to gain fame as an Islamic writer and activist, and three sisters, two of whom, Amina and Hamida, came to attain some prominence in the ranks of the Muslim Brethren. Encouraged by both his parents, Sayyid Qutb swiftly developed a love for learning, and by the age of ten he had completed memorization of the Qur'an at the local primary school. Three years later, the family moved to Helwan, enabling him to enter the preparatory school for the Dar al-'Ulum in Cairo, a prestigious teachers' training college which he joined in 1929. This marked the beginning of his long and fruitful involvement in education and its problems. On graduating in 1933, he was himself appointed to teach at the Dar al-'Ulum, and a few years later entered the service of the Egyptian Ministry of Education.

The year 1933 also saw the beginning of Sayyid Qutb's extraordinarily varied and prolific literary career. His first book was *Muhimmat al-Sha'ir fi 'l-Hayah* (*The Task of the Poet in Life*), and for more than a decade literature remained—together with education—his principal preoccupation. He wrote poetry, autobiographical sketches, works of literary criticism, and novels and short

1

stories dealing with the problems of love and marriage. After embracing Islam as an all-inclusive ideology, he came to repudiate much of this early work. At the time, however, it served to elevate him to the proximity of leading figures on the Egyptian literary scene, such as 'Abbas Mahmud al-'Aqqad (d. 1964) and Taha Husain (d. 1973), whose Western-tinged outlook on cultural and literary questions he initially shared. For example, there are traces of individualism and existentialism in some of Sayyid Qutb's novels, above all *Ashwak* (*Thorns*).

Like his mentor al-'Aqqad, Sayyid Qutb was an active member of the oppositional Wafd party, and he became a prominent critic of the Egyptian monarchy. This brought him into inevitable conflict with his superiors at the Ministry of Education, and it took the strenuous efforts of Taha Husayn to dissuade him from resigning. Sayyid Qutb sought anew, in 1947, to emancipate himself from government employ by becoming editor-in-chief of two journals, *al-'Alam al-'Arabi* (*The Arab World*) and *al-Fikr al-Jadid* (*New Thought*). He lost his position with the former as a result of editorial disagreements, and the latter, which sought in a hesitant way to present the model of an Islamic society free of corruption, tyranny, and foreign domination, was proscribed after only six issues. While continuing to write for a wide range of literary and political periodicals, Sayyid Qutb was thus compelled to continue working for the Ministry of Education.

In 1948, the ministry sent him on a study mission to the United States, doubtless with the assumption that direct acquaintance with America would incline him more favorably to official policies and induce him to abandon the oppositional activities that were increasingly taking on an Islamic aspect. Sayyid Qutb's impressions of America were, however, largely negative, and may even have been decisive in turning him fully to Islam as a total civilizational alternative. While noting American achievements in production and social organization, Sayyid Qutb laid heavy emphasis on materialism, racism, and sexual permissiveness as dominant features of American life. His sojourn in the United States coincided, moreover, with the first Palestine war, and he noted with dismay the uncritical acceptance of Zionist theses by American public opinion and the ubiquity of anti-Arab and anti-Muslim prejudice. After completing a master's degree in education at the University of Northern Colorado in Greeley, Sayyid Qutb decided to forego the possibility of staying in America to earn a doctorate and returned to Egypt in 1951.

One of the most widely read of all Sayyid Qutb's books, *al-'Adalat al-Ijtima' iyyah fi 'l-Islam* (*Social Justice in Islam*) had been published during his absence in America, and with its attacks on feudalism and emphasis on social justice as an Islamic imperative, it earned the approbation of leading figures in the Muslim Brethren. His critical response to Taha Husain's *Mustaqbal al-Thaqafah fi Misr* (*The Future of Culture in Egypt*), a work which sought to present Egypt as an essentially Mediterranean society—i.e., as an appendage of Europe—was also highly appreciated in the same circles. For his part, Sayyid Qutb had been increasingly well disposed to the Muslim Brethren ever since he witnessed the ecstatic reception given in America to the news of the assassination, on February 12, 1949, of Hasan al-Banna, founder of the organization. His perception of the Brethren as defenders of Islam was further strengthened after his return to Egypt when a British official, James Heyworth-Dunne, told him that the Brethren represented the only barrier to the establishment of "Western civilization" in the Middle East.

Sayyid Qutb's cooperation with the Muslim Brethren began almost immediately after his return from America, although his formal membership in the organization may not have begun until 1953. This new allegiance marked a turning point in his political and intellectual life. He had quit the Wafd on the death of its founder, Sa'd Zaghlul, and joined the breakaway Sa'dist Party in 1938, which claimed a greater degree of fidelity to the original ideals of the Wafd. He was also involved in the activities of *al-Hizb al-Watani* (*The Patriotic Party*) and *Hizb Misr al-Fatah* (*The Young Egypt Party*). However, none of these groups engaged his energies and devotions as fully as did the Muslim Brethren, which was, after all, far more than a political party, having aimed since its foundation in 1928 at establishing the hegemony of Islam in all areas of Egyptian life. Conversely, Sayyid Qutb's entry into the ranks of the Brethren provided the organization with its first true ideologue and led ultimately to a radicalization of the whole Islamic movement in Egypt.

In 1951, Sayyid Qutb began writing for periodicals of the Muslim Brethren such as *al-Risala* (*The Message*), *al-Da'wa* (*The Summons*), and *al-Liwa' al-Jadid* (*The New Banner*), and finally realized his ambition of resigning from the Ministry of Education, ignoring the last-minute allurement of an appointment as special adviser to the minister. He then joined the Brethren formally, and in recognition of his talents was made editor-in-chief of *al-Ikhwan al-Muslimun*, the official journal of the organization. In January 1954 the journal was banned, and Sayyid Qutb embarked on the long ordeal of imprisonment and persecution that was to end in his martyrdom some twelve years later.

On July 23, 1952, the Egyptian monarchy had been overthrown in a coup d'etat mounted by a group of soldiers who styled themselves the Free Officers; they were formally led by General Muhammad Najib (aka Naguib), but it soon became apparent that Jamal 'Abd al-Nasir (aka Nasser) was the driving force behind the group. Although the coup was widely popular and its authors grandiloquently dubbed it a revolution despite the absence of mass participation, the Free Officers lacked any organized political base of their own. They therefore turned to the Muslim Brethren, with whom some of their number had already been in contact, for the effective mobilization of popular support. The political counsels of the Brethren were divided, and Hasan Hudaybi, who had succeeded al-Banna as leader, was in addition woefully lacking in political acumen; what is certain is that the idea of taking power at this crucial juncture in Egyptian history did not occur to those who determined the policies of the Brethren. There thus ensued a period of collaboration between the Muslim Brethren and the new regime.

Sayyid Qutb was prominent among the members and associates of the Brethren who collaborated with the Free Officers. According to reliable testimony, leaders of the coup including 'Abd al-Nasir, visited Sayyid Qutb in his home a mere four days before the coup, (Khalidi, 1981, pp. 37-39). About one month after the coup, Sayyid Qutb delivered a lecture on "Intellectual and

Spiritual Liberation in Islam" at the Officers' Club in Cairo, and 'Abd al-Nasir was in attendance. More significantly, Sayyid Qutb was appointed cultural advisor to the Revolutionary Council, established by the Free Officers, and was the only civilian to attend its meetings.

Before long, however, differences arose between the Muslim Brethren and the military rulers of Egypt. As a prelude to eliminating the Brethren as an autonomous force capable of challenging him, 'Abd al-Nasir sought first to coopt the organization by offering cabinet posts to some of its leading members. It was thus intimated to Sayyid Qutb that the Ministry of Education was his for the asking. He was also invited to become director of the *Hay'at al-Tahrir* (Liberation Rally), the newly established government party, and to draw up its program and statutes. Qutb refused all such offers, and most of his colleagues in the Brethren also had the good sense to resist full-scale absorption into the emerging structures of the Nasserist state.

At the same time, it became increasingly apparent that the Revolutionary Council intended to perpetuate its rule indefinitely and was in no mind to listen to the exhortations of the Brethren, either to return to civilian rule based on elections or to call a constitutional referendum. Likewise, it paid no heed to the demand of the Brethren that it should ban alcohol as a first step toward the implementation of the *shari'ah*. Gravest of all was the intention of the Revolutionary Council—carried out in July, 1954—to conclude a new treaty with Britain providing for the retention of a British garrison in the Suez Canal zone and the posting of British troops elsewhere in Egypt whenever Britain deemed its interests in the Middle East to be under attack. This early indication that the nationalist credentials of the Free Officers were not as strong as they proclaimed them to be was profoundly shocking to the Brethren, many of whose members had fought and died in the struggle to evict the British from the Suez Canal zone. The criticisms of the treaty made by the Brethren, and their demand that it be subjected to a referendum, fell on deaf ears.

On January 12, 1954, the Revolutionary Council decreed the dissolution of the Muslim Brethren, and Sayyid Qutb entered jail for the first time. A temporary change in fortune came on March 28 when, thanks to the efforts of Najib, the ban on the Brethren was rescinded and Qutb, together with other leaders of the Brethren, was released. He was now appointed to the Guidance Council of the Brethren, the governing body of the organization, with overall responsibility for its publications.

Soon, however, 'Abd al-Nasir struck back. Having removed Najib from the Revolutionary Council and gained control of the army and police, he reinstated the January decree proscribing the Brethren and moved toward an attempted destruction of the entire organization.

On October 23, 1954, there took place in Alexandria what appeared to be an unsuccessful attempt on the life of 'Abd al-Nasir. There is reason to think that the affair was stage-managed by 'Abd al-Nasir himself. The man said to have fired the shots, Mahmud 'Abd al-Latif, a member of the Brethren, was personally known to 'Abd al-Nasir as an excellent marksman; it is therefore conceivable that 'Abd al-Nasir should have hired him to attempt an "assassination," trusting him deliberately to fire somewhat askew, and then doublecrossed him by executing him to ensure his silence. Significant, too, is the fact that the incident enabled 'Abd al-Nasir to start posing before the Egyptian masses as their embattled hero and thus to inaugurate the adulatory cult surrounding him that continued to infect much of Arab public opinion, even after the disastrous defeat of June 1967. Most compelling of all is the fact that the incident provided 'Abd al-Nasir with a pretext to round up members of the Brethren on a then unprecedented scale. More than one thousand people were swiftly arrested, and show trials got underway with suspicious promptness. On December 4, 1954, seven leading figures, including Hudaybi, were sentenced to death. Hudaybi's sentence was commuted to life imprisonment, but the remaining six were hung.

Predictably enough, Sayyid Qutb was rearrested on this occasion. He was ill at the time of his arrest, but this did not in any way dissuade his jailers from torturing him, in accordance with the still-observed norms of Egyptian justice. Because of extreme physical weakness, Sayyid Qutb was not present in the court in July 1955 when he was sentenced to fifteen years' imprisonment. He was now destined to spend the rest of his life in prison, with the exception of eight short months of relative liberty in 1965.

The ordeal of imprisonment has been a common, almost universal experience for Muslim thinkers and activists in the modern world. For many of them, it has meant not only suffering, but also the opportunity to reflect on past struggles, to review theories and strategies, to deepen and sharpen their insight, to plan and reorganize. It was for this reason that Said Nursi (d. 1960) described prison as the "Josephian School" (*medrese-i yusufiye*), alluding both to his own experience of jail in Kemalist Turkey and the imprisonment of the Prophet Joseph by the Pharaoh.

While in jail, Sayyid Qutb was able to complete a number of his most important writings, including above all the Qur'anic commentary *Fi Zilal al-Qur'an* (*In the Shade of the Qur'an*) he had begun in 1962. Clearly inspired by the circumstances of daily struggle and confrontation in which he lived, this commentary is radically different from traditional exegeses, with their verse-by-verse attention to philological and historical detail and their extensive citation of previous authorities and variant opinions. Emphasizing guidance to correct action as the pre-eminent function of the Qur'an, Sayyid Qutb's concern is to draw out the practical commands and instructions contained in each group of verses of the Qur'an and, beyond that, to demonstrate the coherent structure interrelating the variegated topics found in each section of the Qur'an, an aim inspired, perhaps, by his earlier literary interests. *Fi Zilal al-Qur'an* has been translated in part or in whole into a number of languages, and it is probably true to say that it has been more widely read than any other modern commentary on the Qur'an.

Reflected in several passages of this commentary are the radical theoretical insights which the experience of prison inspired in him. The savagery he and his fellow inmates suffered over the years—including the massacre of twenty-one members of the Brethren at the Liman Tura military jail in June 1957—forced him to conclude that a regime unprecedented in its ruthlessness had come to power in Egypt, and that the primary problem was no longer overt foreign rule or the absence of social justice. It was rather the total usurpation of power by forces intensely hostile to Islam, with the result that the entire life of society was fixed in the non-Islamic patterns into which it had gradually fallen as a result of decay and neglect. Drawing on the terminology and theories of Abu 'l-A'la Maududi and Abu 'l-Hasan Nadwi (although ultimately of course on the Qur'an itself), Sayyid Qutb decided that Egypt, together with the rest of the contemporary Islamic world, was strictly comparable to pre-Islamic Arabia in its disregard for divine precepts, and that its state could therefore rightly be designated by the same term—*jahiliyyah*. Occurring only four times in the Qur'an, the term *jahiliyyah* assumed central significance for Sayyid Qutb, encapsulating the utter bleakness of the Muslim predicament and serving as an epistemological device for rejecting all allegiances other than Islam.

According to Sayyid Qutb, this new *jahiliyyah* had deep historical roots, and it was moreover fostered and protected by all the coercive apparatus of a modern, authoritarian state; it could not, therefore, be easily remedied in the short term. What was needed was a long-term program of ideological and organizational work, coupled with the training of a dedicated vanguard of believers who would protect the cause in times of extreme danger (if necessary by recourse to force) and preside over the replacement of *jahiliyyah* by the Islamic order once circumstances had matured.

Sayyid Qutb first developed these ideas in dialogue with a small number of his fellow inmates, and then included them in notes that were smuggled out of jail to be read by members of his family and others close to them. Many other members of the Brethren, dissatisfied with the uncertain leadership provided by Hudaybi, became aware of the existence of the letters, and, at their request, Sayyid Qutb consented to have the letters made more widely available. Thus there came into being a group of about 250 people who were all affiliated with the Muslim Brethren but were bound together primarily by their devotion to the ideas of Sayyid Qutb.

In December 1964, Sayyid Qutb was released from jail. It is said that his release was due in part to continuing ill health and in part to the intercession of 'Abd al-Salam 'Arif, the president of Iraq,

who invited him to settle in his country. Given the tragic denoue-
ment to this last period of relative freedom in the life of Sayyid
Qutb, it is however possible that the Egyptian government set him
free in order to create the conditions for his rearrest, trial, and final
elimination; although accused of a conspiracy, he was in fact the
victim of one.

In 1964, before Sayyid Qutb's release from jail, a slim volume
entitled *Ma'alim fi 'l-Tariq* (*Milestones*) had been published and met
with instant success; during the first six months of 1965, it went
through five further editions. *Ma'alim fi 'l-Tariq* consisted of some of
the letters Sayyid Qutb had sent from prison and key sections
of *Fi Zilal al-Qur'an*, and represented a concise and forceful
summary of the main ideas Sayyid Qutb had developed: the *jahili*
nature of existing society, government, and culture, and the long-
term program needed for the establishment of an Islamic order.
Continuously read and reprinted down to the present, and translated into most Muslim languages, *Ma'alim fi 'l-Tariq* must definitely
count among the historic documents of the contemporary Islamic
movement.

On August 5, 1965, Sayyid Qutb was rearrested; two weeks
later, his sisters Amina and Hamida were also arrested, together
with Zaynab al-Ghazali, the leading female member of the Brethren. Sayyid Qutb was accused of subversion and terrorism and the
encouragement of sedition. The first charge rested only on the fact
that in 1959 he had been entrusted by Hudaybi with responsibility
for organizing the Brethren in the jails and prison camps of Egypt.
This organization, known as the *Tanzim*, was supposedly linked to
the circles studying his prison letters and dedicated to the immediate and violent overthrow of the Egyptian government. No
evidence was presented in court to show that Sayyid Qutb or any
group linked to him was plotting armed insurrection, and Sayyid
Qutb was even able to establish that on two occasions he had
dissuaded members of the Brethren from attempting such activity,
not least because the needed change, by its very nature, had to be
brought about by popular action. In support of the second charge,
the encouragement of sedition, the prosecution placed great emphasis on *Ma'alim fi 'l-Tariq*, and it became apparent that this book,

with its proven widespread appeal and long-term revolutionary implications, represented the nub of the Egyptian government's concern. In no way deterred by its inability to find in the text of the book any call for the immediate seizure of power, on May 17, 1966, the court condemned Sayyid Qutb to death, together with six other prominent members of the Brethren, including Hudaybi. Four of the sentences were commuted to life imprisonment, but Sayyid Qutb was hanged in Cairo, on August 29, 1966, together with two of his companions, Muhammad Yusuf 'Awash and 'Abd al-Fattah Isma'il.

The trial had been essentially of a book and the ideas it contained. However, certain political circumstances may also have influenced the fate of Sayyid Qutb. In 1965, the principal super power patron of 'Abd al-Nasir was the Soviet Union, and it may be significant that the execution of Sayyid Qutb took place shortly after 'Abd al-Nasir had returned from a trip to Moscow; the influence of the Brethren in general and Sayyid Qutb in particular had, after all, served to block the spread of Marxism in Egypt. Moreover, facts came to light in 1976 suggesting that the affair was in part the result of rivalry between two centers of power within the Egyptian regime: the *Mukhabarat,* the military intelligence, and the *Mabahith,* the intelligence arm of the Ministry of the Interior. Anxious to prove its vigilance in protecting 'Abd al-Nasir and at the same time to discredit the *Mabahith,* leading officials in the *Mukhabarat* manufactured the story of a Qutbist plot against the regime. This, at least, is what can be deduced from the memoirs of Shams Badran, the number-two figure in the *Mukhabarat,* who also took responsibility, without any shade of embarrassment, for having prisoners tortured in preparation for the trial.

It is axiomatic that ideas are more difficult to eradicate than those who formulate and expound them, particularly when the passage of time demonstrates ever more persuasively the congruence of those ideas with reality; the intellectual legacy of Sayyid Qutb is thus very much alive.

It is true that several leading figures of the Brethren distanced themselves from Sayyid Qutb's identification of Egyptian society (and by extension Arab and Muslim society in general) as *jahili.*

Notwithstanding his own experiences in jail, Hudaybi wrote what was in essence a refutation of *Ma'alim fi 'l-Tariq*, under the title *Du'at la Qudat* (*Summoners, Not Judges*). He insisted that the *jahiliyyah* was exclusively a historical phenomenon, not a recurrent state, and that it was therefore inadmissible to designate contemporary Muslim society as *jahili*. Muhammad Qutb, brother of Sayyid Qutb, came to endorse this implicitly non-judgmental position, despite having himself published in 1964 a book entitled *Jahiliyyat al-Qarn al-'Ishrin* (*The Jahiliyyah of the Twentieth Century*). Other Brethren intellectuals who discovered a congenial environment in Saudi Arabia and other Gulf states also foreswore Sayyid Qutb's radicalism.

By contrast, leaders and sympathizers of the Brethren outside Egypt, such as Sa'id Hawwa and Marwan Hadid in Syria, Fathi Yakan in Lebanon, Rashid al-Ghannushi in Tunisia, and Hasan Turabi in Sudan, all assimilated Sayyid Qutb's analysis of the Muslim predicament to one degree or another, and oriented their movements accordingly. Within Egypt itself, the legacy of Sayyid Qutb has helped give rise to a new generation of radical activists no longer affiliated to the Brethren: 'Abd al-Salam Faraj, author of *al-Faridat al-Gha'ibah* (*The Neglected Duty*), a text that supposedly inspired the assassins of Anwar Sadat to act; the group labeled by the Egyptian authorities *al-Takfir wa 'l-Hijrah* (*Identifying Society as Dominated by Unbelief and Migrating from It*); the amorphous but evidently powerful groupings known as *al-Jama'at al-Islamiyyah* (*The Islamic Societies*); and their supposed mentor, Shaykh 'Umar 'Abd al-Rahman, now incarcerated in the United States.

᛭ ᛭ ᛭ ᛭ ᛭ ᛭ ᛭

If the early, literary-oriented writings of Sayyid Qutb are put aside, a handful of important works can be singled out as containing the quintessence of his thought. Three of these have already been mentioned: *al-'Adalat al-Ijtima'iyyah fi 'l-Islam*, *Fi Zilal al-Qur'an*, and *Ma'alim fi 'l-Tariq*. All these books are fairly well known outside Egypt and the Arab world, having been translated in part or entirety into a variety of languages.

It is perhaps the first of this trio, a revised English translation of which we now put before the reader, that has attained the greatest fame, both because of its relative brevity and because of the general interest and relevance of its subject matter. *al-'Adalat al-Ijtima'iyyah fi 'l-Islam* has been translated into numerous Islamic languages, including Persian, Turkish, Urdu, and Malay/Indonesian, and it is the earliest as well as most influential of a cluster of works that have been devoted to the same subject. Sayyid Qutb can thus be seen to have articulated for the first time a major and widely felt concern of the Muslim world. *al-'Adalat al-Ijtima'iyyah fi 'l-Islam,* first published in 1949, was followed two years later by *Ishtirakiyyat al-Islam (The Socialism of Islam)*, a work by Mustafa al-Siba'i, a leading figure in the Syrian branch of the Brethren. The book is similar in content to Sayyid Qutb's work, although the evocation of socialism in its title contravenes Sayyid Qutb's insistence on the uniqueness and autonomy of Islam as a socioeconomic system, defying all comparison with other ideologies or systems. Also in 1951, Hamka, a prominent Indonesian Muslim thinker, published in Jakarta *Keadilan sosial dalam Islam,* the exact Indonesian equivalent of the title Sayyid Qutb had given his book. The influence of Sayyid Qutb is also to be seen in the contents of the work, although Hamka proceeds more systematically and relegates the discussion of historical matters to the last of his book's eleven chapters instead of interspersing them with his main argument. In Iran, the late forties and early fifties saw the activity of Ayatullah Abu 'l-Qasim Kashani, the most politically engaged *'alim* of the period; like his counterparts elsewhere in the Muslim world, he, too, frequently evoked the theme of social justice in the numerous declarations he delivered. Temporarily allied with Kashani was the organization known as the *Fida'iyan-i Islam,* members of which had both personal and ideological links to the Brethren. It is not therefore surprising that radical measures of socio-economic reform designed to produce social justice occupy an important place in the manifesto published by the *Fida'iyan* in 1950 (Algar, 1986, pp. 23-25). The most substantial treatment of the subject of social justice in Islam appeared a decade later with the first publication of Ayatullah Muhammad Baqir al-Sadr's *Iqtisaduna (Our Economics)*. The only one among the authors mentioned to have had a formal and rigorous training in the religious sciences, al-Sadr is the most precise in his philosophical argumentation and the best able to correlate general precepts of social justice with the detailed provisions of Islamic jurisprudence. Nonetheless, there is no mistaking his debt to Sayyid Qutb for the term *al-takaful al-ijtima'i (social solidarity)* of which he makes frequent use, originated in the work of his Egyptian predecessor.

From one point of view, *Social Justice in Islam* is therefore to be evaluated as a document of the first postwar decades in which Islamic movements and personalities were striving to demonstrate the imperative relevance of Islam to concrete socioeconomic problems. This task gained particular urgency from the relative appeal and vitality of Marxism in a number of Muslim countries at the time, not least in Egypt. This helps to explain the frequency of references to Communism and the Soviet Union. Sayyid Qutb's refutation of Marxism often goes together with a critical evaluation of Christianity, presented as essentially an asceticism with no positive implications for worldly life and historically unable to modify Europe's determining legacy of pagan materialism inherited from Rome. In this comparative context, Islam becomes the ideal mean, avoiding both the unrelieved materialism of Marxism and the otherworldliness of Christianity, and balancing the needs of the individual against those of society. Such a comparison was no doubt inevitable, given the (legitimately) polemical and exhortatory nature of Sayyid Qutb's work; it nonetheless contradicts his own warning against describing Islam in terms other than itself, whether by way of similarity or dissimilarity.

Polemical works tend to give short shrift to history, and several of Sayyid Qutb's attempts at explaining historical trends are distressing in their simplicity. The entry of women into the workforce in European countries is attributed to a sudden and unexplained reluctance on the part of European men to continue providing for their womenfolk; no mention is made of the dislocations brought about by the Industrial Revolution. European history is, of course, incidental to Sayyid Qutb's principal theme, and his treatment of early Islam is of much greater significance.

Briefly put, it is his contention that what he terms "the spirit of Islam"—frugal, egalitarian, and pious—ceased to permeate the sociopolitical life of the Muslims with the usurpation of the caliphate by the Umayyad dynasty. He attributes the origins of this disaster to the rule of 'Uthman, the third caliph, whom he subjects to a far more rigorous criticism than any Sunni writer preceding him. Not without justice, he condemns 'Uthman for nepotism and misuse of the public funds, permitting the Umayyads to accumulate the wealth and power they would later use to rebel against Hz. 'Ali and pervert the caliphate into a hereditary monarchy. He is nonetheless reluctant to accuse 'Uthman of total dereliction of duty, and suggests instead that by the time he succeeded to the caliphate he was old and weak, unable to resist the pressure exerted on him by his Umayyad kinsmen. He accordingly expresses the wish that either 'Uthman had become caliph earlier in life, or that 'Ali had been third caliph instead; then the plans of the Umayyads would have been thwarted. That neither of these desirable choices prevailed Sayyid Qutb attributes simply to "bad luck." A more satisfactory explanation would of course have involved a critical examination of all the events that took place after the death of the Prophet. Sayyid Qutb's treatment of the caliphate of 'Uthman nonetheless represents a bold questioning of the idealized image of the whole period of the Four Caliphs that is so commonly encountered.

Some references to events taking place as the book was being written and others to developments Sayyid Qutb anticipated are bound also to evoke a critical response from the present-day reader. The emergence of Pakistan and Indonesia as independent states is twice mentioned by Sayyid Qutb as a sign of the universal resurgence of Islam, an estimate which is difficult to sustain in view of the current disarray in both countries. The forecast of the capitalist West being swallowed up by Communism has also, of course, proved to be the exact opposite of the truth. Sayyid Qutb's failed prophecy may be attributed to a general tendency to overrate ideological factors. He correctly regarded the worldviews of the two competing blocs to be essentially the same in their materialistic bases, but then made the assumption that Marxism, as a purer and more thoroughgoing form of materialism, was bound to win out over its less rigorous counterpart.

Many other insights of Sayyid Qutb have, however, stood the test of time. His assertion that a virulent crusading spirit remains at the core of Western culture, despite a relative decline in active adherence to Christianity, has been tragically vindicated by the genocidal assaults on the Muslims of Bosnia, that were spearheaded by Croats and Serbs but enjoy the complicity of the entire Western world. Similarly, the support instinctively rendered by this crusading spirit to Zionism continues unabated. More importantly, Sayyid Qutb's insistence on the comprehensiveness of Islam as worldview, civilization, and socioeconomic order; his summons to cultural and educational reform; and the moral urgency underlying the whole of his book retain all their validity today, some fifty years after its first publication. For despite all the ink that has been spilled by Muslims and others concerning the "Islamic resurgence," it can hardly be claimed that the Muslim world as a whole is substantially better situated than it was in 1949.

❖ ❖ ❖ ❖ ❖ ❖ ❖

In the course of reading John B. Hardie's translation of *Social Justice in Islam,* first published in 1953 by the American Council of Learned Societies, as a preliminary to writing this introduction, I encountered a number of passages that seemed not to ring true. On comparing them with the Arabic text, I found that Hardie had indeed misunderstood the original. So egregious were the translator's errors that a checking of the entire translation seemed in order, and as a result numerous other mistakes were discovered. Hardie often confused approximately similar words with each other, failed to understand the Arabic syntax, and sometimes resorted to obvious guesswork when confronted with a particularly problematic sentence or phrase. It is remarkable that the serious errors vitiating his translation have gone almost entirely unnoticed, the only exception being a discreet comment by William Shepherd in a valuable article on "Social Justice in Islam" (Shepherd, 1992, p.199, n. 9). This is presumably because the translation was said to have been made with the cooperation of Sayyid Qutb himself. If that was indeed the case, either Sayyid Qutb's knowledge of English was unequal to the task of checking the translation, or he trusted Hardie's knowledge of Arabic sufficiently to content himself with a casual review.

It must be admitted, moreover, that Hardie's version reads deceptively well and that occasionally his renderings of difficult passages are both accurate and felicitous.

I have revised the entire translation to correct all gross errors of meaning. A more thoroughgoing revision to make the wording and structure more closely reflective of the original would, of course, have been possible. The changes I have made suffice, however, to make Hardie's translation faithful to the ideas and arguments of the author, a fair if not perfect reflection of the Arabic original.

❖ ❖ ❖ ❖ ❖ ❖ ❖

The task of revision was complicated by the fact that *al-'Adalat al-Ijtima'iyyah fi 'l-Islam* has gone through several editions that are by no means identical with each other. This, too, is a matter which has largely escaped attention, exception being made again of William Shepherd (Shepherd, 1992, passim). The book has been published at least seven times, but it is not certain that each publication represented a different edition, for the word *tab'a* may mean either "edition" or simply "printing." I have had access only to the fifth edition/printing, published at Cairo in 1377/1958, and it certainly differs significantly from the first edition used by Hardie (even making allowance for his errors of translation). Whole passages found in Hardie are absent from the 1377/1958 printing, to which matters have been added not found in the first edition. Whether the changes were made for the fifth edition/printing or at an earlier date I am unable to tell. Among matters found in the first edition and not in the 1377/1958 printing are the lengthy discussions of *al-masalih al-mursala* and *sadd al-dhara'i'* and the restraint shown by Arab forces in the face of Zionist atrocities during the First Palestine War. Conversely, detailed recommendations on the teaching of Islamic history and on the function of literature in education are missing from the first edition. The *hadith* used for the illustration of various points are not identical in the two editions.

On the basis of a comparison between the first and seventh editions, William Shepherd has suggested that the changes reflect a movement on the part of Sayyid Qutb towards what he calls "radical Islamism," a move caused partly by the ideological influence of Maulana Maudoodi and partly by the unfolding of events in Egypt. This analysis may hold true for the distance Sayyid Qutb travelled between the first and the seventh editions, but cannot be substantiated with reference to the fifth edition, which I have been constrained to use for revising Hardie's translation. As for the differences that do exist between the first and the fifth editions, I have refrained from adding the material found only in the latter and deleting material found only in the former, believing that the first edition has its own particular logic and documentary value.

–Hamid Algar
Ramadan 1420/ January 2000

1 RELIGION AND SOCIETY
IN CHRISTIANITY AND IN ISLAM

I n the world of economics an individual who has private means does not resort to borrowing before he has examined his means to see what resources he has there; nor does a government resort to importing until it has scrutinized its native resources and examined its raw materials and their potential. And so in the case of spiritual resources, intellectual capabilities, and moral and ethical traditions—are not these things on the same level as goods or money in human life? Apparently not; for here in Egypt and in the Muslim world as a whole, we pay little heed to our native spiritual resources and our own intellectual heritage; instead, we think first of importing foreign principles and methods, or borrowing customs and laws from across the deserts and from beyond the seas.

We have only to look in order to see that our social situation is as bad as it can be; it is apparent that our social conditions have no possible relation to justice; and so we turn our eyes to Europe, America, or Russia, and we expect to import from there solutions to our problems, just as from them we import goods for our industrial livelihood. With this difference—that in industrial importing we first examine the goods which are already on our markets, and we estimate our own ability to produce them. But when it is a matter of importing principles and customs and laws, we do no such thing; we continually cast aside all our own spiritual heritage, all our intellectual endowment, and all the solutions which might well be revealed by a glance at these things; we cast aside our own fundamental principles and doctrines, and we bring in those of democracy, or socialism, or communism. It is to these that we look for a solution of our social problems, although our circumstances, our history, and the very bases of our life-material, intellectual, and spiritual alike-are quite out of keeping with the circumstances of people across the deserts and beyond the seas.

At the same time we profess Islam as a state religion, we claim in all sincerity to be true Muslims—if indeed we do not claim to be the guardians and propagators of Islam. Yet we have divorced our faith from our practical life, condemning it to remain in ideal isolation, with no jurisdiction over life, no connection with its affairs, and no remedy for its problems. For, as the popular saying goes, "Religion concerns only a man and his God." But as for ordinary relationships, the bonds of society and the problems of life, and political or economic theory—religion has nothing to do with these things, nor they with it; such is the view of those who are not actively hostile to religion. As for the others, their reaction is: Make no mention of religion here; it is nothing but an opiate employed by plutocrats and despots to drug the working classes and to paralyze the unfortunate masses.

How have we arrived at this strange view of the nature and the history of Islam? We have imported it, as we import everything, from across the deserts and beyond the seas. For certainly the fable of a divorce between faith and life did not grow up in the Muslim East, nor does Islam know of it; and the myth that religion is but a drug to the senses was not born of this faith at any time, nor does the nature of the faith even sanction it. We merely repeat these things like parrots, and accept them second hand like monkeys; we never think of looking for their origin and their sources, nor of learning their beginning or their results. Let us see first, then, whence and how these strange opinions came about.

�֍ �֍ �֍ ✤ ✤ ✤ ✤

Christianity grew up in the shadow of the Roman Empire, in a period when Judaism was suffering an eclipse, when it had become a system of rigid and lifeless ritual, an empty and unspiritual sham. The Roman Empire had its famous laws, which still live as the origin of modern European legislation; the Roman public had its own customs and social institutions. Christianity had no need then—nor, indeed, had it the power—to put before a powerful Roman government and a united Roman public laws and rules and regulations for government or for society. Rather, its need was to devote its power to moral and spiritual purification; and its concern was to correct the stereotyped ritual and the empty sham of ceremonial Judaism, and to restore spirit and life to the Israelite conscience.

Christ (upon whom be peace) came only to preach spiritual purity, mercy, kindness, tolerance, chastity, and abstinence, and to moderate certain restrictions that had been imposed on the Children of Israel or that they themselves had invented. He showed by his behavior and by his opinions that he attached no importance to the narrow traditions of the priests and the scribes; they were concerned only with external acts, while his concern was with the moral and the spiritual realms. Thus he made the Jewish sabbath lawful to his disciples; and thus he allowed them to eat anything which entered the mouth, because it was not that which defiled, but rather that which came forth in the way of "deceit, falsehood, and adultery." Thus, while he made it lawful for his disciples to break the fast on the Jewish fast-days, yet he would not stone the adulterous woman who was brought to him for questioning; for of those who should have been responsible for her stoning, according to the Mosaic Law, not one was free from guilt. He once said, "You have heard that it has been said 'An eye for an eye and a tooth for a tooth'; but I say to you 'Resist not evil; but whoever strikes you on the right cheek, turn the other to him also. And whoever wishes to quarrel with you and to take your undergarment, give him your overgarment also; and whoever forces you to go one mile, go with him two.'"[1]

The same spirit is apparent also in the words, "You have heard that it was said to those of old, 'Do not kill; for whoever kills is liable to judgment.' But I say to you, 'Indeed, everyone who is angry with his brother without cause is liable to judgment; whoever says to his brother "Fool" is liable to the Council; and whoever says "Imbecile" is liable to the fire of Gehenna. So if you bring your offering to the altar, and if you remember there that your brother has some cause of complaint against you, then leave your offering there in front of the altar, go first and settle your quarrel with your brother and then come and present your offering. Be reconciled with your opponent quickly while you are in the way."

Or again: "You have heard that it was said to those of old, 'Do not commit adultery'. But I say to you that whoever looks at a woman with desire has already committed adultery with her in his heart; if your right eye causes you to stumble, pluck it out and cast it from you, for it is better for you that one of your members should perish than that your whole body should be thrown into hell-fire; or if your right hand causes you to stumble, cut it off and cast it from you, for it is better for you that one of your members should perish than that your whole body should be thrown into hell-fire."

Or: "Again ye have heard that it hath been said by them of old, 'Thou shalt not forswear thyself, but shalt perform unto the Lord thine oaths.' But I say unto you, Swear not at all. Not by Heaven, for it is God's throne; nor by the earth, for it is His footstool; nor by Jerusalem, for it is the city of the Great King. Nor shalt thou swear by thy head, for thou cannot make one hair white or black. But let your speech be, Yea; nay, nay. Whatsoever is more than that cometh of evil."[2]

Accordingly, Christianity forgot about "Render unto Caesar the things that are Caesar's, and unto God the things that are God's," and it turned its full strength towards spiritual purity and pious discipline. It took its stand upon the ground that "Religion concerns only a man and his God," while the temporal law is concerned with the relationship between the individual and the state. And this was the more natural since Christianity grew up in the embrace of the Roman Empire, and since it was a reaction against Judaism.

Accordingly, the Christian faith pushed to the uttermost limit its teachings of spiritual purity, material asceticism, and unworldly forebearance. It fulfilled its task in this spiritual sphere of human life, because it is the function of a religion to elevate man by spiritual means so far as it can, to proclaim piety, to cleanse the heart and the conscience, to humble man's nature, and to make him ignore worldly needs and strive only for holy objectives in a world of shades and vanities. But it left society to the State, to be governed by its earthly laws, since to it society was connected with the outer and temporal world, whereas the faith had its realm in the soul and the conscience. In this, Christianity was logical on three counts; first, because it grew up in a strictly limited area; second, because of the particular needs of the Jewish people to whom Jesus was sent in that they formed only a tiny fragment of the totality of the great Roman Empire; and thirdly, because of the limited time allotted to Christianity before the appearance of the new world religion — the faith of Islam.

Then God so willed it that Christianity should cross the seas to Europe, taking with it all its sublimity and purity and denial of the material world. There it met the Romans, inheritors of the pagan and material culture of Greece, and there it met also the peoples of the remoter parts of Europe, its first contact with the barbarian world. They were peoples of immense numbers, fighting bitterly over their narrow territories, ruthless and merciless in nature, mean and selfish in outlook. Among them none could taste the savor of ease for a moment, nor could put away his weapons for a minute, nor could find time in the struggle of life for the speculations of Christianity, this unselfish, excessively self-denying faith. "Whoever smite thee on the right cheek, turn to him the other also; and whoever wisheth to sue thee and take away thy undergarment, give him your overgarment also."[3] Such peoples early saw that religion was of no profit to life, and they concluded that "Religion concerns only a man and his God." Accordingly, they found it natural to seek the refuge of religion while they were in the church and to breathe its air in the sanctuary, and after to return to the battle of life with all their barbarian customs; so they settled their quarrels by the judgment of the sword, or on occasion by that of the local law. And religion was left in pious isolation, to deal only with heart and conscience in the holy sanctuary and in the confessional.

Hence arose that division between religion and the world in the life of Europe; for the actual truth inherent in the nature of things is this, that Europe was never truly Christian. Hence religion there has remained in isolation from the business and the customs of life from the day of its entry to the present day.

But the churchmen, the priests, the cardinals, and the popes were unable thus to guarantee their own prosperity or to preserve their influence so long as the Church remained isolated from the economic, social, and administrative life. So it became inevitable that the Church should become a power comparable to the power of kings and rulers — with an inevitable weakening of its spiritual authority in the sphere of everyday life. Then came the age when the Church had princes with armies and authority not less than the most powerful of kings with their troops and their sovereignty. Thus inevitably there arose the dispute between the Church and temporal power, between the popes and the emperors, with the common people largely on the side of the Church. But to this — again inevitably — there succeeded the alliance between these two powers, for each had a common interest in keeping the masses in subjection and in the exploitation of the common people. This alliance lasted as long as prosperity remained essentially economic and material, and as long as the dispute was basically concerned with temporal power. It was under these circumstances, and because of despots and religious tyrants, that the saying arose that: "Religion is the opiate of the masses." For it was thus that it happened in Europe.

So the Church remained the supreme spiritual power, with full authority over men, in this world and the next. It continued to sell its "plenary indulgences," and to preach its "eternal damnation"; it continued to hold sway over men's bodies and minds alike; further, it even had the power of inquisition to kill or burn anyone who raised his head in revolt, or who even inclined to doubt or heresy. Then came the age of the Renaissance, and the Church was quick to perceive the threat to its power which must result from the enfranchisement of mind and sense after the Dark Ages; there was no slight danger that it would be deprived of its power by the pride of the thought and knowledge now coming into being. So the Church set itself in opposition, striving to muzzle liberty of thought and freedom of speech which contradicted its ancient and threadbare doctrines. And so from that time there has been bitter hostility between the Church and free thought. For the Church was unwilling to limit itself to spiritual affairs, which are the true sphere of Christianity; nor was it content to hold sway merely over the world to come, as is the claim of the Papacy. Therefore, its doctrines have come into conflict with those of science on such matters as the world, the universe, and the nature of existence. But the teachings of science are based on study and trial and experiment, and they are corroborated by experience and by proof, so that the discoveries of science leave no room for doubt concerning the strength of this new weapon; and so there have grown up generations of scientists and thinkers who dislike and even despise the Church, and who have in their hearts only hostility and loathing for Church and churchmen. Hence has arisen the bitterness between religion and science, between the Church and the intellectual world in the life of Europe.

With the advance of time the new science bore its fruits, and there grew from it in the sphere of technology what is known as mass production. Capital increased and in the arena of industry there appeared two sharply divided camps, that of capital and that of labor. The cleavage between the interests of these two soon became apparent, and the real authority passed from the hands of the state to those of the capitalists; and since the Church had no chance of sharing that authority, it joined itself to the capitalist camp.

I should not care to denigrate the whole body of European churchmen. There are some self-seekers who want only power and who devote themselves to its acquisition. To this end they draw from their religion an opiate for the masses of the workers, in order to restrain them from revolution in search of their rights; or they wean them from the pursuit of justice in this world by the promise of compensation in the next. But the majority must be sincere, by reason of their faith in the tenets of Christianity which is essentially acetic. By its nature a denial of worldly life, it is a summons to avoid materialism, to despise the world, and to seek rather the Lord's kingdom in the Heavenly world.

But be that as it may, the laboring classes who contemplate a class struggle have concluded that religion will not serve their cause in that struggle. They affirm that the Church uses religion only as an opiate for the working classes, and they have turned completely against religion, saying of it that, "It is the opiate of the millions." Hence there has arisen the manifest Communist hostility to religion.

❖ ❖ ❖ ❖ ❖ ❖ ❖

On the other hand, what of ourselves; what has all this to do with us? The conditions of our history and the nature and circumstances of Islam have nothing in common with any of these things. Islam grew up in an independent country owing allegiance to no empire and to no king, in a form of society never again achieved. It had to embody this society in itself, had to order, encourage, and promote it. It had to order and regulate this society, adopting from the beginning its principles and its spirit along with its methods of life and work. It had to join together the world and the faith by its exhortations and laws. So Islam chose to unite earth and heaven in a single system, present both in the heart of the individual and the actuality of society, recognizing no separation of practical exertion from religious impulse. Essentially Islam never infringes that unity even when its outward forms and customs change.

Such was the birth of Islam and such its task; so it was not liable to be isolated in human idealism far removed from practical worldly life; nor was it compelled to narrow the circle of its action out of fear of an empire or a monarch. For the center of its being and the field of its action is human life in its entirety, spiritual and material, religious and worldly. Such a religion cannot continue to exist in isolation from society, nor can its adherents be true Muslims unless they practice their faith in their social, legal, and economic relationships. And a society cannot be Islamic if it expels the civil and religious laws of Islam from its codes and customs, so that nothing of Islam is left except rites and ceremonials.

"No, by thy Lord, they do not believe until they make thee judge in their disputes, and do not afterwards find difficulty in thy decisions, but submit to them fully." (4:68) "What the Apostle gives you, receive it; and what he forbids you, refrain from it." (59:7)

"And whoever does not judge by what Allah has sent down—is an unbeliever."(5:48)

One of the characteristic marks of this faith is the fact that it is essentially a unity. It is at once worship and work, religious law and exhortation. Its theological beliefs are not divorced in nature or in objective from secular life and customs. Thus its prayers, which are the highest expression of the theological side of religion, express the turning of the individual and of the congregation towards one single, mighty, and powerful God, and they entail submission to none save to Him. So, too, the direction of prayer[4] is uniform, nor can any deviate from it. Similarly, Muslim prayers infer a kind of equality, since they express one faith to which all are obedient, and in view of which all are equal. Nay, more: "The credo is that there is no god save Allah," which is the most distinctive tenet of the faith, implying as it does for the worshippers a freedom of religion from any kind of servitude. Such a freedom is the fundamental basis of a righteous and dignified community, in which all men are equals.

However we approach the question, there can be no shadow of doubt that the theory of society is obviously reflected in the beliefs and the customs of this religion, and that these latter represent the basic, powerful, and universal theory of all social life. So, if in any age we find a desire to overemphasize the pietistic aspect of this faith and to divorce it from the social aspect, or to divorce the social aspect from it, it will be the fault of that age rather than of Islam.

Now, these statements on Islam are not a new theory which is being propounded, nor is a reinterpretation of the faith here being made; this is Islam as it has manifested itself in history and as it was understood by its first exponent, Muhammad (upon whom be the blessings and the peace of Allah), as well as by his sincere Companions and all those close to its original source. There is a passage in the glorious Qur'an: "O ye who believe, when proclamation is made for prayer on the day of assembly, strive towards remembrance of Allah and leave off business. That is better for you if you are wise. But when the prayer is finished, scatter abroad in the land and seek the bounty of Allah." (62:9-10) Now all of us know how much time in the day is taken up by the statutory prayers and how much remains for business and trade. The time given to prayer is but a small proportion of man's life, while for the needs of society and life there remains the whole length of day and night. So it is said in another place: "We have appointed the night for a cover, and We have appointed the day for a livelihood." (78:10-11) For the major activity during the day is the making of a living, rather than any prescribed acts of worship.

So Islam does not prescribe worship as the only basis of its beliefs, but rather it reckons all the activities of life as comprehending worship in themselves—so long as they are within the bounds of conscience, goodness, and honesty. A man once passed by the Prophet, and the Companions of Muhammad noticed in him an eager intentness on his business which set them talking about him; they said, "O Messenger of Allah, would that this man had been in the path of Allah. Then said Muhammad, "If he has come to work for his young children, then he is in the path of Allah; or if he has come to work for his aged and infirm parents, then he is in the path of Allah; or if he has come to work for himself in all moderation, then he is in the path of Allah. But if he has come to work only for luxury or for self-glory, then he is in the path of Satan." Similarly the two following stories are authoritative indications of the spirit of Islam as understood by its founder, the Messenger of Allah. It is related on the authority of Anas that he said: We were on a journey with the Prophet, some of us having fasted and some having eaten. We alighted somewhere in a day of scorching heat, and he who had a garment gave us its shade, but many of us had to shade ourselves from the sun with our hands. So those who had fasted lay helpless, but those who had eaten arose and went from door to door till they got water for the party. Then said the Messenger, "Those who did not fast have this day carried off the full reward." And again, a certain man, noted for his piety, was mentioned to the Prophet, who said, "Who lives with him? His brother." Then said he, "His brother is then more pious than he."[5]

Now all this does not mean that Muhammad, who surely knew his own religion better than any other, scorned the whole matter of fasting and prayer; it means rather that the essential spirit of this religion is found in this—that practical work is religious work, for religion is inextricably bound up with life and can never exist in the isolation of idealism in some world of the conscience alone. This is what 'Umar ibn al-Khattab had in mind when, seeing a man making a parade of asceticism and enfeeblement, he struck him with his whip, crying, "Do not kill our religion to our face, may Allah destroy you." Or on another occasion, when a certain man was giving evidence before him, Umar said to him, "Bring hither some one who knows you." So the man brought another who praised him highly. Then said 'Umar to the second man, "Are you this man's nearest neighbor, to know his comings and goings?" "No." "Have you, then, been his companion on a journey, whereon he gave evidence of nobility of character?" "No." "Have you perhaps had dealings with him in money matters, wherein he showed himself a man of self-control? "No." "Then I suspect that you have only seen him in the mosque, murmuring the Qur'an, and now and then lowering and raising his head in prayer." "That is so." Then said 'Umar, "Away. You do not really know him." And turning to the man himself, "Go, and bring hither someone who really knows you."

In such stories 'Umar is at one with his Prophet, Muhammad. And such give a reliable indication of the nature of this faith, its opinion of worship and of asceticism, of faith which is hidden in the heart and of work which is apparent to the sight. "In the midst of what Allah hath given you seek the future world, but forget not your portion in this world." (28:77)

And, "Work for this world as if you were going to live forever, but work for the future world as if you were going to die tomorrow." "Whoever among you sees a stranger, let him make provision for him." "And were it not that Allah sets some men against others, the cloisters had been destroyed, and the churches and the synagogues and mosques in which the name of Allah is often repeated." (22:41) "And fight in the way of Allah against those who fight against you, but do not provoke hostility; verily Allah loveth not those that provoke hostility." (2:186) "Piety lies not in turning your faces to East or West; but piety is this, that a man believe in Allah and the Day of Judgment, in the Angels, and the Book and the Prophets; that he give generously and for love alone to kindred and to orphans, to the poor and the wayfarer, to beggars and to those under oppression; that he be constant in prayer and that he give alms; that such men stand to their word when they pledge their word, and that they have fortitude in poverty, in distress, and in time of evil." (2:172)

Such is the position of Islam in regard to works and faith; and hence it is clear that there can be no separation between the faith and the world, or between theology and social practice, as was the case in early Christianity.

Furthermore, in Islam there is no priesthood, and no intermediary between the creature and the Creator; but every Muslim from the ends of the earth or in the paths of the sea has the ability of himself to approach his Lord without priest or minister. Nor again can the Muslim administrator derive his authority from any papacy, or from Heaven; but he derives it solely from the Muslim community. Similarly, he derives his principles of administration from the religious law, which is universal in its understanding and application and before which all men come everywhere as equals. So, the man of religion has no right to oppress Muslims; nor has the administrator any power other than that of implementing the law, which derives its authority from the faith. As for the world to come, all men are making their way to Allah, "and all of them will come before Him singly on the Day of Judgment." (19:95) Hence, too, there can be no quarrel between men of religion and the state concerning the control of the faithful or of their possessions. They cannot contend for economic or spiritual profits, for Islam has no knowledge of one spiritual power and another temporal power. So there is no possibility of disagreement here, as was the case with the emperors and the popes.

Islam is not hostile to learning, nor in opposition to the learned; on the contrary, it accepts learning as a divine and sacred possession which forms a part of religious duty. "The seeking of knowledge is a duty for every Muslim." "Seek learning even if it be found as far as China." "He who treads the path of the search for learning, Allah will facilitate his path to Paradise." So Islamic history has never known those evil, organized persecutions of thinking men or learned men, such as were known in the lands of the Inquisition; the short, scattered periods in which men have been victimized for their theories may be accounted as anomalous in Muslim history. In general, such occurrences were the outcome of political conditions, the result of concealed party differences, and on the whole were not a normal feature of Islamic life. Also, they arose among peoples who neither knew nor comprehended Islam fully.

Such a tolerance was no more than natural in a religion, which did not depend for its proof on wonders and miracles, which did not rely on strange events for the very heart of its message, but which relied rather on the examination and scrutiny of the evidence of life itself and its facts. "Surely in the creation of heaven and earth, in the division of night and day, in the ship which runs on the sea, carrying what is of profit to men, in the water which Allah has sent down from heaven to revive the earth after its death, spreading abroad in it every kind of cattle, in the changing of the winds and the clouds made to do service between heaven and earth—in all these are signs for a people who have intelligence." (2:159) "He bringeth forth the living from the dead, and He bringeth forth the dead from the living; as He quickeneth the earth after it is dead, so will you be brought forth. Among His signs is that He hath created you from dust, and lo, you are human beings, spreading abroad. And among His signs is that He hath created for you wives of your own kind that you may dwell with them, and hath set love and mercy between you; surely in that there are signs for a thoughtful people. Again, among His signs is the creation of the heavens and the earth, and the divergence of your tongues and complexions. Surely in that there are signs for those who know. Among His signs is your sleeping by night and by day, and your seeking a share of His bounty; surely in that there are signs for a people who hearken. Among His signs is that He makes you to see the lightning in fear and desire, and that He sends down water from heaven, and thereby quickens the earth after it has been dead; surely in that there are signs for a people who understand." (30:18-23)

And again, this tolerance is but natural in a religion which associates piety with learning, making the latter the pathway to a knowledge and a reverence of Allah. "Only the learned among His servants truly fear Allah" (35:25); and so He exalts the station of the learned above that of the unlearned. "Say: Are they who have knowledge equal with them who have none?" (39:12) "Surely the learned man surpasses the merely pious man in excellence, as the moon on the night of its fullness surpasses the remainder of the stars." So there is no gulf yawning between religion and learning, either in the nature or in the history of Islam, comparable to that which existed between the Christian Church and the liberal scholars during the Renaissance.

As for men of religion associating themselves with the power of the state or with the power of wealth and thus keeping the workers and the deprived drugged by means of religion, there is no denying that this did happen in some periods of Islamic history. But the true spirit of the faith disavows such persons; the faith indeed threatens them with dire punishments for having exchanged the signs of Allah for a trifling price. And furthermore, history has preserved beside the memory of such men examples of another type of religious scholar, men who without fearing the reproach of anyone confronted rulers and the rich to assert the claims of the poor and the rights of Allah. They encouraged the underprivileged to demand the rights that they expounded to them, and as a result were themselves exposed to the oppression of the rulers as well as occasional banishment and persecution.

✢ ✢ ✢ ✢ ✢ ✢ ✢

We have, then, not a single reason to make any separation between Islam and society, either from the point of view of the essential nature of Islam or from that of its historical course; such reasons as there are attach only to European Christianity. And yet the world has grown away from religion; to it the world has left only the education of the conscience and the purification of the soul, while to the temporal and secular laws has been committed the ordering of society and the organizing of human life.

Similarly we have no good grounds for any hostility between Islam and the struggle for social justice, such as the hostility which persists between Christianity and Communism. For Islam prescribes the basic principles of social justice and establishes the claim of the poor to the wealth of the rich; it lays down a just principle for power and for money and therefore has no need to drug the minds of men and summon them to neglect their earthly rights in favor of their expectations in heaven. On the contrary, it warns those who abdicate their natural rights that they will be severely punished in the next world, and it calls them "self-oppressors." "Surely the angels said to those who died when they were oppressing themselves, 'In what circumstances were you?' They answered, 'We were poor in the earth.' The angels said, 'Was not Allah's earth wide enough for you to migrate?' The abode of such is Hell—an evil place to go." (4:99) Thus Islam urges men to fight for their rights: "And he who is killed while attempting to remedy injustice, the same is a martyr." So, while Europe is compelled to put religion apart from the common life, we are not compelled to tread the same path; and while Communism is compelled to oppose religion in order to safeguard the rights of the workers, we have no need of any such hostility to religion.

But can we be certain that this social order, which was established by Islam in one specific period of history, will continue to have the potential for growth and renewal? Can we be sure that it is suitable for application to other periods of history whose circumstances differ to a greater or lesser degree from those which obtained in the age which gave birth to Islam?

This is a fundamental question. It is not possible to give an exhaustive answer to it here, as it will be answered in detail in what is to follow; first we must examine this social order itself, define its sources and roots, and scrutinize its applications in everyday life. Suffice it here—for we are still in the stage of general discussion—to say that Islam (which is the product of the Creator of the universe, the One who established its norms) has already experienced such an historical process, and the social, economic, and intellectual developments connected with it. This process Islam has traversed by laying down the general, universal rules and principles, and leaving their application in detail to be determined by the processes of time and by the emergence of individual problems. But Islam itself does not deal with the incidental related issues of the principle, except insofar as such are expressions of an unchanging principle whose impact is felt universally. This is the limit of the authority which can be claimed by any religion, in order that it may guarantee its flexibility and ensure the possibility of its own growth and expansion over a period of time.

For this reason the jurists of Islam devoted themselves with a strong and praiseworthy effort to the science of application of the principle, to analogy, and to deduction; most of their work is, in our opinion, in agreement with the spirit of Islam. But in the case of a small proportion, a certain looseness appeared in some of their works, resulting in a greater or lesser divergence from the spirit of Islam. Still, in the majority of cases, it may safely be said that the principles of the faith have kept pace with the needs of the time. To this period of production of jurisprudence there succeeded a long interval during which the growth of law came to a halt, until at the beginning of the present century, new life began to pervade the subject as the Muslim world as a whole started to awake.

The conclusion from this is that we should not put away the social aspect of our faith on the shelf; we should not go to French legislation to derive our laws or to Western or Communist ideals to derive our social order without first trying to reconnect with our Islamic legislation, which was the foundation of our first form of society. Moreover, we should not despair of the ability of the *shari'ah* to govern modern society, because the organic and natural growth of any system within a given environment makes it at the very least more fitted for that environment than a system alien to it or imposed upon it. However, there is a wide ignorance of the nature of our faith as well as the nature of societies and the laws governing life; there is a psychological and intellectual laziness that is opposed to a return to our former resources; there is a ridiculous servility to the European fashion of divorcing religion from life—a separation necessitated by the nature of their religion, but not by the nature of Islam. For, with them there still exists that gulf between religion on the one hand and learning and the State on the other, the product of historical reasons which have no parallel in the history of Islam.

This does not mean that our summons is to an intellectual,

spiritual, and social avoidance of the ways of the rest of the world; the spirit of Islam rejects such an avoidance, for Islam reckons itself to be a message for the whole world. Rather, our summons is to return to our own stored-up resources, to become familiar with their ideas, and to test their validity and permanent worth, before we have recourse to an untimely and baseless servility which will deprive us of the historical background of our life, and through which our individuality will be lost to the point that we will become merely the hangers-on to the progress of mankind. Our religion demands that we should be ever in the forefront. "You are the best nation which has been brought forth for men; you enjoin the good, and you forbid the evil."(3:10)

It may well become apparent to us if we look back on our heritage that we have something to give to this unhappy, perplexed, and weary world, something which it has lost in the present material and unspiritual frame of mind that led to two world wars within a quarter of a century; something which the world is continually trampling under foot in its progress towards a third war, which all the present portents indicate will end in complete ruin.

Such is our position on this question. But, we must not proceed to speak of the value of Islam for modern society until first we have examined the nature of its relation to life and to all human problems; and particularly in the field of social justice, which is the main theme of this book.

2 THE NATURE OF
SOCIAL JUSTICE IN ISLAM

We cannot study the nature of social justice in Islam until we have first examined the general lines of Islamic theory on the subject of the universe, life, and mankind. For social justice is only a branch of that great science to which all Islamic doctrines must revert.

Now the faith of Islam, which deals with the whole field of human life, does not treat the different aspects of that life randomly, nor yet does it split up the field into a number of unrelated parts. That is to say, Islam has one universal and integrated theory which covers the universe and life and humanity, a theory in which are integrated all the different questions; in this Islam sums up all its beliefs, its laws and statutes, and its modes of worship and of work. The treatment of all these matters emanates from this one universal and comprehensive theory, so that each question is not dealt with on an individual basis, nor is every problem with its needs treated in isolation from all other problems.

A knowledge of this universal theory of Islam is necessary because it enables the student to understand its principles and beliefs and to relate the particular to the general; it empowers him to study with pleasure and with understanding its characteristics and its aims. On the other hand, the fact that the basis is religious guarantees that the theory will be both coherent and comprehensive and not departmentalized. For, no theory of life can be of profit unless it comprehends all the departments and all the aims of human life. So the best method of studying Islam is to start by understanding its universal theory before going on to study its views on politics or economics or the relationship between communities and individuals. For, such questions as these are but issues arising out of that universal theory and they cannot be truly or deeply understood except in the light of it.

Now the true Muslim philosophy is not to be sought in Ibn Sina or Ibn Rushd,[6] or such men as these who are known as the Muslim philosophers; for the philosophy which they teach is no more than a shadow of the Greek philosophy and has no relation to the true Islamic philosophy. The faith of Islam has a native universal philosophy which is to be sought only in its own theoretical sources: the Qur'an and the Traditions, the life of its Prophet and his everyday customs. These are the authorities in which the student must delve deeply to find the universal Islamic theory from which come all the Islamic teachings and laws and its modes of worship and of work. Islam as a faith has laid down the nature of the relation between the Creator and His creation, the nature of man's relation to the universe and to the world, and of man's relation to his own soul; it has laid down the relation between the individual and society, between different societies and mankind as a whole, and the relation between one generation and another. All these teachings are the expression in different aspects of the one universal, comprehensive theory which relates to one another all the separate aspects. This is Islamic philosophy, or what I prefer to call the Islamic concept.

The detailed study of this philosophy is no part of this present work; here we shall confine ourselves to the examination of one specific subject. Here we shall merely outline the main headings of the general scheme in order to facilitate our study of social justice in Islam.

÷ ÷ ÷ ÷ ÷ ÷ ÷

Man lived for long ages without achieving a comprehensive theory of his Creator and the universe, or of the universe, life, and mankind. That is to say, man had never been prepared to receive such a universal and comprehensive theory until the birth of Islam.

The relation between the Creator and His creation is to be found in the power of the Word, the Active Will from which all creation came; "His command when He wishes anything is to say, BE; and it is." (36:82) There is no mediating power of any kind between the Creator and His creation, but from His universal and absolute Will proceed all existing things in direct proper order; and by that universal, absolute, and active Will all things are sustained, ordered, and energized. "He manages the affair, sets the signs in order." (13:2) "He grasps the Heavens that they fall not upon the earth, save by His permission." (22:65) "It is necessary for the sun not to overtake the moon, nor the night to outrun the day; but each in its circle they revolve." (36:40) "Blessed be He in whose hand is the kingship; and He over all things hath power." (67:1)

So all creation, issuing as it does from one absolute, universal, and active Will, forms an all-embracing unity in which each individual part is in harmonious order with the remainder. And thus, too, every form of existence embodies a principle which relates it to this perfect and comprehensive order. "He it is who hath created seven Heavens, one above the other; thou canst not see any oversight in the creation of the Merciful. Look again; canst thou see any flaw? Look again and again; thy sight will turn back, dim and wearied out." (67:3-4) "And He set up upon it mountain peaks above it, and blessed it, and arranged its various kinds of food in it." (41:10) "Allah it is who sends the winds to stir up the clouds, and He spreads it in the Heavens as He wills, and breaks it up; so you see the rain coming out of the midst of it; and when He causes it to fall on which of His servants He wills, behold they rejoice." (30:48) Accordingly, it is obvious that all creation must have a fundamental connection with the creative purpose and that the Will from which all creation finally proceeds, and by which it is continually sustained and ordered, is related to creation itself; thus only can that Will give to creation a coherence and beneficial purpose.

Thus, then, all creation is a unity comprising different parts; it has a common origin, a common providence and purpose, because it was deliberately produced by a single, absolute, and comprehensive Will. Therefore it was suitable, adapted, and ready for the appearance of life in the general sense, and for the appearance of man, the highest form of life, in particular. So the universe cannot be hostile to life, or to man; nor can "Nature" in our modern phrase be held to be antagonistic to man, opposed to him, or striving against him. Rather she is a friend whose purposes are one with those of life and of mankind. And the task of living beings is not to contend with Nature, for they have grown up in her bosom, and she and they together form a part of the single universe which proceeds from the single will. Thus essentially man lives in a purely friendly environment, among the powers of a friendly universe. So Allah, when He created the earth, set up upon it mountain peaks above it, and blessed it, and arranged its various kinds of food in it. "And He cast upon the earth mountain peaks, lest it sway with you." (16:15) "And the earth—He established it for mankind." (55:10) "He it is who hath laid the earth low for you, so walk ye about in its regions, and eat of its provision." (67:15) "He hath created for you ,what is in the earth, all of it." (2:29) So the Heavens with their stars are a part of creation; they are connected with the other parts, and everything that is in them and in the earth is friendly, cooperative, and interrelated with all the remaining parts. "And He decked out the lower Heavens with lamps." (67:15) "Did We not make the earth a flat expanse, and the mountains as tent pegs? We created you in pairs, and We appointed your sleep to be a rest. We made the night for a covering, and We made the day for a livelihood. We built above you seven firm Heavens, and We set a lamp ablazing. We sent down from the rain clouds copious waters to bring forth grain and vegetation and luxurious gardens." (78:6-16)

The Islamic creed thus affirms that Allah, the Sustaining Lord of man, has created all these forces in order to aid, assist, and befriend him. For him to attain their friendship it is necessary that he reflect on them, acquaint himself with them, and cooperate with them. If these forces occasionally vex him, it is because he has not reflected on them sufficiently or come to understand the norms that are driving them.

And further, the Creator does not place living beings and men in this world without giving them also His direct care and constant attention, for His perfect Will is constant throughout all the world, constant, too, over every individual part of the universe at all times. "There is no beast in the earth but its provision is a charge upon Allah; He knows its lair and its resting-place." (11:6) "We have created man, and We know what he whispers to himself; We are nearer to him than his jugular vein." (50:16) "Your Lord said, 'Call upon Me, and I shall answer you." (40:60) "And do not kill your children because of poverty; We shall provide for you and for them." (6:151)

Because, then, the Universe is a unity emanating from a single Will; because man is himself a part of the world, dependent upon and related to all the other parts; and because individuals are as atoms, dependent upon and related to the world; therefore, they must have the same dependence upon, and relation to, one another. So, the Islamic belief is that humanity is an essential unity; its scattered elements must be brought together, its diversity must give place to unity, its variety of creeds must in the end be brought into one. For thus and only thus can man be made ready to be at one with the essential unity of creation. "O mankind, We have created you male and female, and We have made you peoples and tribes, that you might know one another." (49:13)

There can be no permanent system in human life until this integration and unification has taken place; this step is a prerequisite for true and complete human life, even justifying the use of force against those who deviate from it, so that those who have wandered from the true path may be brought back to it. "The recompense of those who make war against Allah and His Messenger, exerting themselves to cause corruption in the earth, is that they be killed or crucified, or that their hands and feet on opposite sides be cut off, or that they be banished from the land." (5:33) "If two parties of the Believers fight, then make peace between them; if one of them oppresses the other, then fight the oppressing party until it returns to the command of Allah; if it returns, then make a just peace between them, and act fairly." (49:9) "And if Allah had not resisted one party of the people by means of others, the land would have grown corrupt." (2:251) Accordingly, the fundamental matter is this interdependence and solidarity of mankind, and whoever has lost sight of this principle must be brought back to it by any means. The supreme norms governing existence are more fit to be followed than are the whims of individuals and societies, and mutual solidarity among all corresponds both to the aim of existence as a whole and to the aim of the One Creator.

Now when we come to consider man as a species and as an individual, there is the same comprehensive unity to be observed; man's faculties which are so diverse in appearance are essentially one in purpose. Thus in this respect also man is comparable to the world in its entirety, since its power too is a unity, though diverse in appearance.

Man lived through long ages without arriving at any comprehensive theory of human and universal powers; he continued to differentiate between spiritual and material powers, he denied one of these in order to strengthen the other, or he admitted the existence of both in a state of opposition and antagonism. He organized his life on the basis that such an opposition between these two types of power was natural and that the superiority of one was only to be gained at the expense of the other. He held that such superiority on the one side and inferiority on the other was inevitable, because, as he believed, such opposition was inherent in the nature of the world and of man.

Christianity is one of the clearest examples of this theory of opposition, which it shares to some degree with both Hinduism and Buddhism. For Christianity the salvation of the soul is to be gained by humiliating the body, by punishing it, or even by destroying it, or at the least, by neglecting it and turning away from indulgence. In Christianity and in other similar faiths this is the cardinal principle on which are built their systems of belief; to it can be traced their doctrines on life and its purpose, on the duties of the individual on the one hand and of society on the other, and on man and the different powers and abilities which clash within him.

Thus the struggle between the two types of power continued, with men continually uncertain and perplexed and without any definite assurance as to the true solution. Then came Islam, bringing with it a new, comprehensive, and coherent theory in which there was neither this tension nor this opposition, neither hostility nor antagonism. Islam gave a unity to all powers and abilities, it

integrated all desires and inclinations and leanings, it gave a coherence to all men's efforts. In all these Islam saw one embracing
unity which took in the universe, the soul, and all human life. Its
aim was to unite earth and Heaven in one world; to join the present
world and the world to come in one faith; to link spirit and body in
one humanity; to correlate worship and work in one life. It sought
to bring all these into one path — the path which leads to Allah.

In the same way the world is a unity, composed of things that
are seen and otherwise sensually perceived, and of things that are
unseen and imperceptible. Life is a unity, made up of material abilities and spiritual powers, between which no separation can ever
be made without a resultant disorder and confusion. And similarly,
human personality is a unity of spiritual desires, which rise toward
Heaven, and bodily appetites which cling on earth. No separation
can be made between these aspects of personality because Heaven
and earth are one, because in the world there is a unity of things
seen and things unseen, and because in religion there is a unity of
this world and that to come, between daily life and worship.

But beyond all this, there does exist one eternal and unchanging power, which has no beginning and no end. To it belongs the
government of the world, of mankind, and of life. It is the power of
Allah. The human individual in his transience may join himself to
this power which eternally pervades life and from it seek help in
his misfortunes. He strives after it when he is in the mosque at
prayer, lifting up his heart to Heaven, and he seeks it no less when
he is abroad in the world, busily intent upon his livelihood. So he
seeks to deserve the future life, not only when he fasts and denies
himself all manner of pleasurable indulgence, but also when he
breaks his fast and enjoys all the good things of life — so long as he
does either of these two things with his heart firmly directed
towards Allah. And thus the life of the present world, with all its
prayer and its work, all its luxuries and its privations, is the only
way to the future world, with its Paradise and its Hell, its punishment and its reward.

This surely is the true unity between the sundry parts of the
universe and their powers, between all the diverse abilities of life,
between man and his soul, between his present reality and his

dreams. Such a unity it is which can set a lasting harmony between the world and human life, between life and living men, between society and the individual, and between man's spiritual desires and his appetites. In a word, it means a harmony between the world and the faith, between earth and Heaven.

This harmony is not established in favor of the physical side of man, nor yet in favor of the spiritual side; rather it imparts to both of them an equal freedom, thus bringing both to a healthy position of well-being and growth. Similarly, this harmony is not established in favor of the individual or of society; nor in favor of one nation over another; nor in favor of one generation over another. But each of these is held to have its own rights and its own responsibilities. For, the individual and society, the people and the community, the generation and all other generations—all are bound by one law which has but one aim: namely, that the freedom of the individual and of society should be equally recognized without any mutual opposition and that the generations, one and all, should work together for the growth and progress of human life and for its orientation towards the Creator of life.

Islam is, then, the religion which asserts the unity of all powers in the universe, as well as its assertion of the unity of the divinity, the unity of all the successive manifestations of the one true religion proceeding from Allah, and also the unity of all the prophets in their testimony to this one faith since the dawn of time. "Verily this community of yours is one, and I am your Lord; so worship Me." (23:54) So also Islam stands for the unity of worship and work, of faith and life, of spiritual and material realities, of economic and spiritual values, of the present world and the world to come, of earth and Heaven. From this pervasive unity there issue all the Islamic laws and ordinances, all its exhortations and rules, as well as its teachings on political and economic theory, on the balance of credits and debits, and on privileges and responsibilities. Thus in this fundamental principle of unity there are contained all the various rules of life.

While we are examining this universal theory which takes its rise from the nature of Islamic thought about the world and life and humanity, we may study also the fundamental outlines of social justice in Islam. Above all other things, it is a comprehensive human justice and not merely an economic justice; that is to say, it embraces all sides of life and all aspects of activity. It is concerned alike with perception and conduct, with the heart and the conscience. The values with which this justice deals are not only economic values, nor are they merely material values in general; rather they are a mixture of moral and spiritual values together. Christianity looks at man only from the standpoint of his spiritual desires and seeks to crush down the human instincts in order to encourage those desires. On the other hand, Communism looks at man only from the stand point of his material needs; it looks not only at human nature, but also at the world and at life from a purely material point of view. But Islam looks at man as forming a unity whose spiritual desires cannot be separated from his bodily appetites and whose moral needs cannot be divorced from his material needs. It looks at the world and at life with this all-embracing view which permits of no separation or division. In this fact lies the main divergence among Communism, Christianity, and Islam.

Thus, in the Islamic view, life consists of mercy, love, help, and a mutual responsibility among Muslims in particular, and among all human beings in general. It is apparent, then, that Islam is the eternal dream of humanity, incorporated in a living reality upon earth, whereas Communism is simply the passing rancor of a single generation of men! In the Communist view, life is a continual strife and struggle between the classes, a struggle which must end in one class overcoming the other at which point the Communist dream is realized.

❖ ❖ ❖ ❖ ❖ ❖ ❖

There are, then, these two great facts: the absolute, just, and coherent unity of existence, and the general, mutual responsibility of individuals and societies. On these two facts Islam bases its realization of social justice, having regard for the basic elements of the nature of man, yet not unmindful of human abilities.

The glorious Qur'an says of man that "verily, in the love of gain he is firm" (100:8); the "love of gain" belongs to his nature and to his native endowment. It says also, describing that greed which is of the nature and constitution of man, that "souls are close to avarice" (4:128); it is always near to them. So also there occurs in the Qur'an a wonderfully skillful description of this human trait; "Say: If it were you who had in your power the treasures of the mercy of my Lord, then you would keep a tight hold for fear of spending; for man is niggardly." (19:100) But He is certainly liberal with His mercy in every way; and so, from this liberality of Divine mercy and from that human meanness, it is apparent how great is the extent of avarice in the nature of man if he is left without discipline or exhortation.

Accordingly, when Islam comes to lay down its rules and laws, its counsels and controls, that natural "love of gain" is not overlooked, nor is that deep natural avarice forgotten; selfishness is rebuked, avarice is dealt with by regulations and laws, and no duty is enjoined on man beyond his capacity. At the same time Islam does not overlook the needs and the welfare of society, nor does it forget the great achievements of individuals in life and society in every age and among different nations.

There may sometimes occur that type of social oppression which is inconsistent with justice, when the greed and cupidity of the individual prey upon society; or that same oppression may also take the form of society preying upon the nature and ability of the individual. Such oppression is a sin, not against one individual alone, but against the whole principle of the community. It is an encroachment upon the activity of the individual whose natural rights are infringed; but its evil effects do not merely deprive that individual of his rights; they go beyond him to touch the welfare of the whole community, because it cannot profit to the full from his abilities. So the regulations lay down the rights of the community over the powers and abilities of the individual; they also establish limiting boundaries to the freedom, the desires, and the wants of the individual, but they must also be ever mindful of the rights of the individual, to give him freedom in his desires and inclinations; and over all there must be the limits that the community must not overstep and that the individual on his side must not transgress. Nor must there be interference with great individual achievements; for life is a matter of mutual help and mutual responsibility according to Islam, and not a constant warfare, to be lived in a spirit of struggle and hostility. Thus there must be freedom for individual and general abilities, rather than repression and a restrictive constraint. Everything that is not legally forbidden is perfectly permissible. The individual earns reward for every activity undertaken for the sake of Allah and which gives promise of the highest achievement.

This breadth of vision in the Islamic view of life, together with the fact that it goes beyond merely economic values to those other values on which life depends—these things make the Islamic faith better able to provide equity and justice in society and to establish justice in the whole of the human sphere. It also frees Islam from the narrow interpretation of justice as understood by Communism. For, justice to the Communist is an equality of wages in order to prevent economic discrimination; but within recent days when theory has come into opposition with practice, Communism has found itself unable to achieve this equality. Justice in Islam is a human equality, envisaging the adjustment of all values, of which the economic is but one. Economic equality is, to be precise, equality of opportunity, combined with the freedom to develop one's talents within the boundaries set by the higher purposes of life.

In the Islamic view values are so very composite that justice must include all of them; therefore Islam does not demand a compulsory economic equality in the narrow literal sense of the term. This is against nature and conflicts with the essential fact, which is that of the differing native endowments of individuals. It arrests the development of outstanding ability and makes it equal to lesser ability; it prevents those who have great gifts from using their gifts to their own advantage and to that of the community, and it deprives the community and the individual from the fruits of those gifts. There can be no profit in disputing the fact that the natural endowments of individuals are not equal. And while we may not be as able to see this in the case of mental and spiritual endowments as we can in the sphere of practical life—yet we cannot deny that some individuals are born with endowments of disposition, such as healthiness, or perfection, or stamina; while others are born with a predisposition to sickness, or debility, or weakness. Nor can we deny that others can earn their living by the pleasantness of their conversation, by their pleasing appearance, or by their agreeable nature; thus the gates of undertaking and accomplishment open before them, the same gates which remain closed in the face of others not similarly endowed.

Accordingly, to deny the existence of outstanding endowments of personality, intellect, and spirit, is a piece of nonsense which is not worth discussing. So we must reckon with all these endowments, and to all of them we must give the opportunity to produce their greatest results; then from these results we may take that which appears to be of permanent profit to society. On no account must we close off the outlet for such endowments or discourage them by making them equal in reward with lesser abilities; we must avoid shackling such gifts and stifling them, and thereby depriving of their fruits the community and the human race alike.

Islam does, of course, acknowledge a fundamental equality of all men and a fundamental justice among all, but over and above that, it leaves the door open for achievement of preeminence through hard work, just as it lays in the balance values other than the economic. "Verily the noblest among you in Allah's eyes is the most pious." (49:31) "Allah will raise up in degrees of honor those of you who believe, and to whom knowledge has been brought." (58:11) "Wealth and children are an ornament to life in the world, but the things which endure, the works of righteousness are better in thy Lord's eyes—better for reward, and better for hope." (18:46) From this it is apparent that there are values other than the merely economic; with these values Islam reckons, and of these it makes the means of equilibrium in society, since different individuals have different methods of gaining their livelihood. Islam admits the reasonable causes of these differences as being differences in strength and in endowment. It does not admit differences which depend on rank and station; such it absolutely denies, as will be seen further in Chapter VI, on economic theory.

Islam, then, does not demand a literal equality of wealth, because the distribution of wealth depends on men's endowments, which are not uniform. Hence absolute justice demands that men's rewards be similarly different and that some have more than others—so long as human justice is upheld by the provision of equal opportunity for all. Thus rank or upbringing, origin or class should not stand in the way of any individual, nor should anyone be fettered by the chains which shackle enterprise. Justice must be upheld also by the inclusion of all kinds of values in the reckoning, by the freeing of the human mind completely from the tyranny of the purely economic values, and by the relegation of these to their true and reasonable place. Economic values must not be given an inflatedly high standing, such as they enjoy in those human societies which lack a certainty of true values, or which give to them too slight an importance; in such conditions money alone becomes the supreme and fundamental value.

In Islam money is not given this value; Islam refuses to admit that life can be reckoned in terms of a mouthful of bread, the appetites of the body, or a handful of money. Yet at the same time it demands a competence for every individual, and at times more than a competence, in order to remove the fear of destitution. On the other side, it forbids that unbridled luxury in possessions and desires, which produces social divisions and classes. It prescribes the claims of the poor upon the wealth of the rich, according to their needs, and according to the best interests of society, so that social life may be balanced, just, and productive. Thus it is not unmindful of any one of the various aspects of life, material, intellectual, religious, and worldly; but it organizes them all, that they may be related together and thus furnish a coherent unity in which it will be difficult to neglect any one of their various integral parts. So these departments of life become an organized unity, similar to the great oneness of the universe and to that of life and of all mankind.

3 THE FOUNDATIONS OF SOCIAL JUSTICE IN ISLAM

Islam establishes this social justice, whose nature we have now summarily analyzed, on solid foundations; for the accomplishment of its aims it lays down certain definite methods. It does not leave the matter obscure nor treat it as a general summons. For, by its own nature, Islam is a faith of achievement, of work in the sphere of practical life; it is not a religion of mere words or abstract guidance existing only in the world of the imagination.

As we have already seen, Islam has a basic theory of the universe, of life, and of man. We have seen also that the idea of "social justice" has its roots in that basic theory and enters into its general scheme. We have discovered that the nature of Islamic belief about human life makes social justice essentially an all-embracing justice which does not take account merely of material and economic factors; for Islam does not divide the individual into body and soul, into differing intellectual and spiritual sides. It holds that the values of this life are material and spiritual at one and the same time and that no division is possible in such a unity. It holds also that mankind is essentially one body, its members mutually responsible and interdependent, a body in which there are no clashing and contradictory groups.

Many times it has seemed that reality contradicts this fundamental Islamic theory. So first we must discover what is this reality. The reality which Islam regards as ultimately true is not the state of affairs of any one individual or in any one people or generation, that limited, definite, and temporary reality on which the faculties of frail human individuals are set when they turn away from the search for awareness of the larger and more comprehensive things in human life, the things which endure from pre-eternity to post-eternity. For Islam scans all standards and reckons with all kinds of interests; its aim is the achievement of a purpose which includes all humanity from beginning to end. So, while there may appear to be an inconsistency, this is not the case when we take the comprehensive view, which embraces all men, rather than merely one individual, one people, or one generation.

This comprehensive view of social justice with its far-reaching aims will serve later on to explain the regulations which Islam lays down. These cannot be correctly understood when they are taken individually; nor when they are understood only of the individual in relation to society, or of society only in relation to the people; nor when they are understood only of the people in relation to the generation, or of the generation only in relation to other generations. This comprehensive view will serve to explain the regulations on individual ownership; on *zakat*; on the law of inheritance; on the rules for estates; on the system of rule; on commercial transactions; in a word, it will explain all the regulations prescribed by Islam for individuals, societies, nations, and generations.

At this point we have no intention of dealing with all this; we shall, then, content ourselves to deal with the general foundations on which Islam establishes its regulations for social justice within the limits of its universal theory. And from the nature of these, we will see that Islam believes in the unity of body and spirit in the individual and in the unity of the spiritual and the material in life. Similarly, it believes in an identity of aim in the individual and in society, in the identity of interests of the various societies within a people, and in an identity of purpose among all the peoples of mankind and among all successive generations, despite the difference of their immediate and limited interests.

The following are the foundations on which Islam establishes justice:

1. Absolute freedom of conscience.
2. The complete equality of all men.
3. The firm mutual responsibility of society.

With each of these foundations we shall deal in turn, explaining its nature and its objective.

FREEDOM OF CONSCIENCE

Complete social justice cannot be assured, nor can its efficiency and permanence be guaranteed, unless it arises from an inner conviction of the spirit; it must be claimed by the individual, it must be needed by society; there must be a belief that it will serve the highest purposes of mankind. It must also rest upon some material reality to which the individual may cling while accepting the cost involved and being prepared to defend it. No man will claim justice by law unless he has first claimed it by instinct and by the practical methods that ensure the preservation of instinct. Similarly, society will not persevere with such legislation, even when it exists, unless there is a belief which demands it from within and practical measures which support it from without. It is these facts that Islam has in mind in all its ordinances and laws.

It is the Christian view that freedom of conscience is one of the luxuries of life and that to turn towards the Lord's Kingdom of Heaven and to spurn the life of this world is the true way of guaranteeing to man his freedom and to the soul its happiness. Now this is true, but it is not the whole truth. The needs of life are not paramount under all circumstances, nor do material necessities always predominate; but at most times man must submit to their demands. So, to ignore the material needs of life or to refuse them is not always the better way. It was Allah who created life, and He did not create it for no purpose; nor did He create it for man to neglect it and to check its growth. Certainly it is desirable that man should rise above his material needs and above his bodily appetites. But it is not desirable that because of these aims he should neglect life altogether.

There is a way to achieve the realization of the powers latent in human nature together with the elevation of that nature above submission to the demands of material necessity; it is even the soundest and the safest way. This is what Islam aims to do—to integrate the needs of the body and the desires of the spirit in one unity and to satisfy by freedom of conscience the inner instinct as well as practical reality. So it is not unmindful of either side of the question.

On the other hand, the Communist view is that economic freedom alone satisfies the need for freedom of conscience and that it is purely economic pressure on the individual which prompts him to renounce his legal rights of justice and equality. This too is true but it is not the whole truth. For economic freedom of itself has no guarantee of permanence in society, unless there is also freedom of conscience within the mind. For alone it produces only another form of tyranny—the repression of individual gifts and abilities and inclinations, and these are things which cannot be satisfactorily dealt with by legal methods alone. It produces also a repression of the individual, inasmuch as his natural abilities are unable to find an outlet and have no opportunity of growing in competition with others. Thus, inevitably, the individual is cheated in his desire for that equity which the law has promised him, because he has the inner conviction that he is getting less than others, even if he boasts for a while that he is better than they. The man who has the greatest abilities and who can produce the most will always overcome the law of absolute equality. Or if he cannot do that, he will hate and resent it; in which case, either he will rebel or his intelligence will be extinguished, his abilities will atrophy, and his power of production will be lessened.

But, where equality has its roots in a profound freedom of the conscience as well as in law and its implementation, and if the instinct for it is powerful among the strong and the weak alike, then it will be accepted as a rise in status for the weak and for the strong as humility. It will join in the soul with a belief in Allah, and with the unity and mutual responsibility of the community; more, it will inculcate a belief in the unity and solidarity of humanity. Such is the aim of Islam when it grants complete and absolute freedom to the human conscience; but at the same time it stipulates that first the needs of the body and the material necessities of life must be guaranteed alike by the authority of the law and by the authority of the conscience.

❖ ❖ ❖ ❖ ❖ ❖ ❖

Islam began by freeing the human conscience from servitude to anyone except Allah and from submission to any save Him. There is no supreme authority anywhere except that of Allah, nor can any other grant life or death. None save He can supply provision of anything in earth or heaven, nor can there be any mediator or intermediary between man and Him. Allah is the only possessor of power, and all others are subject to him, without ownership either of themselves or of others. "Say: He is Allah the One, Allah the Eternal. He brought not forth, nor was He brought forth; there is none equal to Him. . . (Sura 112)

Since Allah is One, His worship is also one, and to Him alone must all men turn. There is no object of worship except Allah, nor can men take one another as lords instead of Him. No man among them can excel any other except by his deeds and his piety. "Say: O people of the Book, come to a word which is fair between us and you; namely that we should worship none but Allah, that we associate nothing with Him, and that we do not take one another as lords instead of Allah." (3:57)

Islam has an intense interest in this belief, which the Qur'an emphasizes on numerous occasions. The prophets in their day imagined that their people would turn to them with some sort of worship or with a reverence of some kind or another; but Islam strove to free the human conscience completely from this belief. So Allah says of His Messenger, Muhammad, peace and blessings be upon him, "And Muhammad is only a messenger; messengers have passed away before him. So if he dies or if he is killed, will you then turn back upon your heels?" (3:123) And He addresses the Prophet himself with great clarity, saying: "Thou hast nothing to do with this matter; either He may relent towards them, or He may punish them." (3:123) In the same way, He addresses him in another place with something like a threat: "If We had not made thee stand firm, thou hadst almost leaned towards them a little. In that case We would have made thee taste the double of life and the double of death; then thou couldst not have found a helper against Us." (17:76-77) So, too, He commands him to proclaim openly his true position: "Say: I call only upon my Lord, and with Him I associate nothing. Say: Verily I wield no power over you, either to harm you or to set you right. Say: No one can protect me from Allah, nor can I find a shelter from Him." (72:20-23)

And He speaks of those who deify Jesus, the son of Mary, charging them with unbelief and folly: "They are unbelievers who say that Allah is the Messiah, the son of Mary. Say: Who, then, will control Allah in the least if He wishes to destroy the Messiah, the son of Mary, together with his mother and all those who are in the earth?" (5:19) Or, in another place He says of the Messiah: "He is only a servant whom We have favored, and whom We have made a parable for the Children of Israel." (43:59) He takes him as one of the witnesses of the Resurrection, and in the Qur'an Jesus, the son of Mary, himself answers the assertion which some people make about his divine nature; he establishes his own innocence of this assertion in which he had no part, answering it in a strong, forceful, and impressive manner. "When Allah said: O Jesus, son of Mary, was it thou who didst say to the people, 'Take me and my mother as gods apart from Allah'? he replied: Glory be to Thee, it is not for me to say what to me is not the truth. If I did say it, then Thou knowest it. Thou knowest what is within me, but I know not what is within Thee. Verily Thou art He who knoweth secret things. I said nothing to them save what Thou didst command me: 'Serve Allah, my Lord and your Lord.' I was a witness to them as long as I was among them; but when Thou didst take me away, then Thou Thyself wast a watcher over them. Thou art a witness over all things. If Thou dost punish them—they are Thy servants; if Thou dost forgive them—Thou art the Glorious, the Wise." (5:116-118)

And other passages are similar. The Qur'an places insistent emphasis on this belief, on establishing and clarifying it, in order to ensure freedom of the human conscience from any trace of association with Allah as regards His divinity and His sanctity. For such association would oppress the conscience and would make it worship some created thing among the servants of Allah. If Jesus was a prophet or a messenger, he was still only one of His servants.

And if it is held that no servant is more distinguished in his essence than any other servant in the view of Allah, then all mediation between Allah and His servants is denied; there can be no priesthood and no mediator. So every individual can make his own practical relationship with his Creator and can strengthen his own weak and frail nature with the Power which is from eternity to eternity. So he can draw from that power strength and dignity and courage, can know its mercy and care and kindness, can strengthen his faith and empower his spirit.

Islam insists most firmly on strengthening this link and on the individual realizing that he has the ability to call upon that great Power day and night. "Allah is gentle with His servants." (42:18) "And when My servants ask thee about Me, verily I am near to answer the prayer of him who prays, when he prays to Me. So let them ask an answer from Me, let them believe in Me, and perhaps they may be guided aright." (2:182) "And despair not of the comfort of Allah; verily none despair of the comfort of Allah except the unbelieving people." (12:87) "Say: O My servants who have squandered your own resources, do not despair of the mercy of Allah; verily Allah forgives all faults." (39:54)

Islam has prescribed five times of prayer, in which every day the worshipper stands before his Lord, in which the creature establishes a line with his Creator. These are at stated times, and not merely when it occurs to anyone to stand before his God and to draw near in adoration and prayer. The purpose of these prayers is not only words or movements; rather their aim is to direct the whole man, heart, mind, and body at the same time towards Allah. This is in line with the general theory of Islam on the unity of human nature in its creatureliness and of the unity of the Creator in His divinity. "So woe to those who pray, and of their prayers are careless." (107:4-5)

✢ ✢ ✢ ✢ ✢ ✢ ✢

When the conscience is freed from the instinct of servitude to and worship of any of the servants of Allah, and when it is filled with the knowledge that it can of itself gain complete access to Allah then it cannot be disturbed by any feeling of fear of life, or fear for livelihood, or fear for its station. This fear is an ignoble instinct which lowers the individual's estimation of himself, which often makes him accept humiliation or abdicate much of his natural honor or many of his rights. But Islam insists strongly that dignity and honor are the rights of man and that to be proud of his rights and to persevere in the search for justice is deep-seated in the human soul. By reason of all this—over and above its laws—it insists on the guarantee of an absolute social justice under which man shall not suffer from neglect. Therefore, it is particularly anxious to oppose the instinct of fear, whether of life or of livelihood or of station. For life is in the hand of Allah, and no creature has the power to shorten that life by one hour or by one minute. More, no creature has the power to subtract a single breath from the life of a single soul, nor has any creature the right to inflict the slightest mark or the least injury on any single living being. "But it is not given to any soul to die, except by the permission of Allah, a permission written and dated." (3:139) "Say: Nothing will come upon us save what Allah has prescribed for us; He is our Master." (9:51) "Each community has its appointed time, and when their time comes they will not be an hour behind, nor will they go before their time." (10:50)

In this case there can be no cowardice and no cowards; for life and its allotted span, good and evil are in the hand of Allah, and of no other. "Say: Shall I choose as a patron any other than Allah, the Maker of heaven and earth? He it is Who giveth food, and Who needeth not to be fed." (6:14) "Allah maketh wide provision for whom He will, or He is sparing." (13:26) "And how many beasts do not carry their own provision. Allah maketh provision for them and for you." (29:60) "Say: Who giveth you your provision from Heaven and earth? Or who hath power over hearing and sight? Who bringeth forth the living from the dead, and bringeth forth the dead from the living? And who setteth the affair in order? They will say: Allah." (10:32) "O ye people, remember the favor of Allah towards you. Is there any Creator save Allah, Who giveth you from heaven and earth your provision? There is no god save He. How, then, are ye kept from him?" (35:3) "And do not kill your children because of poverty; We shall provide for you and for them." (6:152) "And if you fear poverty, Allah will enrich you from His bounty if He wills." (9:28) The Qur'an lays it down that the fear of poverty is inspired only by Satan in order to weaken and impede the soul in its trust in Allah and in virtue. "Satan promises you only poverty, and bids you to indecency; but Allah promises you pardon from Himself, and bounty; Allah is bountiful, wise." (2:271)

In that case there is no reason for any man to be oppressed by anxiety about his livelihood, for his provision is in the hand of Allah and in His hand alone; and not one of His created servants has the power to cut off any man's provision or to withhold from him any part of that provision. This belief certainly does not rule out causality and transactions, but it does strengthen the human heart and empower the human conscience; it sets the poor man who is anxious over his livelihood on a level with the man who thinks that his provision is in his own hand, to be won with all his own strength and resource. The instinct of fear does not then keep the poor man from seeking what is his due or from taking pride in himself; it means that he does not have to give up any of his rights or compromise his honor in order to ensure his provision. This is the meaning of the Qur'anic teaching, as it is the objective of Islam; this is the true application of the general Islamic philosophy in hortatory and legal form.

Fear for one's position or station in life often goes together with the fear of death or injury or the fear of poverty or destitution; and Islam is insistent that the individual be freed from this fear also, for no creature can have any power over another creature in this matter, "Say: O Allah, wielder of the kingly power, Thou givest that power to whom Thou willest; and Thou takest the power from whom Thou willest. Thou dost exalt whom Thou wilt, and Thou dost abase whom Thou wilt; in Thy hand is the good. Verily Thou over all things art powerful." (3:25) "Say: In whose hand is the rule over all things? Who giveth protection and seeketh none? If you have any knowledge, you will say: In the hand of Allah. Say: Then why are you bewitched?" (23:90-91) "If Allah help you, then none can defeat you; but if He abandon you, then who will help you after Him?" (3:154) 'Whosoever there be who desires honor, to Allah belongs all honor." (35:11) "To Allah belongs all honor, and to His Messenger, and to the Believers." (63:8)

So here again there can be no fear, for all power belongs to Allah alone, and all honor is Allah's. "And He is supreme above His servants; He is the Wise, the Informed." (6:18)

✣ ✣ ✣ ✣ ✣ ✣ ✣

But sometimes the human spirit is freed from servitude to false objects of sanctity and from subservience to a fear for its life or its livelihood or its station only to fall a prey to social values. Even though it derives from them neither profit nor loss, it still may be under the influence of such values as money, power, rank, or lineage. When the conscience recognizes its practical allegiance to any of these values, its very observance of them renders it incapable of true freedom, so that it cannot feel any real equality with its fellows. So here Islam applies itself to all these values and puts them in their proper place; it pays them neither too little attention nor too much, and thus it restores the true values to their proper and essential status, the true values which are either latent in a man's spirit or given expression in his acts. Thus it minimizes the effect of the material values and checks their impact on their human spirit. So it makes this matter also—together with the practical and legal guarantees it provides—a means towards the complete freedom of the conscience.

"Verily the noblest of you in Allah's eyes is the most pious of you." (49:13) And the noble man in Allah's eyes is he who is really and truly noble. "The Arab has no eminence over the non-Arab except his piety."[7] "And they said: We are the greater in wealth and in children, so we shall not be punished. Say: Verily my Lord maketh wide provision for whom He will, or He is sparing. But the majority of people will not understand. Neither your wealth nor your children are things which bring you near to Us; but only he who believes and who acts righteously will be near to Us. For such men there is a double recompense for what they have done, and they shall be safe in upper chambers." (34:34-36) So let them have their greatness in wealth and children; this is no value which will bring them any prominence or distinction, but "only he who believes and acts righteously." For faith is the permanent value fixed in the conscience, together with righteous deeds in one's life; these are the two real values which can command respect.

At the same time Islam does not depreciate the value of wealth or of family; "wealth and sons are an ornament for life in this world." An ornament. But it does emphasize that such things are not such as to elevate or lower a man's true status. "The things which endure, the works of righteousness, are better in thy Lord's sight — better for reward, and better for hope." (18:44)

The Qur'an deals with material values and spiritual values by coining a parable about them in the souls of two men; it leaves no doubt that one of them is preferable to the other, and paints a clear and appealing picture of the believing soul and of the reality of its values.

"Coin for them a parable. There were two men, to one of whom We gave two gardens of vines which We surrounded with palm trees. And between them We set a patch of arable land. Each of the gardens produced its fruit without failing in any way, and between the two of them We caused a stream to flow. So this man had his fruit, and in dispute with his neighbor he said to him: 'I have more wealth than you, and my family is mightier.' So he went into his garden, sinning against his own soul, and saying: 'I do not think that this will ever pass away, nor do I believe that "The Hour" will come. But even if I am taken back to my Lord, I will surely find something better than this in exchange.' But his neighbor said to him in dispute: 'Have you no belief in Him who created you out of dust, then out of semen, and then formed you as a man? Nay, Allah is my Lord, and I will not associate any other with my Lord. Why did you not say when you entered your garden: "As Allah will; there is no power save in Allah, if you thought me inferior to yourself in wealth and children? It may be that my Lord will give me something better than your garden; and that He will send down on this a thunderbolt from Heaven, so that next morning it will be only smooth, bare soil. Or the next morning the water may have sunk so deep in the ground that you cannot find it. Then his fruit was encompassed, and the next morning he was turning down the palms of his hands in dismay at what he had spent on it, for it had fallen down upon the trellises; and he was saying: 'Would that I had not associated another with my Lord.' He had no party to help him except Allah, and so he was helpless." (18:31-41)

In this there is apparent both the dignity of the believer in his faith, and his contempt for those values of which his neighbor boasted when he disputed with him. What is worthy of attention is that his neighbor, who is so proud of his garden, does not appear to associate any other with Allah. But the Qur'an accounts him as one who does so, and makes him finally admit such an act of association. That is to say, he associated with Allah a purely material value and gave to it a high mental regard; while, by contrast, the true believer would not associate anything with Allah.

So, too, in the story of Qarun the Qur'an portrays two characters in face of the temptation of wealth and property. There is a portrait of that character that is made conceited by such values, the character that is weakened and made mean and which sees itself petty compared to the rich. And, on the other hand, there is the portrait of believing souls which are dignified and strong and that never stoop to smallness or weakness. "Now Qarun was one of the people of Moses, and had authority over them. We gave him so much of the treasures that the keys of it weighed down a band, strong though they were. Then his people said to him: 'Do not exult; for Allah loveth not those who exult. But rather, through what Allah has given you, seek the future abode, without forgetting your part in this world. Do good, as Allah has done good for you, and do not seek to cause corruption in the earth; for Allah loveth not those who cause corruption.' He said: 'This has been given to me solely on account of the knowledge which I possess.' Did he not, then, know that before his time Allah had already destroyed generations which were stronger than him in power, and which had gathered more wealth? The sinners will not be asked about their crimes.

"So Qarun went out among his people in his pomp, and those who were eager for the life of this world said: 'Would that we had something the same as has been given to Qarun. Indeed he is a very fortunate man.' But those who had been given knowledge said: 'Woe to you. The reward of Allah is better for him who believes and acts righteously; but only those attain to it who have had endurance.' Then We cleft the earth for him and for his house, and he had no party to help him except Allah, nor was he one of those who could help themselves. So in the morning those who the previous day had envied his station were saying: 'Ah. How wide a provision does Allah make for His servants as He wills, or how sparing He is. If Allah had not been gracious to us, He would have cleft the earth for us. Ah, how the unbelievers fail to prosper." (28:76-82)

Islam is organized around its view of these teachings; and so Allah forbids His Prophet, Muhammad, to attach any value to those things in which some men find a deceitful enjoyment. "Do not cast your eyes longingly at those things which We have given for the enjoyment of some classes of men, things which are the flower of the life of the world. For We gave them in order to test these men; the provision of your Lord is better and more enduring." (20:131) Some authorities interpret this verse and those like it as meaning merely that the rich should be left to enjoy their riches, while the poor should be content with their poverty. But this is a false exegesis which is inconsistent with the general spirit of Islam. It is the explanation which is typical of those professional men of religion of despotic ages who use it to quiet the public conscience and to divert it from the quest for social justice. Such men must bear the responsibility themselves, for Islam cannot countenance such an exegesis. In point of fact, this verse and others similar to it refer rather to the rehabilitation of the true human values and to the necessity of rescuing the poor from their state of weakness and helplessness under the purely material values of wealth and possessions.

Corroboration of this exegesis is to be found in the fact that Allah commands His Prophet not to attach importance to these values and not to encourage the people to respect them. "Content yourself with those who pray to their Lord in the morning and in the evening, as they seek His presence. Do not let your eyes wander from them, seeking the adornment of the life of this world. Do not obey anyone whose heart We have made careless of Our remembrance, who follows his own desires, and who lives in excess." (18:27) "Do not let their wealth astonish you, nor their children; Allah intends only to punish them in the life of this world, intends that they may themselves perish while they are yet un-believers." (9:55)

In this connection we must also remember the story of Muhammad, peace and blessings be upon him, with the blind beg-gar, Ibn Umm Maktum, and with al-Walid ibn al-Mughira, the chief of his people. It is a story in which Allah delivers a sharp rebuke to His Prophet. "He frowned and turned away because the blind man came to him. What will teach you whether perhaps he will purify himself? Or whether he might let himself be reminded, and the reminder profit him? The man who is rich—to him you give your attention, caring nothing that he has not purified himself. But the man who comes to you earnestly inquiring and in fear—him you neglect." (80:1-10)

A moment of human weakness had assailed Muhammad, peace and blessings be upon him, in his desire that Allah might bring al-Walid over to Islam, and he was intent upon this matter when Ibn Umm Maktum came to him, seeking some knowledge of the Qur'an, calling to him again and again while he was still occu-pied with Al-Walid. The Prophet was annoyed with the beggar, and frowned upon him; but his Lord rebuked him sharply for it in these words which are almost the strongest possible rebuke. Therein He endorses the values for which Islam stands and points out what must be its true path and its constant endeavor—namely, to free the conscience.

❖ ❖ ❖ ❖ ❖ ❖ ❖

So, finally the human soul is freed from its bondage to holy things, is freed from its fear of death and injury, of death and humilia-tion—save for what Allah ordains; it is freed from all regard for outward appearances and for the values of society; yet after all this it still remains in subjection to its own nature, swayed by its plea-sures and its appetites, by its desires and its longings. Thus an inner tyranny replaces the outer which the soul has escaped, and the complete freedom of conscience which Islam desires is not achieved; nor can there be any realization of that supreme human aim, social justice.

Islam is not unaware of this lurking danger for the freedom of the conscience, and it bestows upon it a profound attention. This is evidenced by its care for the innermost depths of the soul, and again by its concern for all the abilities and endowments of the individual. And here Islam comes to the same point as Christianity and makes it its supreme objective. "Say: There are your fathers and your sons, your brothers and your wives; there are your tribes, and the money you have earned, the commerce which you fear may suffer, and the dwellings in which you take pleasure. If these things are dearer to you than Allah and His Messenger, if they are dearer than struggle in His Cause, then wait in idleness till Allah starts on His work. Verily Allah does not guide people who are impious." (9:24) Here in one verse are gathered up all the attractions, the longings, and the desires—all the weak points of the human soul, and they are placed on one side of the balance. On the other side are placed the love of Allah and of His Messenger and the love for struggling in His cause. It is a striking contrast, and it provides a complete escape from strangling desires. The soul that is thus completely freed is the soul that Islam seeks and that it summons to its true destiny. Thus man can rise superior to humiliating necessities, can control the direction of his own course, and can seek after things that are greater and more far-reaching than his own petty ephemeral pleasures.

Again He says: "The love of desires is made to appeal to men in their wives and their children, in hoarded hoards of gold and silver, in excellent horses, and cattle, and land; these things are the treasures of the life of this world. But with Allah is the best place of resort. Say: Shall I tell you of a better thing than these? For those who are pious there are Gardens in the presence of their Lord, through which rivers flow; and long shall they dwell there. There are pure wives for them, and there is favor from Allah; Allah is observant of His servants." (3:12-13) This is not an attempt to drug the mind, nor yet is it a summons to austerity or to a neglect of the good things of life, although in this way some have seen fit to interpret the Qur'an, and in this way others have seen fit to condemn Islam. This is simply a summons to freedom and to an independence from the weakness of desires and passions. Accordingly, there can be no harm in the enjoyment of the good things of life, so long as a man can control them, rather than they him. "Say: Who has forbidden the adornments of life which Allah has made for His servants; or who has forbidden the good things of His provision?" (7:30) "And do not forget your part in this world." (28:77)

To this same line of thought belongs the ordinance of fasting; for its purpose is to raise the soul for a space of time above the powerful needs of human nature. By fasting the will is strengthened and elevated, making man superior to his own essence because he has risen above his necessities.

To this end the Qur'an recommends various methods, among them being the implicit warning about the temptation of wealth and children, which occurs in the phrase, "Your wealth and your children are a temptation." (64:15) In this there is a warning which is sorely needed by human weakness in the face of wealth and children. This is particularly shown in the covetousness which assails a man where his possessions or his family are concerned; he accepts what he would not otherwise accept, submits to what he would otherwise not submit to, and commits sins that he would not otherwise commit. One day the Messenger of Allah, peace and blessings be upon him, came forth holding one of his grandsons in his arms and said: "A child may be an inducement to avarice, cowardice, and ignorance."

✢ ✢ ✢ ✢ ✢ ✢ ✢

Yet even after this, when a man is freed from all the things which would deprive him of his full nobility, he may still be in need. He is in need of food, and so he is humiliated; for there is no need which is more humiliating. The empty belly cannot appreciate high-sounding phrases. Or else he is compelled to ask for charity, and all his self-esteem leaves him, lost forever. This is met in Islam by the law which aims at preventing the causes of such need and at putting an end to them where they exist. Accordingly, it makes the right of the individual to a competence a responsibility of the state and of the rich members of the community; it is a responsibility whose neglect will be punished in the world to come and combatted in the present world. A full discussion of this will follow when we come to treat of social solidarity in Islam. For this reason Islam forbids begging and describes a community of Muslims who have suffered loss by fighting in the cause of Allah and who cannot travel the earth for wealth, on the grounds that "they do not beg importunately from the people." (2:274) So too the Prophet gives a coin to a beggar, and then says: "Verily it is better that one of you should get a rope and collect a bundle of firewood on his back and sell it, so that Allah suffices him thereby; better this than that you should beg from the people that they may give to you or refuse you." Or again he says: "The hand that gives is better than the hand that takes." And he exhorts men to avoid all shameful means of getting money other than begging; for begging is regarded by Islam as a necessary evil. As for the proceeds of the *zakat*, this is the law: It is to be received as a right, not given as charity. "And of their wealth there was a settled share for the beggar and the deprived." (51:19) This share is taken by the state and is spent on the welfare of Muslims to supply their bodily needs, to preserve their dignity, and to protect their power of conscience. If this is not sufficient, provision is made to impose taxes and levies on the wealth of men of means and the richer classes to meet the needs of the poor and the humble.

✧ ✧ ✧ ✧ ✧ ✧ ✧

Thus, Islam approaches the question of freedom from every angle and from all points of view; it undertakes a complete emancipation of the conscience. It does not deal only with spiritual values or only with economic values, but with both together. It recognizes the practical reality of life and equally the capacities of the soul; it attempts to awaken in human nature the highest desires and to evoke the loftiest abilities, thus bringing that nature to complete freedom of conscience. Without such complete freedom human nature cannot prevail against the force of humiliation and submissiveness and servility, nor can it lay claim to its rightful share in social justice, nor can it sustain the responsibilities of such a justice when it has attained it.

This freedom is therefore one of the cornerstones for the building of social justice in Islam. More: it is the principal cornerstone on which all the others must rest.

HUMAN EQUALITY

Suppose, then, that the human mind has come to know all this freedom of conscience; it is free from the least shadow of servility, be it to death or injury, to poverty or weakness, unless what comes by Allah's permission. It is released from the tyranny of the values of social standing and wealth; it is saved from the humiliation of need and beggary, and it can rise superior to its desires and its bodily appetites. It can turn towards its One Sole Creator, to Whom all things must turn without exception and without fail; and in addition to all that it is guaranteed a sufficiency of the necessities of life by legal ordinance.

When the human conscience has come to know all this, it will have no need of anyone to preach equality to it in words, for it will already have experienced the full meaning of equality as a reality in its own life. Moreover, it will not endure the distinctions that arise from worldly values at all. It will seek equality as its right and will strive to ensure that right; it will guard it carefully when it is gained, and it will accept no substitute for it. It will bear the responsibility of guarding and defending its equality, cost what it may in effort and sacrifice.

When the establishment of equality is rooted in the conscience, when it is safeguarded by religious law, and when it is guaranteed by a sufficiency of provision, the poor and the humble will not be the only persons to desire it. Even the rich and the powerful will support it, because their conscience acknowledges those values that Islam is intent on establishing and confirming, as we have already outlined them. This is what actually happened in Islamic society fourteen centuries ago, as will be shown in the course of this book.

But despite this, Islam is not content with simply implying the

concepts of freedom of conscience; rather, it emphasizes the principle of equality in word and text, so that everything may be clear
and firm and explicit. There was an age when some men asserted
their claim to be of the progeny of the gods, while others asserted
that the blood which flowed in their veins was not of the nature of
common blood, but was blue blood, royal or noble blood, and they
were believed. It was an age when there were faiths and religions
which divided the nations into classes; some were created from the
head of a god, and hence they were holy, while others, having been
created from the feet of a god, were despised. A dispute centered
around woman; had woman a soul, or had she not? It was an age in
which a master was permitted to kill his slave or to punish him in
any way, because slaves belonged to a different class of humanity
from that of their masters. In this age Islam was born; it taught the
unity of the human race in origin and in history, in life and in
death, in privileges and in responsibilities, before the law and
before Allah, in this world and in the world to come; it proclaimed
that there was no virtue except in good deeds and no nobility
except in piety. That formed an unparalleled revolution in human
thinking, and it has continued to this day; it was the peak to which
humanity has still not risen. That is to say, what was theoretically
established by human laws during and after the French Revolution
was established as a matter of practice by Islam in a profound and
elevated form more than fourteen centuries previously.

No god can possibly have progeny: "Say: He is Allah the One,
Allah the Eternal. He brought not forth, nor was He brought forth;
there none equal to Him." (Sura 112) "And they said, 'The Merciful has taken a son.' You have committed a terrible thing, at which
the very Heavens almost are torn apart, and the earth cleft asun-
der, and the mountains fallen down in pieces. For they attribute a
son to the Merciful, but the Merciful has no need to take a son.
There is nothing in Heaven or in earth which does not approach
the Merciful as a servant; He has counted them and given to them
an exact number, and all of them must come before Him singly on
the Day of Resurrection." (19:91-95)

Or again, there can be no such thing as blue blood or common
blood; and as for one being created from the head and another

from the foot of a god—" Did We not create you out of mere water which We stored in a secure place until a decreed time? We set the time, and good was Our setting." (77:20-23) "So let man consider: from what was he created? He was created from dripping water, from water issuing from between the loins and the ribs." (86:5-7) "It was Allah Who created you from dust, then from a seed, and Who then set you in pairs. No female conceives or gives birth without His knowing it; none is given long life and none is given short life, unless it be decreed. Verily that is easy for Allah." (35:12) "We have created man out of an extract of clay; when We made him a seed lodged in a secure place; We made the seed a clot of blood, and We created the clot a morsel. We created the morsel bones, and We clothed the bones with flesh. We made him grow as a new creation; blessed be Allah, the best of creators." (23:12-14)

The Qur'an goes on to repeat this teaching in many places to impress on the mind of man the oneness of his origin and his growth. The human race as a whole is made from dust and the individual—every individual—from lowly water. And the Prophet repeats this truth in the Traditions: "Each of you is man; and man is of dust." Thus awareness of the truth is reinforced in man's awareness and perceptions.

When it is thus denied that one individual can be intrinsically superior to another, it follows that there can be no race or people that is superior by reason of its origin or its nature. Yet there are some races that to the present day insist that there does exist such a superiority. There cannot be: "O ye people, reverence your Lord who created you from one soul, creating from it its mate; and He spread abroad from these two many men and women." (4:1) There was originally only one soul; from it came its mate; and from the two of them there spread abroad both men and women. So all are of one origin, all are brothers in descent, all are equal in origin and nature. "O ye people, We created you male and female, and We made you peoples and tribes, that you might know one another. Verily the noblest among you is the most pious." (49:13) These peoples and tribes were not made for the purpose of rivalry or enmity, but for that of mutual knowledge and friendliness; all of them in the eyes of Allah are equal, and there can be no superiority except in piety. But this is another question, unconnected with origin and nature; in these respects, "People are all equal as the teeth of a comb," as says the noble Prophet of Islam.

This equality extends its compass over all mankind and transcends both patriotism and religion; for, since the Messenger said, "All Muslims are of one blood," Islam grants polytheists rights of blood equivalent to those enjoyed by Believers—so long as there is a compact between them and the Muslims. "Whoever kills a Believer by mistake, the penalty is to set free one Believing slave, and to deliver the blood money to the dead man's family—unless they give it as alms. If the killer is of a people who are at enmity with you, but is himself a Believer, then he must set free a Believing slave. If he is of a people with whom you have a compact, then he must deliver the blood money, and set free a Believing slave." (4:94) Thus, the atonement to be made by a polytheist killer whose people have a compact with the Muslims is exactly the same as that to be made by a Muslim killer. The same tendency to equality is shown by the fact that Islam fixes the atonement for an accidental killing as the liberation of a slave; this indicates that it regards freeing a slave as a means of giving life to a soul. Thus this new life is given in exchange for the life which has been taken by the accidental killing; for in the eyes of Islam slavery is akin to death, while emancipation is akin to life.

As for deliberate murder in vengeance or in hatred, the principle is "A life for a life"; and there is no difference between a prince and a pauper, a seigneur and a slave. The Messenger said: "Him who killed his slave we have killed; him who mutilated his slave we have mutilated; him who gelded his slave we have gelded."

Thus Islam was freed from the conflict of tribal and racial loyalties, and thus it achieved an equality which civilization in the West has not gained to this day. It is a civilization which permits the American conscience to acquiesce in the systematic eradication of the Red Indian race, an eradication that is being organized in the sight and hearing of all states. It permits also the South African government to introduce racial laws which discriminate against people of color and the governments of Russia, China, and India to massacre Muslims.

Islam follows up any suspicion of discrimination between men or of superiority of one over another; no matter what its form or guise, no matter what its cause, Islam condemns it. Even in the case of the Prophet Muhammad, the Qur'an constantly reminds his people that he is human like the remainder of mankind; and Muhammad himself reiterates the same fact; he was a prophet, loved and respected by his people, yet always afraid that that love and respect might be led to make him preeminent or superior to others. So here he is, telling his people: "Do not venerate me, as the Christians venerate Jesus, son of Mary; I am only a servant of Allah, and His Messenger." Or again, when he comes into a meeting in which all present rise to their feet out of respect for him, he says: "Whoever takes pleasure in men standing to greet him, let him take his seat in hellfire." And when Muhammad's kinsfolk thought that as a Messenger he would raise their status or their rank and would confer on them a form of aristocracy above the ordinary, Muhammad refused them everything of that kind, save the nobility of good works; and he said to them plainly: "If my people cannot approach me through their good works, shall you, then, approach me through your genealogies? Verily the noblest of you in the sight of Allah is the most pious." So if Muhammad's family enjoyed no superiority except that of good works to raise them above the level of the people, no one ever can enjoy such a superiority. And again, when Muhammad was accosted by the blind man, when he turned away from the poor man, Ibn Umm Maktum, to pay attention to al-Walid ibn al-Mughira, who was the chief of his people, there came swiftly upon him a stern reproof which was almost a condemnation; thus he was brought back to recognize the absolute equality and complete parity of all men. Or when some of the rich nobles looked with contempt on marriage for themselves or for their families with poor men or women, there came the command of Allah: "Settle the unwed among you in marriage, and those who are upright among your male and female slaves. If they are poor, Allah will enrich them of His bounty; Allah is generous and wise." (24:32)

❖ ❖ ❖ ❖ ❖ ❖ ❖

As for the relation between the sexes, Islam has guaranteed to women a complete equality with men with regard to their sex; it has permitted no discrimination except in some incidental matters connected with physical capacity, with customary procedure, or with responsibility, in all of which the human status of the two sexes is not in question. Wherever the physical endowments, the customs, and the responsibilities are identical, the sexes are equal; and wherever there is some difference in these respects, the discrimination follows that difference.

In the spiritual and religious sphere men and women are equal. "Whoever does good works, man or woman, and is a Believer—such shall enter into Paradise and shall not be wronged one jot." (4:123) "Whoever does good works, man or woman, and is a Believer—We shall make them live a good life, and We shall give them their reward for the best that they have done." (16:99) "Then their Lord answered them: I shall not waste the work of any one of you who works, male or female; you belong to one another." (3:193)

Or again in the sphere of possessing and administering money they are equal. "Men shall have a portion of what their parents and their near relatives leave; and women shall have a portion of what their parents and their near relatives leave." (4:8) "Men shall have a portion of what they have gained; and women shall have a portion of what they have gained." (4:36)

In the case of the law about a man getting double the share of a woman in an inheritance, the reason is to be found in the responsibility which a man carries in life. He marries a woman and he undertakes to maintain her and their children; he has to bear the responsibility of the whole structure of the family. So it is no more than his right that for this reason, if for no other, he should have the share of two women. The woman, on the other hand, if she is married, has her livelihood guaranteed through what her husband gives her; if she remains unmarried or if she is widowed, her provision is made from what she inherits. So the question here is one of difference in responsibility, which necessitates a similar difference in the law of inheritance.

Or there is the case of men being overseers over women. "Men are overseers over women because of what Allah has bestowed of His bounty on one more than another, and because of what they have contributed in the way of wealth." (4:38) The reason for this discrimination lies in physical endowment and in use and wont in the matter of oversight. Because a man is free from the cares of maternity, he can attend to the affairs of society over considerable periods and can apply to these affairs all his intellectual powers. On the other hand, a woman is preoccupied for most of her life by the cares of family. The result is that these responsibilities promote in women a growth in the direction of the emotions and the sentiments, while in men growth is promoted in the direction of reflection and thought. So when man is made to oversee woman, it is by reason of physical nature and custom that this ordinance stands. Besides which, the man has the financial responsibility, and the economic sphere is closely linked with that of oversight, which is essentially the acceptance of responsibility. Ultimately, the fundamental point here is one of the balance of privileges and responsibilities in the sphere of the sexes and in that of life as a whole. "The same is due to women as is due from them; but men have a precedence over them." (2:228) This "precedence" is the oversight, the reasons for which we have demonstrated.

Again, there appears to be an instance of discrimination in the question of the giving of evidence. "Call two of your men as witnesses; or if there are not two men, then call one man and two women from those on whom you agree among the people who are present. So if one of the women goes astray, the other may remind her." (2:282) In this verse itself the explanation is made clear; by the nature of her family duties the growth of the woman's spirit is towards emotions and sentiments, just as in man it is towards contemplation and thought, as we have already said. So when she is forgetful or when she is carried away by her feelings, the other will be there to remind her. Thus the question in this case is one of the practical considerations of life rather than one of the inherent superiority of one sex to the other or of a lack of equality.

But the strongest point in Islam is the equality that it guarantees to women in religion as well as in their property and earnings. Also, it gives them the assurance of marriage only with their own consent and at their own pleasure, without any compulsion or negligence; and they must get a dowry. "And give them their stipulated price." (4:28) They must also have all other marital rights, whether they be married or divorced: "Retain them honorably, or send them away honorably. Do not retain them by compulsion in order to transgress." (2:231) "Associate honorably with them." (4:23)

We must notice that Islam guarantees these rights to women and gives them full enjoyment of these privileges in a sincerely humane spirit that is not influenced by the pressure of economic or material interests. Islam declared war on the idea that a girl child was a disaster and that she was better put away while she was still an infant; it was implacably opposed to the custom of burying daughters alive, which was current in the life of some of the Arabian tribes. It fought this custom in the sincerely humane spirit in which it looks at mankind, and it stringently prohibited such murder altogether and without exception. "Do not kill the person whom Allah has forbidden, without justification." (6:152) It specifically forbids the killing of children, though the only children who were killed were the girls: "Do not kill your children out of fear of poverty; We will provide for them and for you." (17:33) In this verse, providing for the children is mentioned first because they are the cause of the fear of poverty; thus it fills the heart of the father with trust in the provision of Allah and in His caring for the children even more than the father. Then as the instincts of justice and mercy gain force, He says concerning the Day of Resurrection, "And when the girl child buried alive shall be asked for what fault she was killed." (81:8-9) So He poses in this passage a clear and decisive question for that terrible Day.

Thus Islam, in granting to women their full spiritual and material privileges, had regard to their human nature and was acting in conformity with its own belief in the unity of mankind. "He created you from one soul, and He created from it its mate to dwell with it." (7:189) Islam's aim was to raise women in status to the point where they would be of necessity half of the one single "soul." For this reason it grants to women, besides the right of spiritual faith and that of material independence, the right of intellectual achievement; more—it makes it obligatory for them. "The search for knowledge is incumbent upon all Muslims, men and women."[8] Similarly, it grants to women the right to pay the *zakat*; more—it lays it down as their duty; for payment of the tax is obligatory for them as it is for men. In the giving of alms also they have the same part as men; "Verily men and women who give alms, and who have lent to Allah a fair loan—they will be recompensed double." (57:17) We must also remember this about Islam—and in its favor—that the freedom that the materialistic West grants to women does not flow from this noble and humane source; nor are its objectives the pure objectives of Islam. It is well not to forget history and not to be led astray by the misleading appearances of this present age. It is well to remember that the West brought women out of the home to work only because their menfolk shrank from the responsibility of keeping them and caring for them although the price was the chastity and honor of woman. Thus and only thus were women compelled to work.

It is to be remembered also that when women did emerge to work, the materialistic West exploited the opportunity presented by a surplus of labor to pay them lower wages; thus employers were able to dispense with men in favor of women, who were cheaper to pay, because the men were beginning to raise their heads and demand their true value. So when women in the West came to demand equality with men, it was first and most essentially an equality of wages that they wanted, so that they might be able to eat and to support life. When they could not gain this form of equality they demanded the right of the franchise, so that they might have a voice to speak for them. And finally they demanded access to parliaments, so that they might have the necessary representation when their equality was being established.

It is well to bear in mind also that down to the time of the Fourth Republic France has not granted to women the right of administering their property—a right which Islam does allow—except by the consent of a guardian. Yet at the same time France grants to women the right of every kind of unchastity, public or private. This "privilege" is the only one which Islam denies to its womenfolk, just as it also denies it to men; thus it guards the honor and the instincts of man, raising sexual relationships above a purely physical level and making them the essential foundation of the family.

And while today we watch the materialistic West preferring women to men in some professions, particularly in commerce, in embassies, in consulates, and in information services such as newspapers and the like, we must not forget the regrettable and unsavory significance of this advancement. It is a form of slavery and servitude in an atmosphere of the smoke of incense and opium. It is the exploitation of the sex instinct of customers by the merchants; and similarly the government appoints women to embassies and consulates, and newspaper editors send women to glean news and information. All of them are merely attempting to make use of women and they know what success a woman can have in these fields. They know, too, what she must give to achieve her success. And even if she gives nothing—which is unlikely—they know what hungry passions and eager eyes encompass her body and her words. But they take advantage of women's hunger for material gain and for some slight success; for humane and noble feelings are far, far from them. As for Communism, it has a wide claim to uphold the equality of women with men; its equality is that of work and that of pay. But when there is equality of work and pay, women become free, and they gain also the right of license, just the same as men. Because in Communism generally the question does not go beyond the sphere of money; whereas in reality all the desires of man and all the instincts of human nature are involved in this one aspect of life. The essential fact is that men refused to support women and hence women were compelled to work like men and in masculine circles in order to live. Thus it is that Communism is the natural and logical outcome of the spirit of the materialistic West—at least in this respect; for the spirit of the West lacks the generous and humane aspects of true human life.

All these things must be borne in mind before the false flame blinds our eyes; Islam has for fourteen centuries granted to women privileges which France has only just granted them. It has always granted them the right to work and the right to earn, which Communism now grants them. But it retains for them the primary duty of upholding the family circle and that for several reasons. In the Islamic view, life is more than merely economic or physical and in itself can offer higher objectives than food and drink. Again, Islam looks at life from many sides and envisages for individuals duties that differ one from the other, but that are all mutually connected and ordered; within this scheme are envisaged the respective duties of men and women, and it lays on each of them the charge of fulfilling a duty primarily towards the growth and the advancement of life as a whole; and it ordains for each of them his guaranteed privileges in order to ensure this universal and humane aim.

✤ ✤ ✤ ✤ ✤ ✤ ✤

And finally the whole human race has a nobility which cannot allowably be lessened. "And We have ennobled the sons of Adam; We have carried them by land and sea, and have given them their provision of good things. We have given them preference over much of that which We have created." (17:72) We have ennobled them, that is, by their nature, and not by their persons or their races or their tribes. And that nobility attaches to all men, with absolute equality, for all alike are Man. It was Man who came of dust; it was Man who was ennobled; therefore all the sons of Man are equal in every respect.

Thus, all alike have a nobility which must not be degraded, and at which none may scoff. "O ye who have believed, let not one people mock another, who are possibly better than themselves. And let not women mock other women, who are possibly better than themselves. Do not scoff at one another, or shame one another with nicknames; it is bad to get the name of evil conduct when you are a Believer; and those who do not repent are evildoers." (49:11) The complete and far-reaching point of the verse is: "Do not scoff at one another." For when a man scoffs at his neighbor he scoffs at himself, for all men come of one soul.

So all men have protracted areas of privacy! "O ye who have believed, do not go into houses other than your own, until you are received as friends and have greeted the inmates. That is better for you; perhaps you will remember. If you find no one at home, do not go in until you receive permission; and if you are told to go away, then go away; that is more innocent for you, and Allah knows what you do." (24:27-28) "Do not spy into one another's affairs, and do not indulge in backbiting against one another." (49:12) The value of these regulations is to make every individual aware that he has a certain sanctity that must not be violated by others; the sanctity of one man is no less than that of another. In this respect also they are equal and all are trusted.

❖ ❖ ❖ ❖ ❖ ❖ ❖

Thus Islam deals with every aspect of human life, spiritual and social alike, in order to firmly establish the concept of equality. There was in fact no need for it to discuss equality verbally and formally for it has already established it in fact and in spirit, through the complete freedom of the conscience from all artificial values, from all outward appearances, and from all material necessities. It has an intense passion for equality; it demands that it be universal and complete, not limited to one race or one nation, to one house or one city. Similarly it demands that equality embrace a wider sphere than merely the economic, to which the teachings of the material West have confined it.

MUTUAL RESPONSIBILITY IN SOCIETY

No form of life can be satisfactory in which every individual is bent on the enjoyment of his absolute freedom without bounds or limits. Such freedom he might be led to expect by his belief in the absolute equality that exists between himself and all other individuals, in respect of all his privileges; but such an expectation is responsible for the destruction not only of society, but also of the individual himself. For there is the important matter of the supreme welfare of society, short of which the freedom of the individual must stop; there is also the private welfare of the individual himself, which entails his giving up his enjoyment of freedom at certain specific limits. Thus, on the one hand, he may not allow himself to be carried to extremes by his passions and appetites and pleasures; and on the other hand, his freedom may not conflict with that of others. For when this latter takes place, it produces unending disputes and makes liberty an unendurable burden; through it the growth and improvement of life are checked by the claims of individual welfare, which is a much narrower interest.

Islam grants individual freedom in the most perfect form and human equality in the most exact sense, but it does not leave these two things uncontrolled; society has its interests, human nature has its claims, and a value also attaches to the lofty aims of religion. So Islam sets the principle of individual responsibility over against that of individual freedom; and beside them both it sets the principle of social responsibility, which makes demands alike on the individual and on society. This is what we call mutual responsibility in society.

Islam lays down the principle of mutual responsibility in all its various shapes and forms. In it we find the responsibilities which exist between a man and his own person, between a man and his immediate family, between the individual and society, between one community and other communities, and between one generation and the other generations that succeed it.

We have the responsibilities which a man has to himself. He must restrain himself from being carried away by his appetites, and he must cleanse and purify these appetites; he must make them follow the path of righteousness and salvation and must not let them go down in degradation. "As for him who has been presumptuous and has sought the life of the world, verily Hell will be his place. But as for him who has feared the greatness of his Lord and has restrained himself from desire, verily Paradise will be his place." (79:37-41) "By a soul and what formed it, made it aware of its wickedness and its piety, he who purifies it prospers, while he who corrupts it fails." (91:7-10) "Do not hand yourselves over to destruction." (2:191) But at the same time man is charged to enjoy himself within those boundaries which will not admit the corruption of his nature; he must give himself his due, both of work and of rest, and he may not exhaust or weaken himself. "Through what Allah has given you seek the future abode, without forgetting your part in this world." (28:77) "O ye sons of Adam, take your adornment in every mosque; eat and drink, but be not immoderate; verily He does not love those who are immoderate." (7:29) "Verily you have a duty to your body."[9]

Thus individual responsibility is complete; every man has his own works, every man is responsible for what he does to his soul, good or evil, benefit or harm; and in his place no other can ever stand, either in this world or in the next. "Each soul is held in pledge by what it has gained." (74:41) "Or has he not been told of what is in the pages of Moses, and of Abraham, who fulfilled his task? That no burden-bearer can bear the burden of another; that man gets no more that he has striven for; that the result of his striving will be seen; and that then he will be fully recompensed." (53:37-42) "What it (i.e., the soul) has gained stands to its credit, and what it has piled up stands against it." (2:286) "Whoever is rightly guided, that is of profit to himself; and whoever goes astray, he does so to his own loss; you are not in charge of them." (39:42) "And he who acquires guilt acquires it only against himself." (4:111)

According to all this, man is ever a watcher over his own soul, to guide it if it goes astray, and to ensure for it its legitimate rights, to call it to account if it sins, and to bear responsibility for neglecting it. In all this Islam postulates two personalities in each individual, keeping watch on one another and observing one another, responsible, the one to the other, for the good or the evil which they share. This fact lies over against the other fact that Islam gives complete freedom of conscience to this individual and complete equality with others; but freedom and responsibility are mutually compatible and mutually necessary.

We have also a mutual responsibility between the individual and his immediate family. "And use kindness with parents; whether one or both of them attain to old age with you, do not say to them, 'Bah'; do not rebuke them, but speak them fair. Lower the wing of humility to them in mercy, and say: 'O my Lord, have mercy upon them, as they brought me up when I was little." (17:24-25) "And We have laid a charge on man concerning his parents; his mother bore him in weakness upon weakness, and he was

weaned in two years. Show gratitude to Me and to your parents."
(31:13) "But blood relations are nearer to each other in the Book
of Allah." (33:6) "Mothers shall suckle their children two full
years, where it is desired that the period of suckling be complete;
and the man to whom the child was born must feed and clothe
them both suitably." (2:233)

The value of this responsibility within the family circle is that
it is the basis on which the family stands and the family is the basic
unit on which society is built; hence there must be a regard for its
value. It rests on the permanent characteristics of human nature,
on the emotions of pity and love, and on the demands of necessity
and welfare. Thus it is the nest in which and around which are produced all the morals and the manners that are peculiar to the
human race; these are essentially the morals of society, which is
raised by them above the license of the animals and above the
anarchy of a rabble.

Communism has sought to condemn the family on the plea
that it fosters ideas that are essentially selfish and produces the
love of private ownership; so Communism itself forbids wealth,
being the control of private individuals by the state. But so far as
may be seen, Communism has failed completely in this matter; for
the Russian people is a domestically inclined people, in whose life
and in whose history the family has a large place. Further, the family is a biological and a psychological institution as well as a social
institution and the idea that a woman should belong exclusively to
one man is biologically sound and is conducive to the reproduction
of healthy children. It has been noted that a woman who is shared
by a number of men becomes barren after a certain time or produces unhealthy children. From the personal point of view the feelings of love and compassion grow better in the atmosphere of the
family than under any other form of institution and the growth of
personality is more complete in the family circle than under any
other form of institution. Tests carried out during the last war
among children in nurseries proved that the child whose upbringing is in the hands of a succession of nurses lacks personality and
has no self-control; nor has he the normal growth of the feelings of
love and affection. So, too, the child who has no father has to

struggle against a feeling of inferiority; from this hard reality he escapes by inventing a father who does not exist, a father to whom he can go in imagination and whom he invents in various shapes and forms.[10]

But biological and psychological factors are not the only ones; we have here also the questions of need and welfare which bind a man and a woman together to set up a home and to rear children. There are also the ties that unite the individuals of one family and make them a social unit; this unit relies upon its own members in good or in ill, and its members are mutually responsible in work and in reward for one generation after another.

Another of the aspects of family responsibility in Islam is the law of material inheritance of property, which is detailed in the following two verses: "With regard to your children Allah commands you thus: The males shall have the portion of two females; if the children are all female, and more than two in number, then they shall have two thirds of what their father has left; if there is only one, then she shall have a half. Each of a man's parents shall have one-sixth of what he has left, if he had any children; but if he had no children and his parents are his heirs, then his mother shall have a third. If he had brothers, then his mother shall have a sixth—after any bequests have been made and any debts paid. Whether your fathers or your sons bring you more advantage you do not know. This is an ordinance from Allah; verily Allah is understanding, wise. You shall have half of what your wives leave, if they had no children; but if they had children, then a quarter of what they left shall be yours, after any bequests have been made and any debts paid. Your wives shall have a quarter of what you leave, if you have no children; if you have children, your wives shall have an eighth of what you leave, after any bequests have been made and any debts paid." (4:12-14) "They ask you for a decision; say: Allah gives you a decision about distant relations. If a man dies, leaving no children, and if he has a sister, then she shall have half of what he leaves; and he shall be her heir if she has no children. If there are two sisters, then they shall have two-thirds of what he leaves. If there is a family, both male and female, then the male shall have the portion of two females. Allah makes it clear for

you, lest you fall into error; Allah has knowledge of all things."
(4:175) Concerning the bequest which is the subject of the first
two verses, He has explained it by saying: "A command is prescribed for you when one of you is near to death and has property
to leave; he must make a declaration, leaving a suitable amount to
his parents and his near kin. This is a duty upon all who are pious."
(2:176) This bequest cannot exceed one-third of the estate after the
payment of debts, and it does not apply to the principal heir;
"There can be no bequest for the heir."[11] This legislation is aimed
only at obviating conditions under which the proper person may
not inherit the kinship gift that the testator wished to give and
bequeath to him. It is aimed also at making available from the
legacy some money for spending for charitable and pious purposes.
Thus this ordinance enacted by Islam is one of the aspects of the
mutual responsibility that connects the individual members of the
same family and successive generations. It is also one of the means
of distributing property, so that it may not become too great and
prove injurious to society. A discussion of this will follow in the
chapter on economic theory. As far as we are concerned here, we
need only say that the Islamic law of inheritance is an equitable
balance between effort and reward, between credits and debits,
within the family circle. The parent who works knows that the
fruit of his labors will not be realized in the short and limited span
of his own life, but will stretch forward to be enjoyed by his children and his grandchildren, who are his natural successors in life.
Such a parent will give of his very best and produce as much as he
can by which the welfare of the state and of the human race as a
whole is served. And besides, there is here an equal balance
between the effort which he puts forth and the reward which he
receives. For as his children are a part of himself, he knows that in
them his life is perpetuated.

On the children's side it is but right that they should profit
from the efforts of their fathers and their mothers; for the connection between parents and children would not be broken even if the
connection in property inheritance were broken. Parents bequeath
to their children traits and endowments in their physical and mental composition; and these qualities remain with them all their lives

and to a great extent determine the course of their future, either for good or for evil. And children have no power either to refuse or to nullify this legacy. However much the state or society tries to give a handsome appearance to a child to whom his parents have bequeathed an ugly appearance, it will be unable to do so; he cannot be given physical health or strength of constitution, because his parents may have given him only weakness and trouble; he cannot be given long life or ample health, because his parents have bequeathed to him only a tendency to swift decay or chronic illness. Therefore, if he must of necessity inherit all this, then it is only his right in society to inherit also the material possessions of his parents; thus there may be some fair balance between credits and debits in his case.

The Qur'an coins a parable of the mutual responsibility of fathers and children, when it tells the story of Moses and "one of Our servants upon whom We had bestowed mercy from Us, and whom We had taught knowledge from Us.. . . . And the two of them set out and travelled until they came to the people of a town. From these people they asked food, but they refused to entertain them. In the town they found a wall which was ready to fall down, and Moses' companion set it up. Moses said to him, 'If you had wished, you could have claimed a wage for that.' But the people of the town still would not give them food . . . .Then his companion explained to Moses his secret reason for setting up the wall, saying, 'As for the wall, it belonged to two orphan youths in the town, and under it was a treasure belonging to them. Their father was a worthy man, and your Lord wished that they might reach full age before finding out their treasure as a mercy from your Lord." (18:59-81) Thus the two sons profited from the virtue of their father and inherited what he left to them, both in the way of property and in the way of virtue. That this is just there can be no doubt.

But when there is a fear that property may be kept in a narrow circle, then the remedy is at hand for the state to set things right. This rectification Islam provides for in its own particular way, as we shall see in the chapter on economic theory.

❖ ❖ ❖ ❖ ❖ ❖ ❖

We must think also of the responsibility which the individual has to society and of that which society has to the individual. On each of these two Islam lays responsibilities, and for each of them it defines the limits to which he may go. In dealing with these responsibilities Islam tries as far as possible to harmonize their interests and to remedy or to punish any loss which either of them may suffer in undertaking the duties which attach to the various fields of life, spiritual and material alike.

Every individual is charged in the first place conscientiously to perform his own work; for the results of individual work are in the long run advantageous and beneficial to the community. "Verily Allah is glad when one of you does work which he performs well."[12] "Say: Work and Allah will see your work, as will His Messenger and the Believers." (9:106)

Again, every individual is charged with the welfare of society, as if he were a watchman over it, responsible for its safety: "Yours is the care of one of the frontiers of Islam, so let none overcome you."[13] Life is like a ship at sea whose crew are all concerned for her safety; none of them may make a hole even in his own part of her in the name of his individual freedom. "Verily some people travelled in a ship, and they were partners, of whom each one had his own place. One man among them struck his place with an axe, and the remainder said to him, 'What are you doing?' He said, 'This is my place, and I can do what I wish in it.' Then if they restrain him, he and they are safe, but if they let him be, he and they all perish."[14] This is a striking picture of the way in which the various interests are inextricably bound up together; over against it stands the selfish outlook that takes account only of the outward appearance of actions, without reckoning their results in practical terms. So here we have an exact indication of what the individual must do and what the community must do in cases such as this.

No individual, then, can be exempt from this care for the general interest, but every one must have a constant care for the community. "Everyone of you is a shepherd, and everyone of you will be held responsible for his flock."[15]

Similarly, the welfare of the community must be promoted by

mutual help among individuals—always within the limits of honesty and uprightness. "Help one another in virtue and piety, but do not help one another in sin and hostility." (5:3) "Let there be a community of you exhorting to good, urging to virtue, and restraining from evil-doing." (3:100) Each individual will be held personally responsible for having urged to virtue; and if he has not done so, then he is a sinner and will be accountable for his sin. "Take him and chain him; then roast him in Hell; then thrust him into a chain of seventy cubits' length. Verily he would not believe in Allah the Great; he would not urge the feeding of the poor. So he has no friend here today, nor any food save foul corruption which only sinners eat." (69:30-37) Not having urged to feed the poor will be accounted one of the signs of unbelief and of repudiation of the faith. "Have you seen him who repudiates the faith? He it is who repulses the orphan and does not urge the feeding of the poor." (107:1-3)

Every individual, again, is charged with the duty of putting an end to any evildoing which he sees. "Whoever among you sees any evildoing, let him change it with his hand; if he cannot do that, let him change it with his tongue; and if he cannot do that, let him change it with his heart; and that is the minimum faith requires."[16] Thus, every individual will be held responsible for every evildoing in the community, even if he has had no part in it. For society is a unity that is harmed by any evildoing, and the duty of every individual is to guard and to protect it.

The whole community is to blame and merits injury and punishment in this world and in the world to come if it passively accepts evildoing in its midst by some of its members. Thus it is charged with the duty of watching over every one of its members. "When We wish to destroy a town We command its luxury-loving citizens, and they deal corruptly in it; thus the sentence upon it is justified, and We destroy it." (17:17) Even though the majority of the people in it were not corrupt, but merely accepted the corruption passively, He still counted their destruction justifiable. "And fear a trial which will not fall only upon those of you who have done wrong." (8:25) There is no injustice in this, for the community in which there is an immoral element and in which evildoing flourishes unchecked is a community which is exhausted and decayed, on the way to its end. The ruin which will overtake it is a natural fate, brought on by its own condition.

So the Children of Israel merited the curse which their prophets laid upon them; their kingdom declined and their spirit left them because they would not change the wrongdoing in their midst, nor did they restrain one another from it. "Those of the Children of Israel who became unbelievers were cursed by the tongue of David and of Jesus, son of Mary. That was because they rebelled and transgressed; they did not restrain one another from evildoing, but practiced it. Bad indeed is what they were doing." (5:82) Or again in the Traditions: "When the Children of Israel fell away into rebellion, their wise men rebuked them, but they would not desist. They sat in company with the evildoers in their assemblies, and they ate and drank with them. So Allah struck the hearts of some of them with others. He cursed them in the words of David and of Jesus, son of Mary, because they rebelled and were hostile." As for the Believers, on the other hand, they are of the number of those of whom the Qur'an says: "And the believing men and women are friends one of the other; they urge to virtue, and they restrain from evildoing." (9:72)

Now concerning the verse: " O you who believe, look after yourselves; he who goes astray will not harm you, so long as you let yourselves be guided." (5:104), some have argued that this verse justifies an abstention from combatting wrongdoing and from changing it. But Abu Bakr (Allah be pleased with him) reminds them that this is a mistaken interpretation. He said: "O people, you read this verse, and you put a wrong construction on it. I myself have heard the Messenger of Allah say: 'Verily people who see wrongdoing and do not change it despite their ability to do so—Allah will speedily bring punishment upon all of them.'" This is the true interpretation, which is in conformity with the aims of Islam. For what this verse actually contains is a statement of individual responsibility. Wickedness, which is negative and which has no positive aspect, is a matter which concerns only him who indulges in it; but it is the duty of others to seek to guide him; if the sinner does not respond, the responsibility is his alone.

The community is also responsible for the care of its weak members; it must watch their welfare and guard them; it has also the duty of fighting in defense of those whom it guards. "It is not for you to refuse to fight in the cause of Allah and in defense of the weak, men, women, and children." (4:77) It must also guard the property of the young until they attain to years of discretion. "Make trial of the orphans until they reach the age of marriage; then if you perceive discretion in them, hand over their property to them. Do not eat it up in extravagance before they grow up. Let him who is rich restrain himself from touching any of it, and let him who is poor use a reasonable amount of it. When you hand over their property to them have witnesses present for them. Allah is sufficient as a reckoner." (4:5-7) Or in the Traditions: "He who strives on behalf of the widows or the poor is like one who fights in the cause of Allah, or like one who rises to pray by night and fasts by day."

The community is responsible for the provision of a competence for its poor and destitute members; it has the care of the money from the *zakat* and of its expenditure on various objects. If this is not enough, the rich are obliged to contribute as much as will meet the wants of the needy; there is no restriction and no condition, except that there shall be a sufficiency. If any individual pass the night hungry, the blame attaches to the community because it did not bestir itself to feed him. "Nay, but you do not honor the orphan, nor do you urge the feeding of the poor; you eat up the inheritance altogether, and you love wealth with an excessive love. Nay, but when the earth is ground down, down, when your Lord comes with the angels rank upon rank, when Hell is brought forth—then indeed man would let himself be reminded; but whence shall he find the reminder? He will say: 'Would that I had sent forward good works during my life.' On that day no one will punish as He punishes, and none will bind as He binds." (89:18-26) Or again in the Traditions: "Whatever people suffer knowingly that a man remain hungry among them, the protection of Allah is taken from them—Blessed and Great is He." And: "He who has an abundance of profit, let him use it on behalf of him who has none." And: "He who has food for two, let him take a third man with him; and he who has food for three, let him take a fourth." And: "He has no faith in Me, who sleeps replete, while his neighbor beside him is hungry, and he is aware of the fact." Where neighborliness is concerned, prosperity obliges a man even to give away one garment out of two. So the story goes that a man came to the Prophet and said to him, "Give me clothing, O Messenger of Allah." He turned away from him, not having the means to comply, and the man said again, "Give me clothing, O Messenger of Allah." Muhammad replied: "Have you no neighbor who has more garments than he needs?" "Certainly I have. More than one." Then said Muhammad: "Then let Allah not put both you and him in Paradise."

The whole Islamic community is one body, and it feels all things in common; whatever happens to one of its members, the remainder of the members are also affected. This is the beautiful, vivid simile which the noble Messenger uses of it when he says: "The likeness of the Believers in their mutual love and mercy and relationship is that of the body; when one member is afflicted, all the rest of the body joins with it to suffer feverish sleeplessness." In the same way he portrays the mutual help and responsibility between one Believer and another in a second finely expressed description: "One Believer strengthens another as one building strengthens another. " And this is the best possible description of the power of mutual help and responsibility in life.

On this foundation the laws against social crimes are firmly built, because mutual help cannot exist except on the basis of the safety of a man's life, property, and honor. "Every Muslim is sacrosanct to a fellow-Muslim—his blood, his honor, and his property." Thus the penalty for killing or wounding is laid down as an exact equivalent: "Free man for free man, slave for slave, female for female." (2:173) The crime of murder is reckoned as equal in punishment to that of unbelief; "Whoever kills a Believer intentionally, his punishment is Hell, and there shall he continue." (4:95) "Do not kill the person whom Allah has made inviolate, except for some justifiable cause; if anyone is unjustly killed, We have given authority to his kinsman." (17:35) "We have prescribed a law for them in this matter; a life for a life, an eye for an eye, a nose for a nose, an ear for an ear, a tooth for a tooth, and for wounds the equivalent." (5:49) He emphasizes the retaliation, seeing in it the life of the community: "In this retaliation there is life for you, O ye who have understanding; perhaps you may be pious." (2:175) And in fact it does mean life; for it safeguards life by discouraging murder and because it preserves the vitality and the power of the life of society.

The punishment for fornication, again, is severe, because it involves an attack on honor and a contempt for sanctity and an encouragement of profligacy in society. From it by a gradual process there come license, the obscurity of family ties, and the loss of those essential feelings of fatherhood and sonship. The penalty for this must be severe; for married men and women it is stoning to death; for unmarried men and women it is flogging, a hundred lashes, which in cases is fatal. "The man or woman guilty of fornication shall be flogged with a hundred lashes; and let no pity for them affect you in the faith of Allah." (24:2)

A punishment of eighty lashes is fixed for those who falsely accuse chaste women, Believers who have been innocently careless; such men are cowardly and falsely impugn the women's honor. In this case the crime of falsehood is closely akin to that of immorality, for it is an attack on reputation and honor, an incitement to hatred and bitterness and dissemination of vice. "As for those who cast imputations on chaste women and then cannot bring four witnesses, flog them with eighty lashes, and never again accept evidence from them." (24:4)

The punishment for theft is likewise severe, because it is an offense against men's sense of security and mutual trust; it is fixed at the cutting off of a hand; for a second offense the other hand is cut off, for a third offense a foot, and then the other foot. "As for the thief, man or woman, cut off their hands as a recompense for what they have piled up—a chastisement from Allah." (5:42)

There are some today who profess to find this a shocking punishment for the theft of property from an individual; but Islam looks at the matter only from the point of view of the safety, the security, and the stability of society. So, too, it has regard to the nature of the circumstances of a crime. This is a crime which is committed secretly; such secret crimes have need of stern punishments, firstly to punish the criminal adequately, and secondly to make him an example through his suffering and his fear of the punishment. And in addition, this stern penalty is not exacted in full if the theft was committed under compulsion, such as the need to ward off the evil of hunger from oneself or from one's children. The general rule is that no guilt attaches to things done under compulsion. "He who is under compulsion, who acts against his will and not of malice, has committed no crime." Thus 'Umar enacted during his Caliphate, as we shall see.

As for those who threaten the general security of society, their punishment is to be put to death, to be crucified, to have their hands and feet cut off, or to be banished from the country. "The punishment of those who war on Allah and His Messenger and who strive to cause corruption in the land is to be put to death, to be crucified, to have their hands and feet cut off on opposite sides, or to be banished from the land." (5:37) For conspiring and coming together to cause corruption and disorder is a greater crime than individual crimes, and they justly merit being followed by a rigorous punishment.

❖ ❖ ❖ ❖ ❖ ❖ ❖

Thus Islam legislates for mutual responsibility in society in all shapes and forms; these forms take their rise from the basic principle that there is an all-embracing identity of purpose between the individual and society, and that life in its fullness is interrelated. So Islam lays down a complete liberty for the individual, within limits which will not injure him and will not damage society on his behalf. It safeguards the rights of society and at the same time specifies its responsibilities on the other side of the balance. Thus it enables life to progress on a level and even path and to attain to the highest ends which can be served by the individual and by society alike.

On these three foundations, then—an absolute freedom of conscience, a complete equality of all mankind, and a firm mutual responsibility in society—social justice is built up and human justice is ensured.

4 THE METHODS OF SOCIAL JUSTICE IN ISLAM

Islam operates on the inner, spiritual side of human nature, rather than on the external; it is from the depths of the conscience rather than on the surface that it seeks to reform man. But at the same time it is never unmindful of the practical situation in the realm of worldly life; it does not forget the true nature of the human spirit, nor the things that influence it for good or evil, for better or worse; it has a care both for the aspirations that soar aloft and for the material necessities which are chained to earth, for human strength that is ever limited and for the perfection that is always absolute. Thus because it has a profound knowledge of the depths of the human spirit, Islam makes use both of laws and of exhortations, it formulates commandments and prohibitions, it lays down limitations and enforces them. But it also encourages the human spirit to exceed such legal responsibilities as far as it can.

Life becomes possible and profitable only as we observe the lowest limit of the legal responsibilities of this faith; but even then it still lacks the perfection at which Islam aims, so long as it is not inspired by the prompting of conscience towards self-control, loftiness, and nobility. So in Islam this prompting of the conscience is complementary to all legal duties; conscience must reinforce these duties, making their performance a pleasure, and thus imparting to human life a value and a nobility which are above the range of compulsion.

When Islam seeks to establish a complete social justice, it sets it on a higher level than a mere economic justice and on a more elevated plane than can be attained merely by legislative measures;

thus it establishes a comprehensive human justice, established on two strong foundations: first, the human conscience, working within the spirit of man; and second, a system of law, working in the social sphere. These two powers it unites by an appeal to the depths of feeling in the human consciousness. "Verily in that there is a reminder for every one who has a heart, or who will lend an ear; he is a witness of it." (50:37) Islam does not overlook the weakness of man or his need for external restraint. As 'Uthman ibn 'Affan said: "Allah restrains man more by means of the ruler than by the means of the Qur'an."

Whoever examines this religion equitably and attentively will perceive the vast efforts it deploys to refine the human soul in all its aspects, dimensions, and dealings. It will be relevant to our subject to look briefly at these efforts, which aim at securing the welfare of society by instituting a permanent supremacy of the conscience rooted in awareness of practical, individual obligation.

Anyone who bestows even a passing and casual glance on this religion must perceive the immense effort that it devotes to the reformation of the human spirit in all its aspects and from every side. And it is not outside our subject to take a brief and summary look at this effort. It is designed for the good of society only to the point at which there can be a permanent control by human conscience; it works to guarantee all human society only until the individual becomes aware of his own practical obligations. "Do not play the spy, and do not backbite one another. Would one of you care to eat his dead brother's flesh? You would abhor it." (49:12) Spying is the worst crime against personal freedom and against the honor and privacy of the individual, just as backbiting is the worst characteristic which can find a lodgment in the weakness of personality; not only does it render a character incapable of praise, but it robs it eventually of all vital and practical courage. "O you who believe, do not go into houses other than your own, until you are received as friends and have greeted the inmates." (24:27) Individual honor must be respected because individual honor is the first requisite of social justice. "O you who have believed, let not one people mock another who are possibly better than themselves.

And let not women mock other women who are possibly better than themselves. Do not scoff at one another, nor shame one another with nicknames; it is bad to get the name of evil conduct when you are a Believer; and those who do not repent are evildoers." (49:11) Mocking one another and scoffing at one another and calling one another by unpleasant nicknames are things which are forbidden alike by the essential values of personality, by human equality, and by social justice. "And do not walk the earth in pride; verily you cannot rend the earth, nor can you reach the mountains in height." (17:39) Vanity and arrogance are characteristics which are unpopular in personality; similarly they are in opposition to the instinct for equality and justice and brotherhood. Islam is a religion in which the highest praise lavished on its Prophet is the verse, "Verily you are of a great character." (68:4) Character is the most essential foundation for the building of a firmly based society, for the joining of earth to Heaven, the temporal to the eternal in the human consciousness with all its finitude and its frailty.

Islam places a great deal of reliance on the human conscience once it is educated; it sets it up as the guardian of the legal processes to see that they are implemented and maintained, and for the observance of the major part of the laws to which conscience alone is accountable. The giving of evidence, for example, is the foundation for the implementation of legal penalties and for establishing certain rights of men; and the giving of evidence is a question that runs back to the individual conscience and to the dependence of society on that conscience. "As for those who cast imputations upon innocent women, and then do not bring four witnesses in corroboration, flog them with eighty lashes and never again accept evidence from them; they are those who deal corruptly." (24:4) "And as for those who cast imputations upon their wives and who have no witness but themselves—let the evidence of one of them be a fourfold testimony in the name of Allah that he is of those who speak the truth. And let the fifth testimony be to invoke the curse of Allah upon himself if he is of those who lie. And punishment may be averted from the woman if she testify four times in the name of Allah that the man is of those who lie; and the fifth testimony shall be to invoke the curse of Allah upon herself if she is not of those who speak the truth." (24:6-9) So, too, even where a written agreement is demanded, it must necessarily be witnessed. "O you who believe, when one of you contracts a debt to another for a stated time, write it down; let a scribe write it down between you justly; let not the scribe refuse to write as Allah has taught him, but let him write, and let the debtor dictate. Let him fear Allah his Lord, and let him not lessen the amount in any way. If the debtor is a fool, or if he is in weak health, or if he is unable to dictate, then let his kinsman dictate for him, justly. Then have the writing witnessed by two of your men; or if there are not two men, then by one man and two women out of those on whom you agree as witnesses; so if one of the women should err, the other may remind her." (2:282) The duty of witnessing is statutory and a matter of principle: "Let not witnesses refuse when they are called." (2:282) Similarly, the giving of evidence is a statutory responsibility in cases of legal dispute: "And do not conceal evidence; for whoever does so, his heart is guilty." (2:283) Thus Islam places reliance on the human conscience in penalties which go as far as flogging or stoning and in matters touching the rights of property. Such a reliance must necessarily ennoble human nature and raise it towards the level for which it longs and searches.

Islam does not leave the human conscience to its own resources; it allots to it these onerous duties, making it the guardian of the observance of the law and of the carrying out of human responsibilities and at the same time challenging it to rise above what law and responsibility prescribe for it. It has set the fear of Allah as a sanction on the conscience and has placed over it the thought of Allah's watchfulness, using uniquely vivid and effective images. "There is no private talk between three, but He makes a fourth, nor between five, but He makes a sixth; and whether there be less than that or more, He is always with them, wherever they are. Then on the Day of Resurrection He will tell them what they have done. Verily Allah is aware of all things." (58:8) "We have created man, and We know what his soul whispers within him; We are nearer to him than his jugular vein. When the two meet and sit, one on the right hand and one on the left, he cannot utter a word without a watcher being beside him, ready." (50:15-17) "Verily He knows what is secret and what is hidden." (20:6)

Thus Islam both gave glad tidings to men and warned them, taking into account not only in this world but also in the next every single human action for which there is no escaping punishment and no avoiding recompense. "We shall set up the balances of justice on the Day of Resurrection, and no soul will be wronged in the slightest degree; even if it is only the weight of a grain of mustard seed, We shall produce it; for We are sufficient as a reckoner." (21:48) "When the earth quakes with a great quaking; when the earth brings forth what has been buried in it; when man says 'What is the matter with it?'; on that day the earth shall tell her tidings, because your Lord has inspired her. On that day men shall come forward separately to see their works; whoever has done the weight of an atom of good shall see it; and whoever has done the weight of an atom of evil shall see it." (Sura 99) Thus runs the constant teaching of Islam, making reverence and piety a sanction upon the conscience; and thus it makes the human conscience the means of advancement by making it responsible for the observance of all that the faith lays down in the way of laws and duties.

✧ ✧ ✧ ✧ ✧ ✧ ✧

In this twofold way Islam proceeded to set the foundations of a social justice, and by this means it succeeded in producing a balanced and interrelated human justice. We shall examine some aspects of this justice in a future chapter; for the moment it will be sufficient to consider one example of this system of law and exhortation. We shall choose the subject of the *zakat* and the alms, because it has an intimate connection with the subject of this book.

Islam makes the *zakat* an obligatory claim on the property of the wealthy in favor of the poor. It is a due which the government can exact by the authority of the law and by the power of its administration; but the public conscience has progressively taken over the enforcement of the payment of this due until such payment has become a natural part of the will of those able to make it.

The *zakat* is one of the pillars of Islam, one of the essentials of the faith. "Prosperous are the Believers who are humble in their

prayers, who turn away from idle talk, and who are active in paying the *zakat*." (23:1-4) "These are the signs of the Qur'an, which is
a Book which makes clear, a guidance and a gospel for the Believers, who observe the prayers, who pay the *zakat*, and who are certain of the world to come." (27:1-3) On the other hand, the act of
withholding the *zakat* is a form of polytheism and of unbelief in the
world to come: "And woe to the polytheists who do not pay the
zakat and do not believe in the world to come." (41:5-6) But, payment of the *zakat* is a method of gaining the mercy of Allah:
"Observe the prayers, pay the *zakat*, and obey the Messenger; it
may be that you will receive mercy." (24:55) Help from Allah
comes to those who pay this due and who discharge their obligations to society, thus deserving to be firmly established in the earth.
"Allah will surely help the man who helps Him; verily Allah is
Powerful, Mighty. Such, if We establish them in the earth, will
observe the prayers, will pay the *zakat*, will urge to good and will
restrain from evil." (22:41-42)

The *zakat* is a human institution of long standing, advocated
by the commands of the prophets before Islam; thus there is no
religion devoid of this important social responsibility. "And make
mention in the Book of Ishmael; he was true to this promise, and
was a messenger, a prophet; he bade his people pray and pay the
zakat, and he was acceptable in the eyes of his Lord." (19:55-56)
So, too, the Qur'an says of Abraham: "We gave to him Isaac and
Jacob as an extra gift; We made them upright men and We made
them patterns to guide men by Our bidding. We inspired them to
good works, to observe the prayers, and to pay the *zakat*; so they
served Us." (21:72-73)

And woe to him who does not discharge this legal obligation.
Said the Messenger of Allah: "The man to whom Allah has given
wealth, and who yet will not pay his *zakat* shall be thus recompensed on the Day of Resurrection; a huge snake with glowing
eyes will encircle his neck on the Day of Resurrection, will grasp
him by the maxillaries—that is to say, by the jaws—and will say, 'I
am your wealth; I am your treasure.'" Which is a fearful, terrible,
and awesome picture.

✧ ✧ ✧ ✧ ✧ ✧ ✧

This *zakat* is a due imposed by the force of the law, an amount of money at a specified proportion. But, in addition to this there is the institution of almsgiving which is imposed on the individual conscience without any fixed rate; it is at the discretion of the will and the conscience. It is the outward sign of charity and brotherly feeling, to both of which Islam attaches a supreme importance; it is an attempt to establish the mutual ties of mankind and social solidarity by means of an individual perception of what is necessary and a personal concept of charity. It serves two purposes: first, to establish an inner refinement of the conscience; and second, to foster a belief in the inherent solidarity of mankind. Islam makes this charity a pure and humane thing, not limited by the bounds of a religious fellowship; for the Qur'an says: "Allah does not forbid you to act righteously and justly towards those who have not fought against you in the matter of religion, and who have not expelled you from your homes." (60:8) And the Messenger says: "You will never be Believers until you show charity." They said to him, "O Messenger of Allah, all of us are charitable." He replied: "It is not a question of your charity to your neighbor, but of your charity to men in general." And thus he sets a lofty pattern of charity which is pure and universal to the point of making it a feature of the faith.

He even takes the final step and includes in the scope of charity all living things. Thus the noble Prophet of Islam said: "Once while a man was travelling he became violently thirsty, so he found a well, went down to the water, and drank. When he came up again he noticed a dog panting and licking the dust in an agony of thirst. He said to himself, 'This dog has the same violent thirst which I had'; whereupon he went down again to the water and filled his boot with liquid. Grasping it in his mouth, he climbed out of the well and gave the dog to drink. And Allah the Exalted gave him reward and pardon." His hearers asked him: "O Messenger of Allah, is there such a reward for us in the case of animals?" He replied: "There is such a reward in the case of every living creature." Or again he said: "There was a woman who went to Hell only on account of a cat; she had tied it up, and had not fed it, nor had she even allowed it to eat of the herbage of the earth."

Such mercy is a fundamental part of faith in Islam, as it is one of its characteristic signs; it indicates the acceptance of religion by the conscience, and it testifies to the existence of that humane spirit without which, in the Islamic view, there can be no religion.

It is on this basis that Islam establishes the custom of alms-giving and charity; it makes one fond of spending voluntarily and freely in anticipation of the approval of Allah, of a return from Him in this world, and of a reward for Him in the world to come. Thus, too, one may escape His anger, His vengeance, and His punishment.

So the good news is for the humble, those who are obedient to Allah, and who spend of their wealth according to His will. "And give good news to the humble whose hearts tremble when Allah is mentioned, who are patient in their afflictions, who observe the prayers, and who expend freely of what We have given them." (22:35-36) This is a picture to inspire the heart of man, and the same idea appears in another connection, where it is written: "Only those believe in Our signs who, when they are reminded of them, fall down in adoration and celebrate the praises of their Lord, and are not puffed up. As they leave their beds they call upon their Lord in fear and in hope; and of what We have given them they expend in alms. No one knows what pleasure is reserved for such, as a reward for what they have been doing." (32:15-17)

And the same generosity is to be found depicted in the beautiful and touching picture of the character of the people of Medina when they received the Emigrants and gave them shelter, sharing with them their property and their houses in cheerfulness and gladness of spirit. "As for those who had houses there and adopted the faith, they loved those who emigrated to them, and they found no desire in their hearts for the share which had fallen to the others; they preferred them before themselves, though there was poverty among them. Those who are preserved from niggardliness of soul shall be prosperous." (59:9)

This is a beautiful and wondrous picture of human nature in

its highest and best aspects. Here is another description which is not inferior to the first in its touching beauty of a community of Allah's servants; some authorities hold that the people in question here are 'Ali and his wife, Fatima, the daughter of the Messenger, and their household:"They fulfill their vows, and they fear a Day the evil of which will fly broadcast. For love of God they give food to the poor, the orphan, and the prisoner, saying, 'It is only for the sake of Allah that we give you food; we want from you neither reward nor gratitude. We fear from our Lord a day which will be grim and forbidding.' So Allah has preserved them from the evil of that Day, and has given them cheerfulness and joy; He has rewarded them for their endurance with Paradise and silk clothing. There they recline on couches, and there they see neither sun nor bitter cold; near over them is the shade of the garden of Paradise, and hanging low around them are its clusters of fruit. They shall be served round with vessels of silver and goblets of glass, with glasses of silver whose measure they have themselves determined; in these they shall quaff a drink tempered with ginger, drawn from a spring named Salsabil. There pass round among them boys of eternal youth, whom to see is to imagine that they are unstrung pearls, and whom to see is to envisage delight and a great kingdom. They are clothed with garments of green satin and brocade, and they are adorned with bracelets of silver; their Lord has given them to drink a pure draught. Verily this has come to you as a reward, and thus your life's striving has been recompensed." (76:7-22)

So the giving of alms is to make a loan to Allah, a loan which is certain to be repaid: "Who is he who will make a fair loan to Allah, and He will double it for him. For such a one there is a noble reward." (57:11) "Verily men and women who give alms and thus make a loan to Allah, He will double it for them. For such there is a noble reward." (57:17) Or it may be regarded as a profitable and remunerative transaction: "Verily those who recite the Book of Allah, who observe the prayers, and who expend in alms of what We have given them, both secretly and openly—such hope for a trade that will not fail. So He may pay them their rewards in full, and may give them increase of His bounty; verily He is forgiving, grateful." (35:26-27) In either case almsgiving is profitable and does not involve loss or injury. "That which you expend in alms of your possessions is to your own advantage, even though you expend it only for the love of Allah; what you expend in alms of your possessions will be repaid you in full measure, and you will suffer no injury." (2:274)

So in the next world Paradise is the worthy recompense of those who expend freely in alms. "And hasten to forgiveness from your Lord, and to a Paradise whose width is as that of the heavens and the earth, a Paradise prepared for those who are pious; they it is who expend in alms both in prosperity and in adversity, who curb their wrath, and who deal leniently with others. Allah loves those who act well." (3:127-128)

Again, almsgiving is a means of purification for one's character and for one's property; the Messenger of Allah commanded that a portion of their property should be taken from people who have sinned and have acknowledged their sins, and that this should be spent on good causes; thus such people might be purified and cleansed. "Others have acknowledged their sins; they have done both deeds that are good and deeds that are evil; it may be that Allah will relent towards them, for Allah is forgiving and compassionate. Take of their property an alms which will purify and cleanse them, and pray over them; verily your prayers will mean a repose for them, for Allah hears and knows. Have they not learned that is is Allah who receives repentance from His servants, and who accepts the alms? Have they not learned that it is Allah who is relenting and compassionate?." (9:103-105)

Thus expenditure on alms is linked to fidelity to the compact with Allah, to reverence for Him, and to fear of an evil reckoning; to give alms indicates wisdom and understanding. But to refrain from almsgiving is to nullify what Allah has commanded to be accomplished; it is a form of violating the compact and of dealing corruptly in the earth. "Only those who have insight are reminded, those who fulfill the compact of Allah and who do not violate the agreement. They accomplish what Allah has commanded to be accomplished, they reverence their Lord, and they fear an evil record. They endure with patience out of regard for the love of

Allah, they observe the prayers, and they expend in alms out of what We have given them, both secretly and openly; they drive away the evil by means of the good. Such shall have the recompense of the Abode, gardens of pleasure into which they shall enter, they and those of their fathers and their wives and their descendants who have been upright; angels shall come in to them by every gate, saying, 'Peace be upon you for your patient endurance; good is the recompense of the Abode.' But as for those who violate the compact of Allah after coming to an agreement with Him, who nullify what Allah has commanded to be accomplished, and who deal corruptly in the earth—for them is the curse, and for them there is an evil abode." (13:19-25)

To refrain from expenditure in the way of Allah is destruction: "Expend freely in the way of Allah, and do not hand yourselves over to destruction." (2:191) The "destruction" of the individual is to lay oneself open to the punishment of Allah in the world to come and to the vengeance of others in this world. The "destruction" of society is the discrimination and the oppression that come in the train of the absence of free expenditure in alms, together with the accompanying discords and hatreds, debility and weakness.

To hinder good works is a form of aggression: "Cast into Hell every obstinate unbeliever who hinders good works, who is hostile and contentious." (50:23-24) "And do not obey any contemptible swearer, any slanderer who goes about maligning, who hinders good works, who is hostile and guilty." (68:10-12) He is hostile to the claims of Allah, to the claims of his own soul as a member of that society.

Charity leads to Paradise, and the charitable man will pass over the hard path that leads thither; the path consists in the setting free of slaves, and in the provision of food in a case of hunger and destitution. "And what has taught you the nature of the 'hard path'? It is to set free slaves, to give food in a day of famine to an orphan who is of your kin, or to a poor man in destitution." (90:12-16) But, to refrain from charity leads to the Fire, and he who merits it will go thither along with the unbelievers. "What made you go into hellfire? They replied: 'We were not among those who prayed, nor were we among those who fed the poor; we plunged into discussion with others, and we scoffed at the Day of Judgment, until the final account came upon us." (74:43-48) "As for those who have been niggardly with what Allah has given them of His bounty, let them not think that it will be well with them; nay, it will go ill with them, for on the Day of Resurrection that which they have stingily withheld will be hung about their necks." (3:175-176) "As for those who have heaped up for themselves treasures of gold and silver, and who do not expend them in the way of Allah, announce for them a painful punishment. On that day their treasures will be heated in the fire of Hell, and they will be branded with them on their foreheads, their sides, and their backs. 'These are the treasures which you heaped up for yourselves, so taste now of what you have heaped up.'" (9:34-35) The treasures which are referred to in this verse are explained in a tradition: "Whoever collects dinars or dirhams, gold in the nugget or silver, and does not pay it over to a creditor or expend it freely in the way of Allah—that is a treasure, and he will be branded with it on the Day of Resurrection." Treasure, properly understood, is not merely money on which no *zakat* is paid, as some have maintained; all money which is hoarded and which is not paid out for these specified purposes is treasure, even if *zakat* has been paid on it. And the other tradition which indicates that money on which *zakat* has been paid is not treasure, is not in opposition to this tradition; for the latter tradition merely makes the former specific.

Indeed, in the case of men who hoard, punishment sometimes overtakes them in this world as a reward for their niggardliness and for their hindering of good works. The noble Qur'an tells a parable of such in a short story concerning a community which had a walled garden from the produce of which they used to feed the poor. Then it occurred to them to be niggardly and to keep the fruit for themselves; but a change of fortune fell upon their garden, and Allah took away their produce, so that the next morning they were regretful. "We have tested them as We tested the owners of the garden when they resolved that they would reap it in the morning, and made no qualification of their resolve. So while they slept a disaster from your Lord encircled it, and in the morning it lay like a garden already reaped. That morning they called to one another, 'Come early to your field, if you intend to reap,' and they went their way, whispering to one another, 'Let no poor man come upon you in the garden today.' So they went out early with this settled purpose, but when they saw it they said, 'Verily we have erred, and we are cheated of our fruits.' The most fair-minded of them said, 'Did I not say to you, Will you not give praise to Allah?' They said, 'Praise to our Lord. Verily we have been evildoers.' So they turned upon one another, blaming one another and saying, 'Alas for us. Indeed we have been presumptuous; it may be that our Lord will give us something better than this in exchange. Verily our desire is towards our Lord.' Such was the punishment; and the punishment of the world to come is yet greater, if only they knew." (68:17-33)

So the Qur'an summons men to be generous before the opportunity is lost to them. "Say to My servants who have believed that they must observe the prayers and expend freely of what We have given them, both secretly and openly, before there comes a Day on which there will be neither bargain nor friendship." (14:36) "And expend freely of what We have given you, before death comes upon one of you, and he says: 'O my Lord, Would that my death might be deferred for a short space, so that I might give alms and thus become one of the righteous.' But Allah will not defer the death of any soul when its time is come." (63:10-11) Similarly the Qur'an cautions men against avarice, that they may guard themselves from it and that they may not be betrayed into it by their desire for wealth and children; for these things are only a trial and a temptation for men. "Your wealth and your children are only a temptation, but Allah has a great reward. So be pious towards Allah as far as you are able, attend and obey. Expend freely in alms; that is better for yourselves. It is those who are protected from avarice of soul who prosper." (64:15-16)

The Prophet makes almsgiving a duty for every Muslim, even though he may have nothing. The explanation of that is this saying of his: "The giving of alms is a duty for every Muslim. They asked him: 'O Prophet of Allah, what of him who has nothing?' He replied: 'Let him turn his hand to labor, and thus profit himself, and then let him give his alms.' They said: 'And what if he can find nothing to do?' He answered: 'Let him find some unfortunate soul who is in need.' They said: 'Suppose he cannot find such a one?' He replied: 'Then let him do some one a service, or let him restrain himself from evil, and that shall be his alms.'" Thus all men have an equal opportunity for generosity, each according to his means, and each according to his ability.

❖ ❖ ❖ ❖ ❖ ❖ ❖

The recipients of charitable expenditure must vary according to varying needs and circumstances; relatives have the prior claim on a man's benefactions, but there are others also who are joined with them and who are mentioned side by side with relatives in the verses of the Qur'an which urge to charity. For charity is a universal human emotion and must take precedence over family consciousness; and indeed the mention of charity in the Qur'an is generally linked with that of faith. More than that—it is an indication of faith, as we have shown. "Serve Allah, and do not associate any other with Him. Show kindness to parents and relatives, to orphans and to the poor, to the stranger under your protection, whether or not he be a relative, to the companion at your side and to the wayfarer, and to those whom your right hand owns. Verily Allah does not love any crafty boaster. Those who are niggardly and who urge others to niggardliness, who conceal what Allah has given them of His bounty—for such unbelievers We have prepared a shameful punishment." (4:40-41) 'They will ask you how they should expend money in alms. Say: What you expend is for the benefit of parents, relatives, orphans, the poor and the wayfarer. Whatever good you do, Allah is aware of it." (2:211)

Thus the neighbor and the companion are placed alongside of parents and relatives, just as the orphan, the poor and the wayfarer are grouped with all of them. All have an equal right to the alms. And this is so, even in the case of those who have committed some evil deed, as in the occurrence connected with Mistah, a relative of Abu Bakr, who shared in the slanderous story about 'A'isha, the daughter of Abu Bakr and wife of the Prophet. Islam ordains that such persons be forgiven, and it forbids that they be punished in this way. Abu Bakr swore that he would cut off the charity which he had been extending to Mistah, for he was exceedingly angry at the calumnies which the latter had been spreading about the character of 'A'isha. But this verse was revealed: "As for those of you who have abundance and ample means, let them not abstain from giving to relatives and the poor and to those who have emigrated in the way of Allah; rather let them pardon and forgive. Do you not wish that Allah should pardon you?" (24:22) Thus Islam seeks to raise human instincts to a high and noble level that does honor to human nature in all ages, that makes human nature a proud thing in the past, the present, and the future, as long as Allah wills.

Islam also elevates the concept of charity itself by making it charity for the sake of Allah the Glorious. It depicts charity in this striking picture that has come down through the Traditions. "On the Day of Resurrection Allah will say: 'O man, I was ill, and you did not visit Me.' Then man will reply: 'O my Lord, how could I visit You, since You are Lord of the Worlds?' Then Allah will say: 'Did you not know that such and such a servant of Mine was ill, and you did not visit him? If you had visited him, you would have found Me there.' 'O man, I gave you your food, but you have given Me no food.' He will answer: 'O my Lord, how could I give You food, seeing that You are the Lord of the Worlds?' And Allah will say: 'Did you not know that such and such a servant of Mine gave you food, yet you gave him none? Surely if you had given him food, you would have found it with Me.' 'O man, I gave you to drink, but you did not give to Me.' Man will say: 'O my Lord, how could I give You to drink, seeing that You are the Lord of the Worlds?' And Allah will reply: 'Such and such a servant of Mine gave you to drink, yet you did not give to him. Had you given him to drink, you would have found it with Me.'"

Islam also establishes certain behavioral norms for almsgiving, thus raising it above the stage where it is merely a mark of the superiority and preeminence of the rich over the poor, and thus raising it also above the stage where it may be only a form of hypocrisy arising from ignoble instincts. For if the impulses leading to almsgiving are allowed to deteriorate, or if charity is followed by imposing a sense of obligation on those who receive it, then it becomes an ungracious business that can only injure the soul, the nature, and the conscience and that can only injure society also by injuring its individual members. There is nothing like attaching a sense of obligation to an act of benevolence for paining people, for humbling them, and rendering them unwilling to accept benevolence. Similarly, there is nothing like hypocrisy in almsgiving for corrupting the conscience and sapping the moral fibre. Accordingly, Islam labors to elevate the nature of both those who give and those who receive, and it is this result that it seeks most strenuously to achieve. "Those who expend their wealth freely in the way of Allah are like a grain which produced seven ears with a hundred grains in each ear; so Allah will give a double return to whom He wills, and verily Allah is powerful and aware. Such as expend their wealth in alms in the way of Allah and do not follow this expenditure with obligations or annoyances shall have their reward with their Lord; no fear shall oppress them, nor any sadness rest upon them. Favorable speech and forgiveness are better than alms followed by annoyance; Allah is rich and clement. O you who have believed, do not make your alms in vain by putting obligation or annoyance upon the recipients, as he does who gives alms for the sake of appearance before the people. He has no belief in Allah or in the Last Day, and he is like a smooth rock with earth on it; if a heavy rain falls upon it, it is left bare. Such men have no power over what they have amassed, and Allah does not give guidance to people who are unbelievers. But those who expend their wealth in alms out of a desire for the approval of Allah and as a support from themselves are like a garden on a hill; if a heavy rain falls upon it, it brings forth its fruit in double measure; and even if no heavy rain falls upon it, yet still there is the dew. Allah is aware of what you do. Would any one of you like this to happen? Suppose he has a garden of palm trees and vines with perpetual water flowing through it, so that he has all kinds of fruits in it; old age comes upon him, and he has only a weak family; then a fiery whirlwind strikes his garden, so that it is burnt up. In such a way does Allah make the signs clear to you; it may be that you will consider." (2:263-268)

For this reason it is desirable that alms be given in secret and privately to the necessitous. Thus, on the one hand, the self-esteem of the recipients is safeguarded, and on the other hand, a check is put upon conceit and pride. "If you give alms in public, that is good; but if you do it secretly and give to the poor, that is better for you." (2:273) And there is a tradition of the Prophet in praise of the man who "gives his alms, but conceals the fact to the point where his left hand does not know what his right hand is giving." This is an outstandingly fine picture of the way in which charity should be kept secret and should not be accounted a matter for pride or publicity.

❖ ❖ ❖ ❖ ❖ ❖ ❖

Islam is aware of the instinct to love oneself and to love money. It is convinced that avarice is always present in the soul, never absent from it. "Souls are ever liable to avarice." (2:127) So it treats all of this psychologically, using the methods which we have seen; it stimulates the will, it warns, it exhorts, it depicts; in this way its aims may be achieved, and thus it can require of this naturally niggardly disposition of man that it be generous with that which he loves dearly and which has a powerful hold upon him. "You will not attain to charity until you expend in alms of that which you love." (3:86) In this way man reaches the height of generosity, the limit of liberality, and the noblest form of beneficence that can possibly arise from the human spirit. Thus man is raised above his own self, and thus the higher side of his nature overcomes the lower, his ethical nature conquers his instinctual nature. By its very nature this is by itself a lofty and universal aim which deserves all effort to attain it. How much more so, then, seeing that it is also an objective for society. The purpose is to create a balance of wealth, to oppose destitution, to establish the responsibilities that exist between rich and poor, and thus to shape a society that has a sense of mutual relationship and mutual help and that is therefore a healthy society.

❖ ❖ ❖ ❖ ❖ ❖ ❖

Islam follows this method, with one example of which we have now dealt in detail. Islam is concerned to persuade the conscience

in the case of every duty which it prescribes. It imposes no more
duties than are demanded by the welfare of society and no more
than can be accepted by the ability of the general mass of mankind.
Beyond that stage it appeals to the conscience, persuading it of its
responsibility and seeking to raise it above its normal scope; thus it
attempts to elevate human life and to draw it ever onward and
upward. It leaves a wide space between the lower level of duty,
which is prescribed by the law and the higher level of conscience,
which is so desirable and towards which individuals and nations
have striven in every age and century.

Thus, for example, Islam prescribes a principle of vengeance,
awarding it as a legal right to the next of kin and permitting him to
exact it in full; yet at the same time it exhorts as strongly as possible that men should forgive, forbear, and pardon. "If any man is
unjustly killed, We have given authority to his next of kin; but let
him not be immoderate in killing; verily he has been helped."
(17:35)

Or again, it prescribes fighting in the way of Allah as a responsibility incumbent on every one who is able for it. But over and
above that, it kindles a love for fighting by inciting the conscience
to accept it, by depicting it in glowing terms, and by emphasizing
its justice and the glories which it brings to a society. "Allah has
purchased from the Believers their persons and their wealth, for
the price of Paradise reserved for them; so they fight in the way of
Allah, so they kill and are killed." (9:112) And were it not that
Allah sets some men against others, the cloisters had been
destroyed, and the churches and synagogues and mosques in
which the name of Allah is often repeated." (22:40) "What is the
matter with you that you do not fight in the way of Allah, and in
defense of the oppressed, men, women and children." (4:77)

It forbids usury and goes on to attack its evil character and the
evil character of its results; thus it seeks to arouse the conscience to
condemn usury and to reject it. "Those who eat up the fruits of
usury will not arise on the Day of Resurrection, except in the same
way as he whom Satan has sent mad by a touch. That is because
they have said: 'A bargain is just the same as usury.' But Allah has
allowed bargaining, though He has forbidden usury. If anyone

receives a warning from his Lord and desists, then he shall keep what he has already gained, and his destiny shall be in the hand of Allah. But if anyone continues to practice usury, then he is one of those destined to Hell, there to abide. Allah will blot out usury, but He will multiply money given in alms; Allah does not love any guilty unbeliever." (2:276-277) "O you who have believed, act piously towards Allah and abandon the usury which is still unpaid, if you are really Believers. And if you do not do this, then know that there will be war from Allah and from his Messenger." (2:278-279)

Islam forbids the drinking of wine and gambling and it links up these things with the custom of divining the future by the casting of lots or sacred arrows; this occurs in one verse which places all these things together as being outside the bounds of common sense and logic. Then it goes on to persuade the conscience of the reasons for this prohibition. "O you who have believed, wine and gambling, sacred lots and arrows are only an abomination, a work of Satan. Turn away from them, then, and it may be that you will prosper. Satan desires only to cause enmity and hatred among you by means of wine and gambling, to keep you from the remembrance of Allah, and from the prayers; so will you refrain?." (5:92-93)

Thus Islam continues through all its commands and prohibitions; the same course is followed. It is the wisest and the most profitable course for human nature, and its results have already been proved in the early history of Islam and throughout the long period of the past fourteen centuries. This method can be repeated for the present and the future, so long as its essential nature is understood, so long as this direction is followed, and so long as men will follow this straight path.

5 POLITICAL THEORY IN ISLAM

Any discussion of social justice in Islam must necessarily include a discussion of political theory in Islam, according to the principle that we have already laid down when we were discussing the nature of Islamic social justice; namely, that it must embrace all the aspects of life and all varieties of endeavor; similarly, that it must include both spiritual and material values, since these are inextricably interwoven. With all of this, political theory is connected; and the more so because in the final resort it is concerned with the implementation of the religious law, with the care of society in every respect, with the establishment of justice and equilibrium in society, and with the distribution of wealth according to the principles that are accepted by Islam.

Any full treatment of political theory in Islam would be lengthy and would require a separate treatise. But our purpose in this work is merely to point out the bearing of such theory on social justice, and therefore we must as far as possible consider only this aspect of the matter. And this is despite the fact that the major difficulty of studying Islam is that the enquirer finds that all its aspects are interconnected, so that one cannot possibly be separated from another. Because this religion is essentially a unity, worship and work, political and economic theory, legal demands and spiritual exhortations, faith and conduct, this world and the world to come, all these are related parts of one comprehensive whole. It is difficult to single out one part for treatment without being led to deal also with the remaining parts. Yet this is what we shall attempt, as far as may be possible.

Some Muslim writers, discussing the Islamic political system, labor to trace connections and similarities between it and the other systems known to the ancient or the modern world, in the ages before and after Islam. And some of them believe that they find a strong support for Islam when they can trace such a connection between it and one of the other ancient or modern systems. In reality this attempt represents nothing but an inner conviction that the Islamic system is inferior to those of the Western world. But Islam does not take pride in any similarities between it and these other systems, nor is it harmed by their absence. For Islam altogether presents to mankind an example of a complete political system, the like of which has never been found in any of the other systems known to the world either before or after the coming of Islam. Islam does not seek, and never has sought, to imitate any other system, or to find connections or similarities between itself and others. On the contrary, it has chosen its own characteristic path and has presented humanity with a complete cure for all of its problems.

It sometimes happens in the development of man-made political systems that they agree with Islam in some respects and differ from it in others. But Islam is in itself a completely independent system that has no connection with these others, either when they agree with it or when they differ from it. Such divergence or agreement is purely accidental and occurs in scattered points of detail; in such coincidence or in such divergence there can be no significance. The truly significant thing is the underlying theory or the philosophy peculiar to the system; Islam has both of these, and it is from these that the details of the system take their rise. These details may either agree with or differ from similar details in other systems, but Islam continues on its own unique way, irrespective of such agreement or divergence.

Thus it is not the task of the Islamic enquirer who embarks on a study of the Muslim political system to look for similarities to, or agreements with, any other system, ancient or modern. Nor do such similarities and agreements add anything to the strength of the Islamic position, as some Muslims believe—especially since they are superficial and in matters of detail only; they arise from chance in merely particular matters and not from any general philosophy or underlying theory. The true method is to turn to the fundamentals of the religion itself in the firm belief that in them lie the complete bases of the system. It makes no difference whether all other political systems agree or disagree entirely. The sole reason for seeking to strengthen Islam through its similarities and agreements with other systems is the conviction of inferiority, as we have said; no Muslim scholar should venture on such a course, but rather should know his own faith with a true knowledge and study it with a true zeal.

In the course of its growth and development the world has known a number of political systems, but the Islamic system is not simply one of these; it is not derived from them nor does it depend on them. It is a system that stands by itself, independent in its theory and unique in its methods. We must necessarily regard it as independent, since it was in independence that it started and since it is the path of independence that it follows.

For these reasons the suggestion of Dr. Haikal is unacceptable, that the Islamic world was "the Islamic empire"; similarly unacceptable is his dictum that, "In fact Islam was an imperial power." Nothing can be further from a true understanding of the spirit of Islam than to call it imperial; and that is so, no matter what distinctions we may draw between the characteristics of an Islamic empire and those of the more familiar imperialism. Again, nothing can be further from an understanding of the true nature of the bonds uniting the Islamic world than to call it the Islamic empire.[17]

Thus it is strange to find Dr. Haikal in his treatment of Islamic rule in *The Life of Muhammad*, or *Al-Siddiq Abu Bakr*, or *Al-Faruq 'Umar* seeking some real and deep-seated difference between the nature of Islam and the nature of the other systems familiar to the world. But he is driven irresistibly to use these two expressions by his belief in the inspired force of foreign institutions. And indeed there are some institutions that are similar in Islam and in imperialism. Perhaps the most convenient instance is that of the Muslim world; this comprises a number of regions of contrasting races and cultures, yet the matter of its government is handled from one capital. This is certainly an imperial custom. But this is only an isolated instance, and, in any case, the points of importance are the way in which the capital regards the provinces and the nature of the relation between it and them.

Anyone who studies the spirit of Islam and its method of administration must recognize clearly that it is as far from familiar imperialism as it can be. Islam holds that there is an equality for Muslims in all parts of the world, and it forbids any racial or regional loyalty; rather, as we have seen, it even transcends religious loyalty in many instances. In accordance with this idea it does not make its provinces into mere colonies or places to be exploited, sources from which supplies may be poured into the capital for its sole profit. Each region is a member of the body of the Islamic world, and its people have the same privileges as the people of the capital. When one of the regions is administered by a governor from the Islamic capital, he can administer it only by virtue of his character as a Muslim who is suitable for the position and not as a colonial governor. But many of these regions that were originally conquered were administered by one of their own people, chosen, not because he was a native, but because he was a Muslim suitable for the position. Again, it is required that what money is collected in any region shall be spent there as a matter of priority. If there is a surplus, it must be contributed to the Muslim public treasury, to be spent on the Muslim world generally according to need. It must not be appropriated to the use of the population of the capital city, even at the cost of destitution in the regions, as is the imperial custom.

All this constitutes a great difference between the Islamic world on the one hand, or the Islamic community to be more exact, and imperialism on the other hand. So the statement that Islam is "an imperial power" is liable to correction, since it is foreign alike to the spirit and to the history of Islam. It is more fitting to say that Islam is universal in its aim, because of its strong belief in the unity of humanity and because of the effort it makes to sum up all this universality in a system of equality and brotherhood.

Dr. Taha Husayn has been more circumspect in his definition; in the preface to *The Great Civil War: 'Uthman* he deals with the Islamic political system and compares it with all the other systems.

His conclusion is that it is by nature fundamentally different from all others. This is undoubtedly correct when we look at the spirit of Muslim administration, not its institutions and details.[18]

Islam, as we have said, proposes independent solutions to human problems; these solutions it derives from its theory of unity, from its fundamental beliefs, and from its distinctive methods. So we must be careful when we describe Islam not to relate it to other principles and theories in order to explain it by means of them or to relate it to them. Islam is a comprehensive philosophy and an homogeneous unity, and to introduce into it any foreign element would mean ruining it. It is like a delicate and perfect piece of machinery that may be completely ruined by the presence of an alien component.

And this is the consideration which I would urge in summing up here; there are many who have introduced into their thought and their reasoning components taken from the machinery of alien systems of government. They believe that they are contributing a new access of strength to Islam when they feed it with these systems. But in reality all that they are doing is an error, spoiling Islam and ruining its spirit so that it cannot operate. And at the same time this is the product of a hidden feeling of inferiority, even though such writers may not openly mention the word inferiority.

❖ ❖ ❖ ❖ ❖ ❖ ❖

The Islamic political system is based on two fundamental conceptions, both of which originate in its general idea of the universe, of life, and of man. One is the idea of the equality of mankind as a species, in nature, and in origin; the other is the belief that Islam represents the eternal system for the world throughout the future of the human race.

The first of these we have already discussed in the chapter on the foundations of social justice in Islam. There we indicated the rights which Islam extends to protected peoples, and to polytheists who have a compact with the Muslims. These are rights which derive from the permanent and fundamental rights of humanity; no difference is made between one religion and another. And the same principle is extended to cover human relationships in general.

When Islam commands war against polytheists, the command refers only to defensive war, which is aimed at stopping aggression. "Permission is granted to those who fight because they have been wronged; verily Allah is able to help them." (22:40) "And fight in the way of Allah against those who fight against you; but do not open the hostilities, for Allah does not love those who open the hostilities." (2:186) This is war solely to defend the Muslims against physical aggression, so that they may not be seduced from their faith; it is war to remove all material obstructions from the path of the summoning to Islam, that it may reach out to all men.

Islam goes far to discharge its obligations to non-Muslims; indeed it goes the length of refraining from helping Muslims against non-Muslims with whom a compact exists. "And if they ask help from you in a matter of religion, it is your duty to render such help; except against a people with whom you have an agreement." (8:73) This is a typical instance of Islam's care to discharge its obligations, and it rests on a view of life which is universal and worldwide in scope. It goes beyond local interests and limited aims, even in matters pertaining to religion.

As to the second conception, namely that Islam represents the eternal system for the world throughout the future of the human race, this originates in the fact that Muhammad was the Messenger of Allah to all men, that he was the Seal of the Prophets, and that his religion is the most correct of all religions. "And We have not sent you unless inclusively to all people." (34:27) "And We have sent you only as a sign of mercy to the worlds." (21:107) ". . . the Messenger of Allah, and the Seal of the prophets. . . ." (33:40) "Today I have perfected your religion for you, have completed My favor towards you, and have approved Islam as your religion." (5:5) "Verily this Qur'an guides you to what is more upright." (17:9) But in spite of this, Islam does not compel others to embrace it: "There is no compulsion in religion." (2:257) Rather, Islam grants to men the utmost freedom and protection to continue in their own religious beliefs. It goes so far in its interpretation of this freedom as to impose the duty of paying the *zakat* on Muslims alone, while it exacts from protected peoples only the polltax; this is demanded because they share in the protection afforded by the

Muslim state, and all the proceeds of this tax are spent on their welfare. But it does not impose the *zakat* on protected peoples, because it is a religious ordinance of Islam and a form of religious service applicable only to Muslims; Islam has no desire to compel protected peoples to perform the religious services proper only to Muslims. So it takes money from them on a purely monetary basis that has no religious significance such as is contained in the ordinance of the *zakat*. Surely this is the height of a discriminating perception of justice in dealing with others.

In granting this extent of freedom to others Islam is prompted by its general and universal spirit; it believes that when they have the opportunity of examining Islam carefully and assiduously, since it will owe nothing to the intervention of material force or of intellectual ignorance, by their very nature men will turn towards it because it insures a perfect balance of all the aims for which previous religions have striven and between all the passions and the desires of human nature. Because under Islam all and sundry are guaranteed an absolute equality and a complete mutual responsibility, and because the aim of Islam is to secure a unity of all men alike in the spiritual and in the political sphere.

The fact that the Islamic political system is based on these two conceptions has had its effect on the nature and the methods of that system. It has made it operate through laws and exhortations, through political and economic theory, and through all the other systems which it includes. Thus it does not legislate for one race or for one generation, but for all races and for all generations; it followed universal and comprehensive principles when it laid down its laws and its systems of government; it laid down general principles and broad fundamentals only, leaving the application of these to the process of time and to the emergence of specific problems. This reliance on general principle is most clearly perceptible in the field of political theory, which is the specific concern of this chapter.

❖ ❖ ❖ ❖ ❖ ❖ ❖

Political theory in Islam rests on the basis of justice on the part of the rulers, obedience on the part of the ruled, and consultation between ruler and ruled. These are the great fundamental features from which all the other features take their rise.

There must first be justice on the part of the rulers. "Verily Allah commands justice." (16:92) "And when you judge between the people, you must do so with justice." (4:61) "And when you speak, act justly, even though the matter concerns a relative." (6:151) "And be not driven by hatred of any people to unjust action; to act justly is closer to piety." (5:11) "Verily on the Day of Resurrection he who is dearest of all men to Allah, and he who is nearest to Him will be the just leader; but he who is most hated by Allah on that Day, and he who is most bitterly punished will be the tyrannical leader." [19]

This refers to that impartial justice which is absolute and which cannot be swayed by affection or by hatred; the bases of this justice cannot be affected by love or by enmity. Such justice is not influenced by any relationship between individuals or by any hatred between peoples. It is enjoyed by all the individual members of the Muslim community, without discrimination arising from descent or rank, wealth, or influence. In the same way, such a justice is enjoyed by other peoples, even though there may be hatred between them and the Muslims. This is a high level of equity to which no international law has so far attained nor any domestic law.

Those who doubt this should examine that form of justice that depends on the strength or the weakness of communities, which is the mark of those who are regularly at variance one with another. That is, they should examine that form of justice that the white man administers to the red man and the black man in the United States or that the white man administers to the colored man in South Africa. There are other similar instances from contemporary conditions with which everyone is familiar.

The principal care of Islamic justice is that it shall not be purely theoretical, but that it shall be applied in the realm of practical life. The historical development of Islam supplies a succession of illustrations of this, which we shall consider in their proper place; here we are concerned to consider only the theoretical aspect, as it is revealed to us in the ordinances of Islam.

And secondly, there must be obedience on the part of those who are ruled. "O you who have believed, obey Allah, and obey the Messenger of Allah and those who hold authority among you." (4:62) The fact that this verse groups together Allah, the Messenger, and those who hold authority means that it clarifies the nature and the limits of this obedience. Obedience to one who holds authority is derived from obedience to Allah and the Messenger. The ruler in Islamic law is not to be obeyed because of his own person; he is to be obeyed only by virtue of holding his position through the law of Allah and His Messenger; his right to obedience is derived from his observance of that law and from no other thing. If he departs from the law, he is no longer entitled to obedience, and his orders need no longer be obeyed. Thus the Prophet says that, "There can be no obedience to any creature which involves disobedience to the Creator." Or again: "Hear and obey—even if your ruler is an Abyssinian slave with a head like a raisin, so long as he observes the Book of Allah the Exalted." It is made very clear by this tradition that to hear and obey is conditioned by the observance by the ruler of the Book of Allah the Exalted. An absolute obedience such as this is not to be accorded to the will of the ruler himself, nor can it be a binding thing if he abandons the law of Allah and of His Messenger. "If anyone sees a tyrannical power which is contrary to the will of Allah, which violates the compact of Allah, and which produces evil or enmity among the servants of Allah, and if he does not try to change it by deed or by word, then it is Allah who must supply the initiative."[20] This tradition indicates the necessity of getting rid of a ruler who abandons the law by deed or by word, but with the minimum use of force. This is another necessary step beyond the mere withholding of obedience, which is in itself a purely negative measure.

We must make a distinction between the fact that a ruler derives his authority from his implementation of religious law and the theory that a ruler draws his authority from religion. No ruler has any religious authority direct from Heaven, as had some rulers in ancient times; he occupies his position only by the completely and absolutely free choice of all Muslims; and they are not bound to elect him by any compact with his predecessor, nor likewise is there any necessity for the position to be hereditary in the family. Further, in addition to this, he must derive his authority from his continual enforcement of the law. When the Muslim community is no longer satisfied with him his office must lapse; and even if they are satisfied with him, any dereliction of the law on his part means that he no longer has the right to obedience.

In this we see the wisdom of the Prophet, who did not specify anyone as his successor; had he done so, such a man might have laid claim to some religious authority, as having been appointed by the Messenger.

Thirdly, there must be consultation between ruler and ruled. "Take counsel with them in the matter." (3:153) "And their affair is a matter for consultation among them." (42:36) Consultation is one of the fundamentals of Islamic rule, although no specific method of administering it has even been laid down; its application has been left to the exigencies of individual situations. The Messenger used to take the advice of the Muslim community in matters concerning which no revelation was received; thus he would ask their opinion in wordly affairs in which they had some skill, such as positions on a field of battle. Thus he listened to their opinion at the battle of Badr, and encamped at the well of Badr, though originally he had been some distance away from it; similarly, he listened to them in the matter of digging the trench,[21] and also, against the advice of 'Umar, in the matter of prisoners, though in this case there eventually came a revelation which supported 'Umar's point of view. [22] Whenever revelation was received, of course, in the very nature of the case there was no room for consultation, in accordance with the very foundations of the faith; the matter then pertained exclusively to the Messenger, the Trusty One.

In the same way the Caliphs continued to consult with the Muslims. Abu Bakr did so in the case of those who withheld the zakat; he held strongly that war should be declared on them, and though 'Umar at first opposed him, he finally came to agree with Abu Bakr most fully, Allah having opened his mind to understand that Abu Bakr was set on such a course. Again, Abu Bakr took counsel with the Meccans concerning the war in Syria, against the opposition of 'Umar. And 'Umar. himself took advice in the matter of going into a plague-stricken country; he came to his own conclusion, and subsequently found a precedent in the custom of the Prophet which confirmed him, and thus he kept to his course. Such was the method of consultation; it did not follow any well-marked or definite system, because the needs of that age never demanded more than this type of informal counsel. But the wide variety of questions which now arises leaves ample room for a wide range of systems and methods; hence no system is specified by Islam, which is content rather to lay down only the general principle.

⁘ ⁘ ⁘ ⁘ ⁘ ⁘ ⁘

A ruler, then, has no rights other than those that belong to any individual of the Muslim community—except that he can claim obedience to his command, advice, and help in the enforcement of the law.

Although the Prophet was not merely a ruler but also a law-giver, he yet established the customary limitations that must be observed by any ruler as governing the rights that Islam grants to him. And Muhammad's successors followed his example in this respect, as we shall see when we deal with the historical development of Islam. Thus he allowed every man to defend his rights, but added that the aggrieved party might show forgiveness. so when a creditor of his came to him on one occasion and upbraided him, the Muslims were concerned about such a happening; but Muhammad advised them to let the man be, because a creditor had the right to speak his mind. Or again, one day as the camels carrying the alms passed him he stretched out his hand towards a woolen garment carried by one of the beasts and said: "I have no more right to that garment than has any other Muslim." He once said to 'Ali and Fatima, who were the most beloved of all people to him, "I cannot give to you while leaving the poor members of the community with their bellies racked by hunger." Or once he said to the members of his own clan, the Hashemites, "If my people cannot approach me through their good works, shall you, then, approach me through your genealogies?"

A ruler, therefore, has no extra privileges as regards the law, or as regards wealth; and his family have no such privileges either, beyond those of the generality of Muslims.

No ruler may oppress the souls or the bodies of Muslims, nor dare he infringe upon their sanctities, nor touch their wealth. If he upholds the law and sees that religious duties are observed, then he has reached the limit of his powers. At that point his power over his people has reached its end; Allah Himself protects them from his power, in soul and body, in their sanctities and their wealth. For the Muslim faith safeguards them in these respects by clear and unmistakable commands. This it does in a way that leaves no room for doubt of the intensity of its desire to safeguard faith and peace and honor to all and sundry. "O you who have believed, do not enter houses other than your own without first being received as friends and giving a greeting to the inmates." (24:27) "It is not good to approach your houses from the back . . . but approach your houses by the doors." (2:189) "Do not play the spy." (49:12) "Every Muslim is sacrosanct to every other Muslim, his blood, his honor, and his property . . . A life for a life, and retaliation for wounds."[23]

✦ ✦ ✦ ✦ ✦ ✦ ✦

But while Islam sets a strict limit to the power of a ruler so far as he is personally concerned, it gives him the broadest possible powers in looking after matters of welfare that pertain to the community; such matters are those in which there is no guiding precedent in existence and that evolve with the processes of time and with changing conditions. The general principle is that "a ruler may make as many new decrees as he finds new problems." This is the application of the Qur'anic principle "and He has put no limitation on you in the matter of religion." (22:77) and of the Messenger's phrase, "There must be no hardship and no contention." It also confirms the general aims of this faith, namely, to improve the status of the individual, as well as that of society and that of man in general; this must be done in accordance with the principles established by Islam and must be conditioned by the personal justice of the ruler.

It is the responsibility of the ruler to put an end to anything that occasions hardship in the community no matter what it may be; it is, similarly, his duty to encourage anything that is of any kind of profit to the community. But, at all times, he must be careful not to depart from the ordinances of Islam.

These are wide powers, which touch every aspect of life; and the establishment of social justice in all its aspects is a matter that is bound up with these powers. A ruler may, for example, go beyond the legal requirements in the matter of money; in addition to the *zakat* he may introduce other taxes by which to encourage equality and justice; by these he may check malice and ill-feeling, and by these he may remove from the community the evils of luxury and penury, as well as that of artificially high prices, all of which evils are the product of the growth of excessive wealth. And, similarly, with all the other matters that are within the disposal of the ruler.

The historical development of the life of the Islamic community has provided many examples of this care for the public welfare. Illustrations can be given from every period, and a discussion of this will follow in due course. The important thing for the moment is to establish the fact that Islam is not a stagnant system and that its practical applications are to be found not merely in one age of history, nor only in one quarter of the world.

✢ ✢ ✢ ✢ ✢ ✢ ✢

To continue: This discussion so far has been only of the statutory aspect of political theory in Islam. But beyond this there lies the voluntary aspect in which exhortation passes beyond what the law dictates; this is the Islamic custom in dealing with all its responsibilities and all its requirements. It leaves the minimum level of achievement to the law, while to exhortation it prescribes the achievement of the supreme level; thus it leaves for man a wide space between these two, a gap that he can overcome as best he may.

Political theory in Islam stands on the foundation of conscience in addition to law. It stands on the conviction that Allah is present at every moment alike with the ruler and with the ruled, watching over both. "Whatever servant there may be to whom Allah gives the care of his subjects, if he does not guard them carefully, he shall never see a trace of Paradise." "And do not consume your wealth among yourselves vainly; do not display it before rulers in order guiltily to consume a part of the people's wealth, while you are aware of it." (2:184)

The ruler and his subjects together must bow to the authority of Allah in all things; reverence for Allah is the final guarantee of the establishment of justice. We have already discovered that Islam lays upon the reformed human conscience great responsibilities in the matters of politics and economics. But when reverence for Allah is not in that conscience, then there is no safeguard; for the law can always be deceived or evaded, and the ruler, the judge, or the people be cheated.

We shall see later that this conscience which Islam fosters and reforms has achieved momentous things and has produced results which appeared to be impossible and amazing in Muslim life through the passage of the centuries.

6 ECONOMIC THEORY IN ISLAM

Atreatment of economic theory is perhaps the most essential part of any discussion of social justice, and it may be that many readers have thought the promise of this book slow of realization as they have read through the opening chapters to this point. But this delay has been deliberate; for, social justice in Islam is a greater thing than mere economic theory, as we have already seen, and it seemed necessary first to expound the comprehensive teaching of Islam on social justice. It was necessary also to discuss the nature, the foundations, and the methods of this justice in the broadest sense. And only now are we ready to turn to the matter of money itself, though it is this matter that takes pride of place in the materialistic philosophies that emphasize economic values at the expense of all others.

Islam enters the field of economic theory under the influence of its universal philosophy and guided by its general ideology. Its interests are the welfare of the individual and the ensuring of the welfare of society. In these interests it holds a position of doing injury neither to the individual nor to society; it does not oppose human nature nor, on the other, hand does it seek to impede the fundamental customs and the high and far-reaching objectives of life.

In order to implement this ideal, Islam makes use of its two fundamental methods: legislation and exhortation. By the former, it achieves the practical objective of being responsible for the maintenance of a healthy community, capable of growth and improvement; by the latter it aims at raising men above the level of pure necessity to achieve a more developed form of life. Its objective is to improve life in general to that ideal state, which admittedly all men cannot achieve under all conditions, but to the height and perfection of which Islam ever keeps the way open.

First, then, we shall discuss one illustration, the matter of property, and after that we shall proceed to treat of economic theory in detail.

Islam has always imposed one claim upon property and that is the payment of the *zakat*; this is one ground on which a ruler may use force against his subjects if they withhold this tax, and similarly it is one thing which he can impose on them by legal right, in a fixed and established amount. Further, Islam has given to a ruler the right of exacting in addition to the *zakat* as much as will prevent hardship and do away with penury and preserve the well-being of the Muslim community. This, when there is need of it, is a claim similar to that of the *zakat*, a claim whose exercise depends on the communal welfare and on the justice of the ruler.

So far the law can go; thereafter exhortation has commended to the people the practice of getting rid of all wealth, expending it entirely in the way of Allah. This is the meaning of the tradition related by Abu Dharr concerning Muhammad, as follows: The Messenger of Allah went out one day in the direction of Uhud, and I went with him. He said, "Abu Dharr," and I answered, "At your service, O Messenger of Allah." He said, "Those with the most shall be those with the least on the Day of Resurrection, except for the man who spends thus and thus"; and he gestured to right and left, in front and behind; "And how few shall they be." Afterwards he said, "Abu Dharr," and I replied, "Yes, Messenger of Allah; you are dearer to me than my father and mother." He said, "It gives me pleasure to have something such as my possessions at Uhud, which I can expend in the way of Allah, so that when I die I shall leave only two pennies' worth of it." I said, "Nay, but rather you should leave two thousand, O Messenger of Allah." He replied, "No; it will be but two pennies' worth." Then he added, "Abu Dharr, you desire the most, I the least."

So when Muhammad came to the last hour to which all men must come, when he was acutely ill and near to death, he remembered that he had six or seven pounds in his possession. He commanded his household to give this away in alms; but immediately a fainting fit overtook him, so that his household were too busy attending him to carry out his order. When he recovered from his faint, the first thing he asked was, "What has happened to that money ?" Discovering that it had not yet been given away, he fell into a fit of anger and commanded that 'A'isha be brought in; then he took the money in his hand, saying, "How could Muhammad face his Lord if he were to meet Allah with these in his possession?" And at once all the money was given as alms.

Thus there are these two things, legislation and exhortation, which together are the groundwork of economic theory, as they are the groundwork of all Islamic theory.

And now we may start on our detailed explanatory study.

✦ ✦ ✦ ✦ ✦ ✦ ✦

THE RIGHT OF INDIVIDUAL OWNERSHIP

Islam ratifies the right of individual ownership—by legal means of acquisition which will shortly be explained—and to this ratification it adds the corollaries that will ensure this right to its possessor. It guards him from theft, from being plundered or robbed, and from being cheated by any means whatever. To accomplish all this, it lays down restrictive legislation; but in addition, it provides reformatory exhortations to prevent men coveting what is not their own but belongs to other people. Upon the same basis are laid the other corollaries, such as the right to dispose of personal property by sale, rental, mortgage, or contract, by presentation or bequest or legacy. And so on through all the legal methods of property disposal within the established limits.

There is no doubting this clear and definite ratification of such rights, as it is made by Islam. "Men shall have a portion of what they have earned, and women shall have a portion of what they have earned." (4:36) "Give to orphans their money, and do not exchange the good for the evil." (4:2) "As for the wall, it belonged to two orphan youths in the town, and under it was a treasure belonging to them. Their father was a worthy man, and your Lord wishes that they might reach full age before finding out their treasure as a mercy from your Lord." (18:81)

The stern Islamic punishment for theft is an indication of the sanctity of this right of possession, of the way in which it is guarded, and of the necessity for preventing its being infringed. "As for the thief, man or woman, cut off their hands as a recompense for what they have piled up—a chastisement from Allah." (5:42) Or in the case of usurpation, the man who perpetrates such a crime is accursed; the Messenger of Allah said: "Whoever usurps the property of another on the earth shall have seven earths hung about his neck." And the same with plundering: "He who plunders is not one of us." "Surely no man's property is lawful for you, save only with the good will of the owner." "Every Muslim is sacrosanct to every other Muslim—his blood, his honor and his property."

Similar to the right of possession is that of receiving and giving an inheritance. "Men shall have a portion of what their parents and their near relatives leave; and women shall have a portion of what their parents and their near relatives leave." (4:7) "Allah commands you concerning your children that a boy shall receive the same share as two girls." (4:11) "They will ask you for a decision. Say: Allah gives you a decision about relationships. If a man dies without a son and if he has a sister, then she shall have half of what he leaves." (4:176)

This ratification of the right of individual ownership and the guarding of it ensure an equality between effort and recompense. This is over and above the fact that it is in accordance with human nature and in agreement with the fundamental inclinations of man's soul; for it is with these inclinations that Islam reckons when it establishes its whole social system. But, at the same time this conception is in accordance with the welfare of society, because it encourages the individual to give his utmost to the advancement of life.

Every man is created with a natural love of wealth for its own sake; "Verily the love of wealth is strong." (100:8) He is naturally endowed with a love of possession and with a desire to retain what he possesses: "Say: If you had possessed the treasures of the mercy of my Lord, then you would have been gripped by the fear of spending." (17:100) "And souls are near to avarice." (4:128) There is no harm in the competition that arises from these natural inclinations; for it encourages every man to give of his best so that he is zealous to work and to earn; and such work he both wants and needs. He is not conscious of being forced to work, and hence he does not expend his labor grudgingly or hopelessly. But in the end it is society that profits from his labor and his toil; and so Islam lays down principles that will ensure that profit to society and that will make it certain that no harm can arise from such complete freedom of the individual or from the ratification of his right of personal possession.

Justice demands that the social system shall conform to the desires of the individual and satisfy his inclinations—at least so far as will not injure society—as a return for his contribution to it in the way of ability and labor; in the sweat of his brow, in the labor of his thought, and in the exertion of his nerves. Justice is the greatest of the foundations of Islam; but justice is not always concerned to serve the interests of the individual. Justice is for the individual, but it is for society also, if we are willing to tread the middle way; and so we must have in our life justice in all its shapes and forms.

Over and above all this, none can affirm that the breaking down of natural and accepted barriers will bring some benefit to the individual and to society; but it is a low estimate of human nature that would make such barriers the one and only method of achieving justice. It is only fanciful theories, not rooted in practical experience, that would suppose that such bounds can be imposed from without through systems of government or law, in one nation or in a number of nations. Islam has no such low estimate of human nature; but, at the same time, it has no intention of building all its social structure on such fanciful theories which ignore all the depths of experience.

Similarly, it is possible to say that the sanctity of human nature claims the profoundest and greatest respect from us, because of its intrinsic value and deep-rootedness; when we seek to exhort that nature or to legislate for it, we must do so with great wisdom, with passionate honesty, and with penetrating insight. For it is unthinkable that the experience of millions of years through which man has lived should be spent in vain; or that we should construct mere hypotheses regarding man's character and nature and ways, and then implement these theories by violence and force.

With the ratification of the right to receive or give an inheritance we have already dealt in the section on mutual social responsibility. This right is in conformity with the nature of man that we are discussing here, just as it is in conformity with justice on its highest level; it is equally in conformity with the welfare of the community, using that term in the widest sense, which knows no barriers between one nation and another throughout the human race. In addition this right of inheritance is one of the methods of dispersing wealth, as we shall see.

THE RIGHT OF THE DISPOSAL OF PROPERTY

But Islam does not establish the right of personal ownership absolutely, without bounds or limitations; it certainly ratifies that right, but along with it are ratified other principles that almost make it theoretical rather than practical. They almost strip a man bare of his right to possession by the time that he has met all his essential needs. Islam establishes such limitations and bounds as almost render a man bound rather than free in his disposal of his property, whether he increases, spends, or administers it. But it is consideration for the welfare of society that lies behind all this; it is also consideration for the welfare of the individual himself with regard to the universal objectives by which Islam orders its view of life.

The cardinal principle that Islam ratifies along with that of the right of individual possession is that the individual is in a way a steward of his property on behalf of society; his tenure of property is more of a duty than an actual right of possession. Property in the widest sense is a right that can belong only to society, which in turn receives it as a trust from Allah who is the only true owner of anything.

Thus the glorious Qur'an says: "Believe in Allah and in His Messenger; and spend of that of which He has given you the stewardship." (57:7) The text of this verse needs no explanation to bring out the meaning; for its meaning is apparent, namely, that property which is in the hands of men belongs to Allah and that men are its stewards rather than its masters. Or, in another verse, which concerns those who give certificates of manumission to slaves, "Give them of the property of Allah, which He has given you." (24:33) They are not giving to the slaves this property out of their own possessions, but out of the property of Allah; they thus act as intermediaries. Or clearest of all in a third verse, "Allah has favored some of you more than others in the matter of a competence. Yet those who have been thus favored will not give back such provision to the slaves whom they possess; in that respect they are equal. Will they thus deny the goodness of Allah?" (16:73) Here we have the definite affirmation that when those who have been favored in their competence give to their slaves, it is not only an equitable division between some who are rich and others who are poor. Not that in the least. This share is nothing more than the basic right of the latter, who have just as good a claim to it; and so they are equal in it. There is only one solution: one party has exactly the same right to receive as the other has to give. Then follows the disapproving question, "Will they thus deny the goodness of Allah?" Property is "the goodness of Allah"; it is not man's own possession.

There can be no clearer indication of the true nature of the possession of property than to describe it as the power of disposal and use. The outcome of this definition is that there can be no real place for personal possession unless it carries with it the rights of disposal and use. The condition on which this right must stand is that of wisdom in the disposal; if the disposal of property is foolish, then the ruler or society may withdraw this right of disposal. "Do not give to fools the property which Allah has given you to manage, but rather provide for them out of it, and clothe them." (4:4) Thus the right of disposal depends on being mature and being able to fulfill one's duties; when the possessor does not meet these requirements, then the natural fruits of ownership come to an end; that is, the right of disposal is annulled. This is also clearly shown in the fact that if a man dies without an heir, his legal heir is the

Imam (the ruler of the community); thus it appears that the property belongs to society and is merely administered by an individual, so that if he leaves no issue, the property reverts to its original ownership by the community.

I have not emphasized this principle in order to teach any communistic doctrine of property, for the right of personal ownership is firmly established in Islam. I have emphasized it because it is significant in the creation of a true understanding of the nature of personal ownership, and an understanding of how these two ideas are reconciled in the general Islamic view of property. In other and clearer words: The individual must realize that he is no more than the steward of this property, which is fundamentally the possession of society; this must make him accept the restrictions that the system lays upon his liberty, and the bounds that limit his rights of disposal. On the other side, society must realize its fundamental right to such property and must thus become bolder in prescribing the regulations and in laying down the laws which concern it. Thus only may we arrive at principles that will ensure complete social justice in the profitable use of property, which cannot be an end in itself nor a subject of actual ownership. The clearest instance of this is the matter of the tenure of land; thought cannot conceive that any man should be the owner of the land itself; all that he can possess is its irrigation and its crops, which means that the matter is one of the profitable use of a possession rather than one of actual ownership.

Another principle that Islam ratifies is that of the undesirability of personal ownership when it remains in the hands of a small group or circulates among them, so that others can have no part in it. "In order that it may not be passed around between the rich among you." (59:7) A story attaches to this text, which gives us the full meaning of this general Islamic principle.

The Emigrants had gone with the Prophet of Allah from Mecca to Medina; the poor had no property to take with them, and the rich had left their property behind them, so that they were as poor as the poor. But the Helpers were of generous mind, and they rose above the natural avarice which lies in the human soul; so they took the Emigrants as brothers in everything that they possessed. Out of the goodness of their hearts and of the nobility of their minds this action extended as far as their most intimate personal belongings. "They loved those who had emigrated to them, and they found no desire in their hearts for the share which had fallen to others; they preferred them above themselves, though among themselves there was poverty." (59:7) Thus they provided a pleasing example of the effect of religious belief on individuals, and thus they gave a perfect pattern for the attaining of freedom from worldly desires and the achievement of freedom to seek higher things.

Yet there continued to be a wide gap between the rich of Medina and the poor Emigrants; the Prophet saw the generosity and liberality of the Helpers, but saw no need to ask them to give more or impose a fixed payment upon them since they had adopted the Emigrants as brothers in everything they possessed. Then came the affair of the Banu Nadir,[24] when there was no warfare because they surrendered peacefully to the Prophet. Accordingly, the booty in this case belonged rightfully to Allah and His Messenger in its entirety; it is not so in a case of active war, where four-fifths of the booty belongs to those who have done the fighting, and only the remaining fifth to Allah and to the Messenger. In this case, the Messenger decided to restore some form of equality to the Muslim community as regards the possession of wealth; accordingly, he presented the booty of the Banu Nadir to the Emigrants for their personal use. With them he included two of the poorer Helpers in accordance with the reason given for the decision that the entire booty was to be given over to the Emigrants.

Concerning this event the Qur'an says: "What Allah has given to His Messenger as booty from the people of the towns belongs to Allah and the Messenger, to the relatives, the orphans, the poor, and the wayfarer, in order that it may not be passed around between the rich among you. Take what the Messenger gives you, and refrain from what he forbids; show piety towards Allah, for Allah can punish severely. The booty shall be for the Emigrants who were expelled from their dwellings and their property, seeking favor and approval from Allah. They helped Allah and His Messenger; they are the upright." (59:7-8)

This disposal of property by the Messenger and the causes given for that disposal in the Qur'an provide a clear and self-evident proof of the correctness of the Islamic principle that it is undesirable to have wealth concentrated in the hands of a few members of the community. It means also that there must be a readjustment of the foundations underlying this custom, so that here also there may be some form of equity. "In order that it may not be passed around between the rich among you."

That is to say, an excess of wealth on one side and a lack of it on the other produces a profound corruption, greater even than that produced by hatred and rancor. Wherever an abundance of wealth is found, it is like an abundance of vital strength in the body; it must find outlets, and there can be no permanent guarantee that such outlets will be moral and worthy. Thus wealth also must take its course, sometimes in the form of a luxury which corrupts the soul and enervates the body, sometimes in the form of desires which have to be satisfied. The effect of these desires is to be found on the other side of the community, which lacks wealth; here this effect takes the form of the sale or barter of personal honor, or the form of flattery, or falsehood, or the destruction of personality—all simply to satisfy the desires of the wealthy and to pander to their false vanity; for necessity easily overcomes opposition. The overwealthy man on the other hand is concerned only to find an outlet for his excess of vitality and for his excess of wealth. And thus moral degradation together with its appendages—drinking, gambling, slave trading, procuring, the spoiling of manhood, and the loss of honor—is only the outcome of an excess of wealth on one side and a lack of it on the other. And the unequal balance of society is a product of this discrimination.

All this takes no account of the personal hatreds and the individual jealousies, roused by those who have immoderate wealth, in the hearts of the poor who cannot find enough for their needs. The reaction here is sometimes hatred, sometimes a feeling of degradation and debasement; such men feel that their status is lowered in their own eyes and their honor sullied in face of the power and influence of wealth. Thus they are reduced to a small and humble manhood that knows nothing but the desire to please the rich and the powerful.

Islam, despite the emphasis that it lays on the spiritual values, is not unmindful of the importance of economic values; and no matter how much it seeks to raise men above the material considerations of this world, it never lays greater obligations on them than their human nature is able to bear. Therefore, it disapproves of money being circulated only among the rich, and so it makes the avoidance of this one of the principles of its economic theory.

Thus we have here the concept of a communal wealth that cannot be restricted to individuals, a wealth of which the Messenger enumerated three aspects, water, herbage, and fire. "All men share in three things, water, herbage, and fire." In these terms he described the essentials for the life of the community in his native Arabia; and so the profitable use of these things must be for the community as a whole. Now, the necessities of communal life vary from one country to another and from one age to another; but the analogy—for this is one of the fundamental laws of Islam—is easily applied to all other things that fall into the category of necessities. But this is another subject, which will be discussed in its proper place in the course of this book.

There is, then, a proportion of all wealth that belongs by right to the needy members of the community; this proportion is prescribed as the *zakat*. "And of their wealth a portion belongs by right to the beggar and the destitute." (70:24-25) Nor is this concept restricted to personal possessions; it covers communal possessions also, and the money arising from it must be used in specified ways. "The alms money is only for the poor and the destitute . . ."etc.

A true statement of the Islamic view of individual possession would therefore be this: The fundamental principle is that property belongs to the community in general; individual possession is a stewardship which carries with it conditions and limitations. Some property is held in common, and this no individual has any right to possess. A proportion of all property is a due that must be paid to the community, in order that the latter may disburse it to specified individuals of its own number; these constitute cases of need that may thereby be remedied so that the community may preserve its health.

THE MEANS OF INDIVIDUAL ACQUISITION

On the basis of this theory of the nature of ownership Islam organizes its logical results; it lays down the conditions of acquisition and the limitations of disposal; it establishes customary limits for profitable use in such a way that it does not deviate from considerations of social welfare and of individual welfare, which can never be separated from it.

Thus it emphasizes first of all that ownership in the sense of profitable use of property is made possible by the authority of the law, which is the guardian of social affairs. "It is the lawgiver who really gives to men their possessions, because he gives them legal status." And the same thought occurs among the definitions: "Possession is a legal concept relating either to an object or to usufruct; and he who has the profitable use of anything or who accepts an equivalent value for anything needs the ratification of the law."

"This definition means that ownership cannot be permanent unless it is legally declared to be so and ratified; and this finding is confirmed by all the jurists of Islam. For all rights, that of ownership among them, are lacking in permanence except by legal process and ratification of the transaction. Right of ownership is not an intrinsic quality of things, but arises from the sanction of the law, which alone can give legal effect to the preceding transactions."[25]

This ruling must be borne in mind by anyone who tries to explain the Islamic theory of the right of ownership; it represents the handing over by the law, acting for the community, to an individual of some particular thing to which the individual has no right except by virtue of this legal act. For the principle is that everything belongs to the community, and therefore, all permission for personal ownership must come from the law, virtually or actually.

The only method in Islam of gaining the right of ownership is by work of any kind or variety. Here again we see the idea of just relation between effort and reward. To explain this we may say that the methods of acquisition of wealth which are recognized by Islam are as follows:

First, hunting. This was the original primitive method of livelihood in human history; and it still exists as a means of gaining a form of wealth by more advanced and modern methods; for fishing and pearl diving, coral fishing and sponge diving are profitable pursuits both for governments and for individuals. There is still also the hunting of birds and animals, both for sport and for profit.

Second, cultivating waste lands which have no owner, by any method of cultivation. Here the individual must continue his irrigation of the land for a space of three years after he has put his hand to it. If he does not, then his right of possession lapses, because the purpose of cultivating waste land is to ensure general prosperity through its full employment. Three years is a sufficient test of the ability of any man who puts his hand to the task; if such ability has not then shown itself, the land reverts to the community and no individual can sequestrate it. "The land belongs to Allah and His Messenger, and after that to you; if any man cultivates waste land, then it shall be his, and none shall have the right of sequestration after three years."

Islamic law here is wiser than the secular law, which is derived from French law. For in secular law, "setting the hand to it" must be followed by a period of fifteen years before the land can pass into the possession of him who sets his hand to it. And the result is the same whether he has cultivated the land or left it waste during that period and the ensuing period. Such a result is of course incompatible with the Islamic emphasis on the true nature of ownership, for what we find here does nothing more than legitimize a fait accompli. So great is the difference between Islamic theory and common law.

Third, the extraction of minerals hidden in the earth, or mining. This occupation leaves four-fifths of the value of the minerals extracted as the possession of the worker; the other fifth is *zakat*, since such mining is allowable, and the individual earns by his own labor and toil. But here we must reckon with this saying: All the mining which had been done up to the time with which this statement deals has been of metals which are little used, such as gold and silver, not things which are necessary for the whole of the community, such as petroleum, coal, and iron. Can petroleum and coal and iron and similar things be compared with the common necessities such as water and herbage and fire? Or can they be compared with that mining which was known in the first days of the Islamic era? We shall leave our discussion of this to its proper place in this book.

Fourth, raiding. From this comes the possession of plunder, which consists of everything possessed by an unbeliever who has been killed by a Muslim. "The plunder of an unbeliever who has been killed belongs to the man who killed him." Again there comes under this head the possession of booty; four-fifths of this go to those who have done the fighting, while the other fifth goes to Allah and the Messenger. "And know that whatever you take as booty, one fifth of it belongs to Allah and the Messenger, to the relatives, the orphans, the poor, and the wayfarer." (8:42)

Fifth, working for a wage for others. Islam gives regard and honor to this type of work and calls for the prompt payment of wages in full and without deductions. The Qur'an advocates such labor, making it a source of honor in the eyes of all who see it and a matter for regard and esteem. "Say: Work, and Allah will see your work, as will His Messenger and the Believers." (9:106) In this there lies an incitement to true and faithful work. There is also honor for work, because it is worthy of regard and consideration and esteem. So in another place the Qur'an urges men to effort and exertion in the earth for this same cause: "So walk about in the earth in all its regions, and eat of what it provides." (67:15)

The Messenger also went far to give sanctity to labor when he accepted a hand swollen with constant toil, saying: "This is a hand which is beloved of Allah and His Messenger." And many other traditions have come down to us that reiterate this religious sanction. "He who in the evening is weary from manual labor shall receive pardon for his sins that very same evening." "Verily Allah loves the servant who practices a trade. " "Whatever food any one of you eats, let it be nothing but the fruit of his hands." And we have already seen how Islam makes work a form of worship and how indeed it rates it above all formal worship. Thus it estimates that the man who works and supports a brother renowned for his piety is actually the more pious of the two.

On the basis of this theory that sanctifies labor, Islam also sanctifies the claim of the worker to his wage. It demands first of all that he be paid in full; it warns any employer who acts unjustly towards his men that he is earning for himself the enmity and the hostility of Allah. The Messenger of Allah once said: "Thus saith Allah, the Great, the Glorious: Three there are whom I will hate on the Day of Resurrection—a man to whom I have been generous and who has betrayed My generosity; a man who sells a free man into slavery and lives off the price; and a man who hires another at a stipulated wage, takes full advantage of his labor, and then will not give him his due." The collocation of these three forms of disobedience and the identity of their punishment have a particular significance. The first is deceit because it is a betrayal of the protection of Allah, the second is an unavenged crime against the essential nature of a free man for motives of profit, and the third is living off the sweat of a hired man. This last is similar to living off the price of a free man sold into slavery, thus betraying his essential humanity; it is similar to breaking an oath that has been sworn in the name of Allah, thus betraying the protection of the Creator. All of these things merit the enmity and the hostility of Allah because of their infamy and because of the disgraceful nature of such a betrayal.

In the second place, Islam demands that the payment of wages be punctual. It is not enough that they should be paid in full; they must also be paid on time. The Messenger says: "Pay your hired man his wages before the sweat is dry on him." Islam here seeks to meet both a psychological and material need in the life of the worker. The psychological need is that he must know that he is an object of care and concern; promptness in the payment of wages conveys this knowledge and makes him realize that his labor is valuable and his place in society assured. The material need is that the worker is generally in need of his wage from day to day in order to provide the material necessities for himself, his wife, and his children. So late payment harms him by denying him the fruits of his labor and toil at the most necessary time, and it lessens his zeal and willingness to work. Whereas, Islam is insistent that all should work who are able and that they should do as much as they can; thus from work they may gain a psychological satisfaction and a material sufficiency at the same time.

Again Islam prohibits any worker from allocating any part of his wages to anyone such as an overseer, as if there could be here any "workers' leader" who does not work himself but who demands a share of the wages of every worker. The Prophet said: "Beware of allocations." When we asked, "What are allocations?" he replied: "A man controls a party among the people, and he exacts a due from this one and a due from that one." This is contrary to one of the principles of Islam, that there must be no pay without work, no wealth without labor. And over and above this, such a system contains the possibility of oppression and ruin for the worker.

In return for this care for the rights of the worker, Islam requires of him that he on his side shall perform his work fully and faithfully; for every right carries a corresponding responsibility in Islam. "Verily Allah is pleased when one of you does a piece of work which he performs well." This is but natural as a consequence of the equality between effort and reward; it is natural also from the point of view of the character on which Islam insists as the basis of true life. For dishonesty and careless work indicate a corruption of the spirit of man and a deadness of his conscience. To indulge in such laziness and to become habituated to it tends to make the spirit of man idle and his conscience void. And beyond that, the welfare of society as a whole is disturbed and menaced by poor work.

Sixth, assigning by the ruler of a piece of land that does not belong to anyone. Such is land pertaining to the Muslim public treasury taken from the polytheists who cannot have the right of inheritance; its custodian is the Imam. Or, it may be uncultivated land; it again has no owner. The Prophet assigned land to Abu Bakr and 'Umar, and the Caliphs after him did the same, as a reward for meritorious effort or service to Islam. But, this was always done within narrow limits and always of land that had no owner or was uncultivated. When the Umayyads came to power they plundered the people and assigned lands to their relatives, but they were oppressive tyrants rather than righteous Muslim rulers, as we shall see.

Seventh, money necessary to sustain life. Islam prescribes the use of money drawn from the *zakat* in specified ways. "The *zakat* is only for the poor and the destitute, for those employed in collecting it, for those who have to be won over to Islam, for the ransom of slaves and the relief of debtors, for spending in the way of Allah, and for the wayfarer." (9:60) Any man who comes into any one of these categories is eligible for a share of the *zakat*. There are some who will not work and who draw the *zakat* as being in need; but need is an urgent substitute for work. It is work that Islam sanctifies, and which thereby becomes the first and the best means of acquiring the right of possession.

These are the methods that Islam recognizes as the methods of legal acquisition; anything outside of these is rejected and condemned. Thus plundering, theft, robbery, and misappropriation do not confer the right of possession. Neither does gambling, which is forbidden: "Wine and gambling, the use of lots and arrows are only an abomination, a work of Satan. Turn away from them, then, and it may be that you will prosper." (5:92) Money that comes by a forbidden method is also forbidden, for gambling is not work but simply robbery. In addition, it gives rise to enmity and hatred among the gamblers themselves and is therefore incompatible with the original plan of Islam, which was to spread the spirit of love and mutual help and fellowship. "Satan only wishes to cause enmity and hatred among you by means of wine and gambling." (5:93)

The reason for the acceptance of these seven methods of acquisition is clearly the fact that they are all based on the expending of effort; this effort must be rewarded, for it is one of the supports of life; in it there lies power for the cultivation of the earth, the profit of society, the reformation of the spirit of man, and the purification of his conscience. There is nothing like work for reforming the soul, strengthening the body, and guarding the whole nature of man from the diseases of flabbiness and weakness.

So long as work remains the prime cause of the right of acquisition it will also be of itself the ratification of the right of individual possession—but always within limits already described, to
ensure that no one is harmed by it. Indeed it will provide an incentive to the individual to give his utmost effort, so that his natural
desire for possession may be satisfied. But, he must always work in
legitimate ways and must harm no other by his work. When he
departs from these ways, in order to achieve justice he must be
brought back to them without losing his zeal for work and becoming one of the idle and profitless weaklings.

Along with the Islamic theory of the ownership of property we
must enter into the method of passing on possessions. Here no
absolute freedom is granted, a fact is clearly seen in the regulations
governing inheritance and bequest. Gifts and presents alone are
free of all restraint; in these matters the individual is given full liberty to give away or donate as much of his property as he wishes,
while he is still alive. The reason for this freedom is that there is an
inherent personal restriction on such giving, inasmuch as a man of
property will give away only part of his money, so that his heir will
not suffer as he well may in the case of bequests. If he does
nonetheless go to extremes, then he exposes himself to restrictions
being placed on him by the withdrawal from him of the function
of ownership.

But when a man dies, his control ceases and his money passes
to those who succeed him as heirs or as beneficiaries under his will,
the passing on of such money being liable to regulations under a
system that is laid down on certain wise bases. There can be no
bequest to the heir, and there can be no bequeathing of more than
one-third of the total estate; this is the extreme limit. Bequests have
been provided for, as we have said, in order to deal with circumstances which may arise; for example, it may happen that near relatives are unable to inherit, though their relationship entitles them
to a share, because their degree of relationship lets other heirs take
precedence over them in the estate. So bequests function addition-
ally as a form of generosity or almsgiving.

The passing on of property by inheritance is governed by the
specific regulations contained in the two verses of the Qur'an

dealing with this question; these we have already quoted in the section on mutual responsibility in society. (4:12-14)

The general principle of the division of an estate is this: A man shall have the same share as two women, the reason for which we have already explained. An heir from the paternal side of the family takes precedence over one from the mother's side, even though there may be circumstances under which the latter should have the larger share; this is the result of a balancing of responsibilities against rights. For, the inheritor on the paternal side was charged with greater responsibilities to the testator. In the same way, the son in a family inherits everything after the grandparents have received their portion; for it was he who was primarily responsible for maintaining his father during the lifetime of the latter, if need arose. A full brother takes precedence over a half brother, because it was on him that the legal responsibility fell of maintaining his brother if he was unable to earn his own living. Similar principles apply to the settlement of debts left behind by the deceased. Thus, by a just system of division a balance is struck between obligations and rewards, between responsibilities and privileges.

The reason for this principle of inheritance has already been sufficiently discussed in the section on mutual responsibility in society; there we showed its connection with the basic principles of Islam as they apply to this mutual responsibility and as they apply to the ties of relationship and between generations. We also showed the interest which Islam has in this regard for the nature, the inclination, and the needs of the individual and of society alike.

Here we must only discuss the reason for the inheritance regulations as touching society. As we have already seen, Islam is opposed to the heaping up of wealth and to its being confined within a limited circle. The inheritance regulations are a means towards decreasing the swollen fortunes that accumulate in succeeding generations. For, the one property passes at the death of its owner to a multitude of children and relatives and so becomes a number of fortunes of medium or small dimensions. It is seldom that such a fortune retains its original unity under this system, except under rare and anomalous conditions; for example, a man may die leaving only one son to inherit the whole estate, because he has neither father nor mother, wife nor daughter. But in the majority of cases the fortune is divided up between a number of individuals.

When we compare this with the English system, under which the whole estate goes to the eldest son, the wisdom of Islam is apparent in dividing up the one single fortune; it is equally clear that the system is just to the various heirs, for it does not give them any ill-feeling for the eldest son.

WAYS OF INCREASING POSSESSIONS

Along with the Islamic theory of the ownership of property we must consider the question of the way of increasing it and trading in it. The owner is not allowed absolute freedom to dispose of his money in this way as he may wish. For beyond his individual interests there are those of the society with which he interacts.

Every individual has freedom to increase his wealth, but only within legally prescribed limits. He is permitted to till the ground, he is allowed to transform raw materials into finished products, he may carry on retail trade; but he may not swindle, hold a monopoly on any of the necessities of life, put out his money at interest thus to grow and increase, or cheat the worker out of his wage. All these things are forbidden. Reputable methods of increase are the only methods that Islam countenances for the growth of wealth, but these do not generally produce that degree of capital that sets a wide gulf between the social classes. Capital only reaches the disgracefully swollen proportions that we see today when it is amassed by swindling, usury, oppression of the workers, monopolies or exploitation of the needs of the community, robbing, plundering, despoiling and pillaging—and by all the other criminal methods involved in contemporary exploitation. This is what Islam does not permit. We shall now consider these in turn; and we start with an explanation of the wisdom of Islamic law on the methods of increase.

❖ ❖ ❖ ❖ ❖ ❖ ❖

Islam forbids dishonesty in business; "He who swindles is not one of us." "When two make a bargain and are not at variance, so long as they tell the truth and deal openly, blessings shall attend their bargain; but if they deal covertly and falsely, all blessing is denied to their bargain." So you must buy and sell without dishonesty, both in commodities and in currency. If your article has a blemish, you must point it out; if you do not do so, then you are being dishonest and your profit is unlawful. Nor can you escape the punishment of your dishonesty by giving away the unlawful profit as alms; for alms cannot be reckoned to your credit unless they are given from your lawful possessions. It is told on the authority of Abdullah ibn Mas'ud that the Messenger of Allah said: "No servant of Allah who makes unlawful wealth can give it away in alms and expect it to be received; nor can he spend it and expect to receive a blessing from it; nor even can he leave it behind his back without its pushing him forward into hellfire. Verily Allah does not blot out one evil by another; rather He blots out evil with good. So wickedness cannot blot out wickedness." Again he said: "Flesh fattened upon unlawful profit shall not enter Paradise, but Hell shall have possession of all such."

In this matter Islam is following its essential principles, just as it does in preventing injury to men and in emphasizing the need for mutual help between all men. For, dishonesty in business is a defiling of the conscience; it involves the harming of others and the destruction of the trusting nature of men; and there can be no mutual help without trust. Besides, the proceeds of dishonesty represent an access of wealth without legitimate effort, and the general Islamic principle is that there can be no gain without effort, just as conversely there must be no effort without reward.

✦ ✦ ✦ ✦ ✦ ✦ ✦

Monopolies on the necessities of life are not recognized by Islam as one of the legal methods of gain or of the increase of wealth. "He who imports goods shall be given his provision, but he who monopolizes goods shall be accursed." "The monopolist is a sinner." That is to say, a monopoly is an infringement of the right to trade and to manufacture, and the monopolist permits no one but himself to import or to manufacture his chosen goods. Thus he can control the market and can impose on the people what prices he wishes, inflict on them hardship and distress, and injure them through their livelihood and through their necessities. In addition, he closes the door of opportunity against others who desire to gain their living as he gains his, or to succeed more than he has. It sometimes happens even that the holder of a monopoly will cut off the supplies or destroy a glut of goods, so that he may be able to impose an exorbitant price. This represents stopping or lessening the flow of supplies that are for general use and that Allah has ordained for the use of all men on the earth. Thus we have seen how loads of Brazilian coffee were burned in order to prevent a drop in the market price of coffee; but at the same time millions of people could not buy coffee to meet their needs. Similarly, we find the medicine markets monopolized by Jews and others; so the sick undergo suffering or are left to die, while the monopolists make their scandalous profits and thereby amass their unlawful wealth.

In its desire to check this method of increasing wealth Islam goes so far as to put outside the pale of the faith all who hold monopolies. "He who holds a monopoly on food for forty days is clear of Allah and Allah of him." Such a man is no Muslim, who can thus injure society by engendering in it fear and lack of its necessities, solely in order to make an unlawful gain, and thus to increase his private wealth at the expense of the general welfare.

✥ ✥ ✥ ✥ ✥ ✥ ✥

Usury is another method of increase that is unlawful; Islam is strongly opposed to this custom and condemns it outright, warning those who practice it of the most terrible consequences. "O you who have believed, do not live on usury doubled and redoubled; but act piously towards Allah, and it may be that you will prosper." (3:125) This is not a case of prohibiting merely doubling and redoubling, while allowing smaller gains; the mention of doubling is no more than an emphasis on actual fact, a description of what takes place. This prohibition strikes rather at the very root and principle of usury, a fact that is made clear in other verses. "Those who live off usury will only arise at the Day of Judgment as those arise whom Satan has overthrown by a touch. This is because they have said, 'A bargain is just the same as usury.' But Allah has allowed bargaining, though He has forbidden usury. If anyone receives a warning from his Lord and desists, he shall keep what he has already gained, and his affair shall be in the hands of Allah; but anyone who continues on his way is destined for hellfire, long to stay there." (2:276) "O you who have believed, show piety towards Allah, and leave alone what remains unpaid of your usury, if you are true Believers. If you do not, then be warned of enmity from Allah and from His Messenger. But if you repent, you may keep your capital, no wrong being done on either side." (2:278-9)

In its loathing of the practice of living on usury Islam goes so far as to make its shamefulness even greater than that of adultery; and this it holds to be something that destroys honor, violates true relationships, and is a disgrace to society. Thus the Messenger says: "A pennyworth of usury which a man uses knowingly is worse than thirty-six acts of adultery."

In all this Islam is true to its fundamental beliefs on wealth, morality, and the welfare of society. Property is a trust in the hands of its possessor, who is thereby obliged to use it for the general good of society; it must not be subverted and used as an instrument to oppress and plunder the people. No man of wealth may pounce on the hour of his fellow's need as an opportunity for taking advantage of his position in order to demand a return of more than he has given. Sometimes such need is for necessary food, for medicine for the treatment of disease, for expenses on education or other things; then the alternative is either that all these things be left unattended to or that the wealthy man have his way with the needy, giving them a little and demanding a large return. Thus he injures them by the financial power that he wields, so that either they have to slave unremittingly to pay the usurer his interest, or their debt doubles itself year after year.

This is the excessive wealth enjoyed by the rich man; he does not work other than being a man of property; he drinks blood and sweat in his greed, voracious in his idleness. But it is work that Islam sanctifies, making work the primary ground of possession and profit; and it does not permit wealth to grow through idleness, nor will it allow wealth to beget wealth. Only effort can beget wealth, otherwise such wealth is unlawful.

Islam has an interest also in the effect on the purity of the individual's nature and on the fellow feeling between the members of society. No man can live off usury and still have a true nature and conscience; and usury on the other side does not encourage or perpetuate fellow feeling and sympathy in society. Anyone who gives me one dinar in order to demand a return of two dinars from me is my enemy; I cannot have any friendly feeling for him, nor can I bear him any affection. Mutual help is one of the fundamental principles of the Islamic society, but usury destroys mutual help and vitiates it at the very root. Therefore, Islam is opposed to this practice.

Furthermore, in this present age there is apparent another reason for prohibiting usury, a reason that was not formerly apparent. This is that usury represents a method of amassing a vast amount of capital wealth that does not depend on effort or labor; this is brought about by the existence of nonworkers who rely only on this means of increasing and multiplying their wealth. Thus idleness and luxury are encouraged at the expense of the toiling masses, who need money and have to borrow it at interest in the critical hour. From this situation there arise two dangerous social ills: one is the amassing of unlimited fortunes, and the other is the division of society into two classes, an upper and a lower. So there appears an idle, lazy, and luxury-loving class that does no work and yet has everything. The money that they possess is like a net to entrap more money, except that there is no necessity to put a bait in the net; for the poor fall into it only too readily; their steps, driven by necessity, lead them straight into it.

Money should be loaned to those in need freely and without interest; this is the way to increase affection, cultivate generosity, and create a sense of mutual responsibility between rich and poor, between powerful and weak. For there is no intrinsic excellence in property, but only an enjoyment and an effort. And the mere possession of money does not entitle a man to make a profit out of it alone. It is the borrower who must put out the effort, and therefore all profit resulting from that effort should accrue to him who makes the effort; the capital of the loan should be returned alone, that is to say, without interest, to its owner.

According to Islamic usage, it is right that loans should be made for either consumption or production. In the former case, where the loan is to be used for the provision of material necessities, the borrower must not be oppressed by having to pay interest on the loan, and the custom is that the principal sum shall be repaid alone when the borrower is in better circumstances. In the latter case, the principle is that the profit is made rather by the effort expended than by the money borrowed; for money cannot make profits except by effort, and it is that effort that is the important thing in the eyes of Islam. Accordingly, Islam forbids usury in all cases; but it holds that a loan must be made freely to anyone who has to meet essential needs of any kind.

When a man borrows money and then falls on evil circumstances, "Then let there be indulgence until better times." (2:280) It seems that this conditional sentence in fact implies a command: "If he be in adverse circumstances, then let there be indulgence until better times." This gives it the form of a command rather than that of an exhortation. And besides this, affection is encouraged by help and forbearance, as the Messenger said: "Allah will be merciful to a man who is forbearing when he buys or sells or exacts payment." Forbearance in collecting a debt preserves the self-esteem of the borrower and encourages in his heart an affection for the lender; it gives him an incentive to work hard in order to repay his loan as far as he can. So Muhammad said: "Anyone who would rejoice in Allah saving him from the pains of the Day of Resurrection should attempt to ease the pain of another who is in evil circumstances, or should remit his debt." Or again: "He who grants indulgence to one in evil circumstances or who remits a debt — Allah will grant him shelter."

On the other hand, Islam commands the borrower to spare no effort to pay back his debt, clear his obligations, set against the grace of a loan the equal grace of repayment, and thus foster mutual trust in dealings between individuals. "If anyone takes the money of others with the intention of repaying it, Allah will repay it for him; but if anyone takes such money with the intention of destroying it, then Allah will destroy him." Anyone who accepts money with the intention of repaying it works unceasingly to earn and to support himself; thereby he gains for himself generally true greatness and strength of character. But anyone who accepts money with the intention of not repaying it desires to live on the money of others; so he ceases to work altogether and becomes lazy, till ultimately his ambition fails and he degenerates into destruction and ruin of character. The Messenger once said: On another occasion a man asked him: "O Messenger of Allah, is it your judgement that if I am killed in the way of Allah He will forgive my sins?" The Messenger, peace and blessings be upon him, answered: "Yes, if you are killed while patient and vigilant, facing the enemy, not with your back turned to them." The Prophet then asked the man to repeat his question, and this time he answered: "Yes, except for a debt remaining unpaid, for this what Jibril has just conveyed to me." Thus, for a debtor who is able to repay, it is not enough to fight in the way of Allah and to be killed, not enough to be a man of endurance, patient, always advancing in battle and never retreating; despite these things a debt still hangs about his neck; for it is a duty, not only to Allah, but also to others, so long as he is able to repay. One who has no means to discharge his debt is permitted to do so by the use of *zakat* which he receives. Abu Sa'id al-Khudri said: A contemporary of the Messenger came into difficulties through his commercial transactions, and had a huge debt. So the Messenger commanded: Give alms to him. The people gave him alms, but still the amount could not discharge the debt. Then the Messenger said to the man's creditors: "Take from him what you can get, and let that be enough for you."

The Prophet also took another step forward when wealth accrued to him after the conquests, in that he formed the habit of settling the outstanding accounts of debtors after their death out of the public funds. It is related on the authority of Abu Huraira as follows: When they brought to the Messenger of Allah the case of a man who had died owing money, he would ask, "Has he left enough to pay his debt?" If he was told that such was the case, he would pray for the man; otherwise he would say to the Muslims, "Pray for this, your comrade." But after Allah granted him the conquests, he stood up in public and said, "I am more worthy of the love of the Muslims than their own selves; but if any Muslim dies owing money, the discharge of the debt shall be my duty. Even if any such man leaves sufficient money for repaying the debt it shall remain for his heirs."

In this way Islam insists that every man be paid in full; it demands this with the same insistence with which it demands that the needy be helped and that there be indulgence in the matter of repayment. Thus it takes a comprehensive view of all the aspects of the matter, in order to guarantee the general welfare, and holds an impartial balance between privileges and responsibilities.

WAYS OF SPENDING

Such are the limitations that Islam lays down for the increasing of wealth by business dealings. In the case of spending money, the matter is likewise not left unregulated; the wealthy man is not free to lock up his wealth or to spend it as he wishes, even though there may be a natural appearance of such freedom of disposal. In Islam the individual is not left to himself to do with his property as he wishes; he has his degree of freedom, but it is bounded by a hedge of limitations. In addition, there can seldom be a purely personal disposal of property that does not in some way affect other people, even though such effects may not be material or in any way apparent.

The man who is niggardly is similar to the man who is wasteful; neither of these is approved by Islam, because both of them are harmful to themselves and to society. "And do not keep your hand chained to your neck that it cannot spend; neither spread it wide open to squander, so that you are left censured and in poverty," (17:31) "O sons of man, take your adornment at every mosque; eat and drink, but do not be wasteful; verily He does not love those who are wasteful." (7:29)

"Chaining the hand" in niggardliness is forbidden to people, so far as concerns the legitimate enjoyment of their property; Islam commands the individual to enjoy what he possesses within legal limits, and it is opposed to people who forbid that which is not forbidden. For life should be made pleasant and agreeable and cheerful, without wantonness or waste; and Islam does not command austerity or asceticism or abstinence from the good things of life. Therefore, in the above verse He commands the sons of man to adorn themselves with suitable adornments; and the Qur'an goes on after this verse to say in disapproving accents: "Say: Who has forbidden the adornments of Allah, which He has provided for His servants, and the good things which He has provided? Say: On the Day of Resurrection these will be exclusively for those who have shown belief during the life of this world. Thus do We make the signs distinct for people who have knowledge. Say: My Lord has forbidden only indecencies, both open and secret, crime, and unjustified greed; He has forbidden that you should associate with Him anything for which He has revealed no authority, and that you should say against Allah things which you do not know." (7:30-31)

Islam desires that all men should have enjoyment of the reasonable pleasures of life, old and young, rich and poor alike; hence the form of address in this passage, "Sons of man." So when it happens that Islam summons men to endurance and obedience, this summons does not entail asceticism or self-denial; rather it is a summons to keep oneself in tranquility of mind and to endure adversity until it passes away or is removed. Beyond this, every individual is called upon to enjoy all permissible things, and society wants to encourage its members to enjoy such things. So it will never forbid them to enjoy the things which Allah calls them to enjoy in this life.

Accordingly, it is laid down that a portion of the *zakat* shall be given to the poor; by the "poor" are meant those whose possessions are not sufficient to make them liable to pay the tax. By this donation they may be given a comfortable living, rather than the bare livelihood which they already possess. That is to say, Islam advocates not merely a bare existence, but rather an enjoyment of life that is better than a bare existence. So when Islam awards something to a poor man out of the *zakat* money, it is giving him comfort and the enjoyment of more than the bare necessities; it is better for him to spend what he has, to enjoy the reasonable pleasures of life, and not to forbid himself the many goods things of life. Thus his life may become pleasant and agreeable, and thus the soul may find a freedom from purely material cares to think great thoughts, formulate lofty ideals, ponder the problems of the universe and human nature, and take up the search for perfection and beauty. So the Messenger says: "Allah loves to see the results of His beneficence to His servants." Hardship and poverty constitute the greatest possible denial of the beneficence of Allah, and He disapproves such a denial.

All this is from only one point of view; but there is another point of view which Islam has in mind, namely, the undesirability of money being kept out of circulation and never being spent. Such restriction of money nullifies its function; for society requires that money be kept in general circulation, so that the various aspects of life may be encouraged, so that the widest productivity may be guaranteed in all fields, so that work may be provided for the workers and an incentive kept before human nature. The restriction of money nullifies all of this, and therefore in Islam such restriction is forbidden, because it militates against the welfare of the individual and of society in general.

At the opposite extreme from niggardliness we have wastefullness, which is a corrupting influence alike on the individual and on society. But, let us first hasten to emphasize that the spending of money—even the whole of one's money—in the way of Allah is not waste. The basis of this belief is in the tradition about the Messenger and the mountain of gold, in which he desired that if he had the value of two cents left, he might spend it all in the way of Allah. Waste is constituted only by wasteful spending on oneself, and such is the meaning Islam gives it.

Waste in this sense means that luxury of which Islam disapproves so strongly; it hates wealth to be confined to the rich, lest its accumulation prevent it from being spent in the way of Allah; this it holds to be a source of injury both to the individual who possesses the wealth and to the society in which he lives. Such misuse is, therefore, an evil thing that it is incumbent on society to change in order to avoid its own ruin by this means.

The passages of the Qur'an and the Traditions of the Prophet that disapprove and forbid luxury are frequent and numerous; they are clear and definitive, teaching that this is among the worst of unlawful things in the eyes of Allah and His Messenger. Islam certainly urges men to enjoy the good things of life and disapproves of men denying themselves those things that are lawful for them; it calls on men to make life pleasant and agreeable, and not gray and drab. Yet it is the same Islam that disapproves of waste and luxury so strongly and even violently.

The Qur'an characterizes luxury-loving people sometimes as those whose aspiration fails, whose strength disappears, and whose liberality vanishes. "When a Sura is revealed which contains the command, 'Believe in Allah, and fight along with His Messenger,' those who have long purses call on you; they say, 'Let us be among those who stay at home.'" (9:87) When we remember how Islam insists on *jihad* and urges men to share in it and honors those who volunteer for it, we see how much it must despise, by contrast, those who have the long purses for turning away and refusing to join the ranks of those who fight. This is not in the least strange; for the lover of luxury is flabby and weak-willed, soft, and with little virility; he cannot rely on his strength, his ambition has failed, and his generosity has vanished. To take part in a *jihad* would hinder the gratification of his petty desires and forbid him his animal pleasures for a time; he recognizes no value in life except these corrupt and disgraceful things.

Furthermore, many times in history mention is made of the lovers of luxury as always impeding not only themselves but also their followers in pursuing the way of truth; for so long as there are such, there will also be weaklings who will flatter their pride, minister to their desires, and lose their personality like insects. "We have never sent anyone as a warner to a town, but the men of luxury have said, 'We do not believe in your message.'" (34:33) "Then said the chief men of his people, who disbelieved and dismissed as false the idea of meeting the Last Day, men to whom We had given luxury in the life of this world: 'This is only a man like yourselves; he eats what you eat, and he drinks what you drink. If you obey a man like yourselves, surely you will lose by it.'" (23:34-36) "And they said: 'O our Lord, we obeyed our chiefs and our great ones, and they led us from the Way; O our Lord, bring upon them a double punishment, and lay on them a mighty curse." (33:67-68) Nor is there anything strange in this; for lovers of luxury must have their easy, perverse, and sickly life; they must gratify their desires and have their pleasures; they must have around them followers and courtiers who are submissive. But truth and religion and faith forbid them most of the things that they must have and limit the number of their permissible possessions to a quantity they find slight and insignificant, in which their weak minds and jaded appetites can find no pleasure. Truth and religion and faith raise the status of the common man, so that the luxurious can no longer have an absolute authority over their weaklings and cannot make out of them obedient instruments and willing tools. Truth and religion and faith forbid the superstitious illusions and legends with which they have surrounded themselves and which they exploit in the misguided, ignorant, and subservient societies. Thus they are hostile to all truth and to all knowledge. All this takes no account of the effect that luxury has on the conscience or of the atrophy of the senses that is produced by excessive indulgence. "And on the Day of His gathering the peoples, together with that which they have worshiped apart from Allah, He will say: 'Did you lead these My servants astray, or did they by themselves err from the Way?' They will say: 'Glory be to Thee. It was not right for us to take any patron apart from Thee; but to these and to their fathers Thou hast given a perpetual enjoyment, till now they have forgotten Thy reminder, and are become a ruined people." (25:18-19) So, wealth and excessive property inherited from a previous generation make one forget the reminder of Allah, and thus issue in barrenness and drought. For the explanation of the phrase, "They have become a ruined people" is one which is illustrative, vivid, and full of significance; land which is "ruined" is barren land which cannot produce or bear fruit; similarly, the hearts and souls and lives of such people are barren, smooth, and hard; in them no real life can flow.

The Messenger describes the houses of the luxurious as houses of the Satans, because of the corruption which springs up in them and because of the temptation which issues from them.

"There are camels which belong to the Satans, and houses which belong to the Satans. The former I have seen when one of you brings out his pedigreed camels which he has been fattening, and on which he will not mount; he passes by one of his fellows who is exhausted, and he will not invite him to mount. The latter I see only in the lattices which people have screened with brocade." The Messenger of Allah saw belonging to the Satans camels that their owners had no need to ride, while exhausted wayfarers could not afford a beast to carry them. We see the same thing here in the shape of the huge automobiles which come and go on small and trifling errands, while thousands cannot afford a tram fare; and other hundreds have not even the use of their legs to travel, having lost them in some calamity. As for the houses Muhammad saw in the lattices that people screened with brocade, we still see them and in them forms of luxury that never occurred to the mind of man in that earlier age.

Undoubtedly, luxury is the cause of destruction in the course of history, as it is the cause of insolence. "How many towns have We destroyed which were insolent because of their prosperity. These are their dwellings, almost uninhabited since then." (28:58)

And equally certainly, luxury is a reason for punishment in the world to come, because it results in grave sin. "Those on the left hand, what are they? They live now in hot wind and scalding water, in the shadow of black smoke, neither cool nor elegant; yet they were previously in luxury and persisted in grievous sin; they would say: 'When we are dead and turned to dust and bones, can we really be raised up again? And also our fathers and the men of old?'" (56:40-47)

But, it is not only the individual who loves luxury who will suffer destruction and punishment; the community that permits the existence of such luxury will be similarly afflicted. "And when it is Our will to destroy a town, We command its luxury-loving citizens, and they deal corruptly in it; thus the sentence upon it is justified, and We destroy it utterly." (17:17) The "will" here referred to is not predetermination in the commonly accepted sense, but rather the law of cause and effect, or of reason and result. If there are luxury-loving individuals in a community and the community suffers them to remain so, doing nothing against them; if it refrains from checking the causes of luxury; if it leaves the luxury-loving to pursue their corrupt way; then all these factors, because of their very existence, are causes that will inevitably result in the destruction and the downfall of the community. Such is the meaning of "will" in this verse. That is to say, the results are related to the reasons, and the effects must follow where the causes occur; for such is the normative pattern which Allah has laid down for the universe and for all life.

The community will be held responsible for this evil that exists in its midst; for luxury must inevitably lead to evil by reason of its very existence in the community. As we have already seen, there must be some outlet found for excessive resources. Here in Egypt we have excessive wealth, which is a resource. We have also an excessive physical vitality, which is again a resource. We have an excess of spare time, not filled by work or thought, and this too is a resource. Accordingly, young men and women who love luxury, who have youth and leisure and wealth, inevitably go astray and seek extra outlets for their excess of resources in body, wealth, and time. Generally, these outlets are trivial and take their form from the period and the social environment; but there comes a time when they pass this limit of triviality and take the form of license and depravity, both physical and mental.

And on the other side, there is exploitation, profiteering, and destitution; these produce the slave traders, the toadies, the courtiers, and hangers-on of the wealthy, all of whom spread the spirit of laxity and dissipation; they cheapen the true values of life, which do not appeal to luxury-loving men and women. Thence, the disease extends outwards to all the other classes of the community until finally there comes the inevitable result, namely, the wide spread of immorality throughout the community, the growth of license, the weakening of body and of mind, and the decline of moral and spiritual powers. At this point the command of Allah is fully executed and such a community is utterly destroyed.

This is what Islam sees in the crime of luxury; it is a crime that is basically individual, but when the community acquiesces in it and does not check such an evil with hand and voice and heart, then it is a crime that produces its own fruits. The disease extends to the whole body of the community and issues ultimately in its destruction; for, the results are dependent on the reasons, the effects on the cause. "And you will not find any change in the custom of Allah." (33:62)

But what, then, is the limiting factor in both luxury and privation, and what is the just middle course between them? It is our belief that environment and common usage provide the most equitable criterion. So if we go back to the first age of Islam, we find a poverty-stricken country in which hardship and penury were common; it is for this reason that we find the Messenger saying, as he limits luxury, "No son of man has any claim to possess more than three things: the house in which he lives, the garment which covers his nakedness, and a crust of bread (that is, with nothing to accompany it) and water." So too he forbids the wearing of silk: "He who wears silk in this world will not wear it at all in the next." And 'Ali relates that the Messenger forbade also the use of Egyptian cloth and of clothes dyed yellow. He forbade also the wearing of gold rings. All these were forbidden to men. But women were permitted the use of silk and gold, although he himself disliked his daughter Fatima to wear gold. But this was a personal matter, in that the Prophet enjoined it on his own household, but did not apply it to the people in general.

It is our belief that we do not permit anything that should be forbidden when we say: This was the logical outcome of the Prophet's environment; but Islam does not demand hardship so long as that hardship is not necessitated by the conditions of the environment or by the state of the community. It is true, nonetheless, that the wearing of silk and saffron-dyed clothes or of embroidered garments is harmful to the status of men; it encourages them to become soft and cowardly in time of war; and such softness cannot exist in a community where the economic level does not permit it. But, the Messenger did not carry the idea of hard living to the point of neglecting and overlooking one's dress. Jabir told this story of him. The Messenger of Allah came to visit us once, and seeing a dishevelled man with untidy hair, he said, "Could this fellow find nothing to keep his head in order?" Then, seeing a man wearing dirty clothes, he said, "Could this fellow find no way of washing his clothes?" In the same strain Abu al-Akwas al-Jashmi tells this story on the authority of his father: The Prophet once saw me wearing old clothes, and said, "Have you any property?" I said, "Yes." He asked, "Where did you get your property?" and I said, "From all that Allah has given me in the way of sheep and camels." He said, "Then, since Allah has given you property, let Him see you wearing some of the results of His favor and generosity."

We have already noticed Allah's commandment to the sons of man to take their adornment and not to forbid the good things which He has permitted them. The meaning that we take from all of this is that the condition of one's environment is the criterion in this matter, and that it is the general standard of living in the community that must be the limiting factor in both luxury and privation. For, when Allah granted to the Muslims the conquest of the neighboring countries, when the general wealth increased and the standard of living rose, clothes became more elaborate, and the Muslims enjoyed things that they had never known before. Yet no one reproved them for such conduct so long as they did not exceed a reasonable limit.

We can find many illustrations of this in the conditions of our present age. For, when the American workingman, for example, has his house with hot running water, electricity and gas, his radio set and his private automobile, when he may, if he is able, make a weekly excursion with his family or visit a cinema; when these things are so, it is not luxury that the White House should be the home of the President. But when millions of a nation cannot find a mouthful of pure water to drink, it is undeniably luxury that some few people should be able to drink Vichy and Evian, imported from overseas. And when there are millions who cannot afford the simplest dwelling, who in the twentieth century have to take tin cans and reed huts as their houses; when there are those who cannot even find rags to cover their bodies, it is an impossible luxury that a mosque should cost a hundred thousand guineas or that the Ka'ba should be covered with a velvet covering, embroidered with gold. And it makes no difference that it is the Ka'ba or that it is a mosque. For, people are more deserving of the money that is spent in this way.

From such examples it is possible to lay down limits for luxury and for privation. The conditions of our environment must be the criterion; and such conditions will generally prove a reliable guide. The general wealth of the community and the standard of living in each period and in each district will limit the incidence of luxury by showing it up; for the social conscience seldom errs in its estimation of such things. Such is the Islamic limitation for all changing conditions and in every age.

❖ ❖ ❖ ❖ ❖ ❖ ❖

THE ZAKAT

Now let us consider the *zakat*, which is the outstanding social pillar of Islam; a discussion of the *zakat* is the most essential part of the economic theory of Islam.

Payment of the *zakat* is a duty that is laid on property; in one aspect it is a form of worship, in another it is a social responsibility. When we remember the Islamic theory of religious and social affairs, we may say that the *zakat* is a social responsibility with a religious significance. The word *zakat* means purification and growth. It is a purification of the conscience and of the moral sense, because it means paying the ordained due. It is a purification of the soul and the heart from the natural instinct of avarice and from the disposition to love one's self; for, money is dear and possession is an enviable thing, so that when a man can give away his money generously to others, he cannot but be purified, elevated, and improved. And it is a purification of property itself, because it means paying what is due on the property, after which its possession is legal. Again, because there is a religious significance in the *zakat*, it is a mark of the sympathetic understanding of Islam that protected people who are "scriptuaries" are not required to pay it; instead of it they pay a land tax, so that they may contribute to the general expenditure of the state without being liable to a religious duty which is specifically Islamic unless they choose.

The *zakat* is a right that the community claims from the individual, either to guarantee a competence to some of its members or to provide some little enjoyment over and above a bare livelihood. Islam accomplishes, thereby, part of its general principle: "In order that property may not be passed around between the rich among you." In other words, Islam disapproves of people being in poverty and need; it decrees that every man earn his living by his own work so long as he can, but that he receive his share from the public monies when for any reason he is unable to work.

Islam disapproves of people being in poverty or need, because it wishes to preserve them from the material cares of life and give them leisure for better things, for things are more suitable to human nature and to that special nobility with which Allah has endowed the sons of man. "We have given nobility to the sons of man, and have carried them by land and sea; We have given them provision of good things, and have given them great preference over many of the things, which We have created." (17:72)

And indeed He has given men a nobility through their minds and their emotions and through their spiritual yearnings for what is higher than mere physical needs. But, when men have only the bare necessities of life, they cannot gain any respite from labor in which to satisfy these spiritual yearnings or these intellectual capacities; then they have been robbed of their nobility and are reduced to the level of animals. More than that, even. Even animals generally find their food and drink, and some animals can have pride and energy and cheerfulness. Some birds can sing and can rear a brood into life, since they have a sufficiency of food and drink. How then is the state of a man, the noblest creation of Allah, whom the material needs of food and drink keep too busy to rise even to this level that the birds and animals achieve, much less to the level that is proper to man, to whom Allah has given nobility? And even when he has done his allotted work, he does not receive a competence; this is the disaster which makes him many degrees lower than the state that Allah purposed for him; this is the disaster that also ruins the community in which such a man lives. For such must be a degraded community, which does not ratify the nobility that Allah has given and which by that fact is disobedient to the will of Allah.

Man is the vicar of Allah on His earth; He appointed him as such to encourage life in the earth, elevate it, and make it a beautiful and pleasant thing; He appointed him to have the enjoyment of its beauty and loveliness and give thanks to Allah for His favors. But, man can never achieve any of this so long as his whole life must be spent in the pursuit of his daily bread—even if through this pursuit he gains a sufficiency. How, then, can he fare if he has to spend his life in labor and cannot even then earn a sufficiency?

Islam disapproves also of the existence of class distinctions in a community where some live on a standard of luxury and others on a standard of hardship; it disapproves even more of hardship becoming privation and hunger and nakedness. Such a community cannot be truly Muslim; for the Messenger says, "He does not believe in me who sleeps full-fed while his neighbor is hungry and he knows it." Or again, "Not one of you will be a Believer until he loves his brother as himself." Islam disapproves of such class distinctions because of the rancors and hatreds that lie behind them, sapping the very foundations of society, because they contain elements of selfishness and covetousness and harshness that will corrupt the soul and the conscience, and because they compel the poor either to steal and rob, or to humble themselves and sell their honor and their nobility. All these are degrading things, from which Islam would deliver a community.

For all these reasons the *zakat* is prescribed as a compulsory duty on property; it as much the right of those who receive it as it is the duty of those who pay it. Islam lays down a statutory level of property, and all who are above that level must pay the tax. This means that the most that a man can have and still be exempt is four ounces of gold, which is equivalent to twelve guineas in current money, or twenty-five ounces of silver, which is equivalent to twelve Egyptian pounds. The computation of this must be over and above a man's living expenses and must also be over and above any debt or obligation. This is essential, because no man must be called on to pay the *zakat* when he is in fact eligible to claim from it. Crops and fruits are estimated and assessed at the time of harvesting and come under the heading of merchandise, being valued in gold or silver. The case of livestock is governed by specific percentages that are equivalent in monetary terms to approximately one-fortieth of their face value.

Those who may claim from the *zakat* as laid down in the Qur'an are as follows:

First, the poor. That is, those who possess less than the statutory amount or those who have that amount but are overburdened with debt. It is held that such people do possess something, but that it is very little, whereas Islam holds that everyone should have a competence and something more, so that as far as possible all may enjoy some of the good things of life.

Second, the destitute. That is, those who possess nothing at all. By the nature of their case they are more worthy recipients than the poor. But my personal opinion is that the poor are mentioned before the destitute in the Qur'anic verse because the little that the poor do possess is not nearly enough, and therefore they are on a level with the destitute. For, the aim of Islam is not merely a bare material living, but something above that, as we have seen.

Third, those employed on the tax itself. That is, those who collect it. These, even though they may be rich, are given a proportion of the proceeds. This is the salary attaching to their position, and hence it must come under the heading of labor and pay, rather than under that of need and its remedy.

Fourth, those whose hearts are to be reconciled. That is, those who have recently entered Islam. Here the purpose is to strengthen their convictions and to rescue them from their enemies. But this practice has fallen into desuetude since Allah gave strength to Islam after the Wars of Apostasy[26] in the days of Abu Bakr, and Islam has never since then known the need of making converts by means of money. Nonetheless, such persons are mentioned in the text of this verse from the Qur'an and 'Umar saw nothing wrong with such a practice. So we may bear this example in mind and use it if need arise.

Fifth, slaves. That is, slaves to be ransomed. These desire to regain their freedom in exchange for a sum of money that has been arranged with their owners in order to facilitate that freedom. This practice also has now disappeared, owing to the circumstances of our time.

Sixth, debtors. That is, those whose wealth is submerged by debt. This holds so long as such debt is not sinful and so long as luxury or some similar thing is not the cause of it. To give to bona fide debtors out of the poor-tax is just, because it means the cancellation of their debts; it means that they are freed from their burden and are helped towards a more ample form of life.

Seventh, in the way of Allah. This is a universal outlet for wealth, the conditions of which must be dictated by circumstance. It entails equipping a military expedition, caring for the sick, teaching the ignorant, and performing all the other tasks of which the Muslim community stands in need. Expenditure under this head covers all social work in every country and under all conditions.

Eighth, the wayfarer. That is, one who carries no money and who has nothing to spend. Such cases today are refugees in time of war, raiding, or persecution, who have had to leave their money behind them and who have no way of recovering it.

These classifications, both private and public, cover all the aspects of social security in life. Islam assigns to these groups a share of the *zakat*—but only after they have exhausted their private means of support. Islam is insistent on the nobility of human nature; yet despite this, it gives allocations from the *zakat* as a right, and not as a gift or favor; for, it is still mindful that "The hand that gives is better than the hand that receives." Inevitably the giver confers a favor and the recipient accepts a favor. Hence Islam insists that men cannot dispense with the method of work, and hence it lays on the community the prime responsibility of providing work for each of its individual members. Once a beggar came to the Prophet for charity; the latter gave him a small coin and bade him buy a rope to use for collecting firewood, so that he could live by the work of his own hands. And as he gave it he said: "It is better for one of you to get a rope and collect firewood, carrying it on his back and selling it, than to beg from the people, who may give to you or may refuse you."

Such assistance from the *zakat* is a protection held in reserve and constitutes a guarantee for the man who is without resources; such a man may have exhausted his powers and gotten no return;

or he may have gotten a return that is under the subsistence level; or he may have gained a bare subsistence. In this matter Islam has a synthesis of two points of insistence; first, that every individual shall work as far as he can and shall not rely on social assistance while remaining idle himself; and second, that the needy must be helped in order to avoid destitution, in order to relieve him of the weight of necessity and the pressure of need, and in order to set him free for a nobler form of life.

OTHER STATUTORY TAXES

But the *zakat* is not the only duty on property.

We must here look at the almost general agreement among those who discuss the *zakat* in these times that it represents the extreme limit of the demands which Islam can regularly make on capital. For this reason we must examine this agreement to which the professional theologians have come.

For, in fact, the *zakat* is the lowest limit of the statutory duties on property, and it stands alone only when society does not require any additional income. But when the *zakat* is not enough, Islam need not feel that its hands are tied; on the contrary, it gives the ruler wide powers to assign levies on capital—that is to say, forced contributions from capital at a reasonable rate—subject always to the permanent limitations of its own welfare.

The subject of "public interest" and of "blocking of means,"[27] the limitations of which we shall trace later, is a broad subject; it includes the care of all the aspects of communal welfare, and it guarantees the prevention of all want in any form.

And we shall see that the occurrence of the problem in the history of Islam has provided examples in this field, as the community has from time to time felt the need. For the basic principle on which it rests is flexible enough to embrace all states and conditions.

7   THE HISTORICAL REALITY OF JUSTICE IN ISLAM

The material under consideration here may safely be called "The Spirit of Islam." This spirit will be immediately perceived by anyone who studies the nature or the history of Islam; it is to be found implicitly in all Islamic law and exhortation. Yet, although this spirit must be very clear in such a way that no one can help being affected by it, it is difficult to define in precise terms, as indeed must be the case with every deep universal feeling and every lofty universal philosophy. It is clearly discernible in objectives and aims, in incidents and occurrences, in customs and norms, but it is difficult to define in exact terms.

It is this spirit that dictates the very high standard required by Islam as the objective to which its adherents must strive and seek; not merely by the observance of obligations and rites, but even more by that inward obedience that is greater than any obligation or rite. This standard is difficult of achievement and still more difficult of permanent retention. For, the tendencies of human life and the tyranny of human necessity do not permit most people to achieve such a high standard, or, if in a moment of high ambition and aspiration they do reach it, to remain long on it. For, such a standard involves difficult responsibilities, duties of life and property, of beliefs and conduct. But perhaps the heaviest of these duties is the constant watchfulness which Islam enjoins on the individual conscience and the keen moral sense which it evokes in a man; it gives him a clear view of his rights and his responsibilities to himself and to the community in which he lives, to the human race to which he is related, and to the Creator Who watches over him in small things and great, and Who knows his most secret and inner thoughts.

Nonetheless, the difficulty of such achievement and the impossibility of long maintaining it do not mean that Islam is a purely abstract and imaginative philosophy or idealism to which men's desires may reach out, but short of which their achievements must always fall. For, the achievement of this standard of which we have been speaking actually is not the obligation of all men at all times. Rather it is the prescribed objective for men to aim at today, as they will tomorrow, and as they did yesterday, the objective which they have sometimes attained, sometimes missed. There is in this an example of the Islamic faith in man, in his conscience and in his ability, which is of great scope; it is also a proof that there need be no despair of the human race in the near or distant future. There is, besides, a wide range for the labor and the life of the great majority; "Allah lays no responsibility on any man beyond his capacity." (2:286) Thus the tolerance of Islam accepts gladly from all men what they can achieve within their own limits, below which the level of their life must not fall; "all men have degrees of accomplishment," (6:132) but the road to the highest standard is always open.

This spirit to which we have referred has left its mark on the historical reality of Islam; this faith, which is at once a philosophy and a theology, has taken on various personalities in the course of history but never has it been merely a set of barren theories, a collection of maxims and warnings, of stories and fables. Rather, it has taken the form of living human examples and actual historical events, customs and habits, which can be seen by the eye and heard by the ear, and which have left their traces on the reality of life and on the events of history. It is as if that spirit infused itself magically into all the personalities Islam has assumed in its history, transforming them and renewing them.

This is the most acceptable explanation of that galaxy of remarkable characters whose recollection Islamic history has preserved as it grew through the ages. It is also the explanation of those events and occurrences that one would almost regard as legends created by some fertile imagination, were it not that the records of their happening have been accurately kept and preserved by history. History can scarcely record all the examples of spiritual purity and moral courage, of moving sacrifice and of death for an ideal, all the flashes of spiritual and intellectual greatness, and the actual deeds of heroism in the various fields of life.

There must be a connection between all these deeds of heroism and achievement that are scattered through the pages of history and the spirit of Islam, which supplied a motive for them. It was this spirit that provided the source for the power discernible in all these manifestations. The study of these deeds of heroism and achievement is mere confusion if they are not connected with one fundamental source; and it is to be feared that it is unsatisfactory and false to the real truth of the universe and of life to refer the secret of all greatness in personality to some individual genius, and thus to neglect the primary spirit that impels and inspires a man. Such a spirit it was that influenced not only the course of the times and the nature of events, but also the spirits of heroes, sending them forth as a living wave of powerful armies, in the deeps of which all personal virtues and all events and circumstances were submerged.

We shall not go far wrong if we refer the occurrence of all these personal virtues and all these deeds of heroism to the action of that powerful spirit, which was a universal and all-embracing movement. It inspired all those abilities that appeared on the surface to be personal, but which were essentially universal. And the measure of all individual genius is its ability to bear comparison with that universal inspiration. The supreme form of greatness is without any doubt the prophethood of Muhammad b. 'Abdullah. It was that office of prophecy that enabled him to receive and to sustain continually that inspiration; it was strong enough to keep him at his high standard throughout his whole life. Essentially his was a universal strength rather than an individual ability.

Other examples of greatness are thus to be graded downwards from the standard of the Prophet, as they occurred in his Companions of Muhammad or in the adherents of his faith during the course of history. Each example corresponds to the individual's degree of receptivity to the underlying spirit of Islam.

It is a wide view such as this that can give us an understanding of how the spirit of Islam has touched mortal spirits, how it has awakened geniuses and inspired heroic deeds, and how it has, in the broadest sense, changed the course of human history.

The results of the activity of this spirit are to be clearly seen alike in the great events of history and in the happenings of everyday life. Spiritual greatness is not to be judged in terms of quantity or measure, but rather in terms of quality and influence. Thus the greatness shown in the conquest of the empires of Persia and Rome by a handful of Arabs in an incomparably short space of time loses none of its value when it is compared with the greatness displayed in the endurance of Bilal, the Abyssinian slave. The Quraish persecuted him beyond mortal endurance to make him abjure his religion, but he would not; they burned him with red-hot stones placed on his stomach and chest, they left him hungry and without water, and they tortured him; yet even in the heat of that unbearable torture he would say no more than, "Allah is One, Allah is One."

It is the same spirit which inspires the "man in the street," without wealth or influence, to stand before the mighty and all-conquering Caliph and boldly to speak the word of truth to him, not fearing to incur censure in the cause of Allah. It is to be seen again in the case of the Righteous Caliph, who could receive the submission of empires and yet remain unmoved, who could be exalted and yet humble. Both of these cases draw their inspiration from the same source, the powerful, influential, and profound spirit of Islam.

In the matter of the Arab conquest of the Persian and Roman Empires, we must reckon with the influence of that spirit and with its conquest of the awesome material powers that lay athwart its path. These powers were mustered in the two great Empires, and they were such that the Arabs could never have matched them had they lacked that spirit of Islam. The victory of Islam here was the victory of a spiritual philosophy embodied in mortal men, and this fact gives powerful support to the spiritual interpretation of history before which materialistic interpretations cannot stand, for they cannot possibly explain such a surprising victory.

It was a far-reaching spiritual change that Islam made in the Arabs of the peninsula, in their thought and their behavior, in their aims and their objectives, in their social and their economic organization. The evidence of this change is not less clear than is that of the conquests; rather it is clearer and stronger. What economic revolution, taking place in the life of Arabia between the call and the death of Muhammad, could possibly have effected this complete change in thought and mind, in organization and direction? The only thing that could possibly have had these amazing results is a spiritual philosophy.

It is difficult for us on this occasion to depict this change fully; it will be enough to refer to the following description, which was given by a witness from among the Arabs of that very time, and which was given in the presence of other witnesses who were opposed to this faith; yet this speech was neither challenged nor contradicted. This incident took place when some of the Muslims emigrated to Abyssinia, taking their faith with them. They were fleeing from the persecution of Quraish, during the early days of the propagation of Islam. The Quraish were afraid that this emigration might provide a breathing space to the Muslims, and so they dispatched two of their number as envoys to the Negus of Abyssinia to bring back the emigrants; these two were 'Amr ibn al-'As and 'Abdullah ibn Abi Rabi'a. These two spoke something as follows: "O King, there have recently taken refuge in your country some foolish youths who have abandoned the religion of their people without joining your religion. They have brought with them a religion that is of their own making, one with which neither we nor you are familiar. So we have been sent to you in this matter by the chiefs of their people, who include their fathers and kinsfolk and relatives; so you may restore them to their families who are more highly regarded than they and fully knowledgeable of the shame and disgrace they have inflicted upon them."

Then the Negus asked the Muslims, "What religion is this, on account of which you have left your people, for which you will not enter my religion, and which is a faith strange to all known faiths?"

The reply was given by Ja'far ibn Abi Talib thus: "O King, we were a people of ignorant barbarity. We used to worship idols and eat carrion flesh; we practiced fornication, we disregarded family ties, we neglected the duties of hospitality, and the strong among us ate up the weak. Thus we continued until Allah sent us a Messenger of our own number, of whose descent we know, and whose truthfulness, faith, and chastity are unquestioned. He summoned us to Allah, to believe in Him as One God, to worship Him, and to repudiate what we and our fathers worshiped apart from Him in the way of stones and idols. He bade us tell the truth in our conversation, observe good faith and ties of kindred, be faithful to our hospitable duties, and refrain from the eating of forbidden foods and blood. He forbade us to practice fornication and to use false speech, to eat up the property of orphans, and to slander chaste women. And he bade us worship Allah and associate nothing with Him, he ordained for us the prayers, the *zakat,* and fasting . . ."

Now the two Quraish envoys were present and one of them was 'Amr, who was neither unable to speak nor deficient in shrewdness; yet neither of the envoys contradicted Ja'far's description of the state of Arabia before Islam, or of the nature and form of the new religion. Therefore, this must be a true and reliable description of the former state of affairs and of the new.

That is evidence from history itself, the history of Arabia. And here is another piece of evidence from one who is not a Muslim, and who lives in the modern age. J. H. Denison speaks of the world in general at that time when he says in his book, *Emotion as the Basis of Civilization*: "In the fifth and sixth centuries the civilized world was on the brink of total collapse, because the cultures which had made the establishment of civilization possible had already collapsed, and there was nothing else to take their place. It was then apparent that the great civilization, the rearing of which had occupied the labor of four thousand years, was on the point of dissolution and disintegration, and that mankind would be forced to return to its former barbaric state wherein one tribe fought and killed another, where law and order were unknown. The system set up by Christianity was creating division and destruction, rather than unity and order.[28] Civilization was like a huge tree with spreading branches whose shade extended over the whole world; now it stood tottering, eaten away to the core by rot. And in the midst of such an aspect of general corruption there was born the man who was to unify the whole world."

✦ ✦ ✦ ✦ ✦ ✦ ✦

But we must proceed; for this discussion grows too long, and the subject of this book is not "Islam," but "Social Justice in Islam." It is our purpose now to turn to examples of this question taken from history.

✦ ✦ ✦ ✦ ✦ ✦ ✦

Yet we shall not commence our examples of social justice until we have first looked at some examples of another matter still more essential in Islam and upon which all the foundations of Islam depend.

We spoke a short time ago of the constant watchfulness that Islam enjoins on the individual conscience, and of the keen moral sense that it inculcates. The course of Islamic history has preserved examples of these qualities in larger numbers than we can quote here, but a few typical examples will serve to represent the whole field.

The following story comes from Buraida. Ma'iz ibn Malik came to the Prophet, saying, "O Messenger of Allah, purify me." "Woe to you," answered the Prophet. "Turn and ask pardon of Allah, and repent towards Him." So Ma'iz went a short distance apart, then came back and repeated his request. The Prophet reiterated his former instructions, and again Ma'iz followed them. But at the fourth time of asking the Prophet said, "From what am I to purify you?" "From adultery, " he answered. The Prophet asked, "Is this man mad?" and was told that he was not; "Has he been drinking wine?" he asked; whereupon one of those present arose and smelled Ma'iz' breath, but could detect no trace of wine. Muhammad said to him then, "Have you really committed adultery?" "Yes," he answered. So the Prophet gave the order, and Ma'iz was stoned to death. Two or three days later the Messenger said in public, "Seek pardon of with Allah for Ma'iz ibn Malik; for he has made such a repentance that if it had been on behalf of a whole community it would have been effective for all." Thereupon there came to him a woman of the Ghamidi clan of Azd, and said, "O Messenger of Allah, purify me." "Woe on you," he said to her. "Go and ask pardon of Allah, and repent towards Him." She said, "Do you intend to repulse me as you did Ma'iz ibn Malik? For I am with child by fornication with him." "You!" said the Prophet, and she answered, "Yes." Then he commanded her, "Wait till you have brought forth your child," and one of the Helpers volunteered to care for her until the time of the birth. When this happened, he came and told the Prophet, "The Ghamidi woman has had her child." Then said the Prophet, "We cannot stone her, and leave her helpless child without a nurse"; but one of the Helpers at once said, "I will be responsible for a nurse, O Prophet of Allah." So they stoned the woman to death. Another version of the story relates that Muhammad said to the woman, "Go away until your child is born"; then, when the child was born, he said, "Go and nurse your child until it is weaned. " When the child was weaned, the woman came back with her child, and with a piece of bread in her hand, saying, "Now, O Prophet of Allah, I have weaned him and he can eat solid food." So he gave the child to one of the Muslims, then gave the command, and she was buried up to her breast; then Muhammad commanded the people to stone her. Khalid ibn al-Walid took up a stone and threw it at her head, so that the blood bespattered his face, and he cursed her. But the Messenger of Allah said to him, "Softly, Khalid. For by Him in whose hand is my life, she has made such a repentance that had it been made even by a taxgatherer, all would have been forgiven him." Then he gave orders about the woman and prayed over her; and she was buried.

Now neither Ma'iz ibn Malik nor his partner in crime were ignorant of the dreadful penalty that they would have to pay or of the shameful end that they would have to face. No one had seen them, to establish the fact of their crime. Nevertheless they pressed the Messenger importunately, no matter what was dictated by his mercy and by that of Islam, to deny them the benefit of any doubt; they closed all possible ways against their own escape; indeed the woman even confronted Muhammad, the Messenger of Allah, with wanting to repulse her as he had repulsed Ma'iz. She almost accused Allah's Messenger of neglecting his own religion.

Why did they do these things? The answer lies in their request, "Purify me, O Messenger of Allah." This betrays the true impulse that was strong enough to overcome the love of life—a watchful conscience and a keen moral sense. It was the desire to be purified of a crime of which none save Allah was cognizant; it was the shame of meeting Allah unpurified from a sin which they had committed.

This is Islam. Its keen moral perception appears in the conscience of the offender, and its profound mercy appears in Muhammad's repulsion of these two people and in his effort to provide a way of escape for them. Its resolution appears in the carrying out of the stipulated punishment when the charge had been proven, despite the nobility of the confession and the intensity of the repentance; for on this point the sinner and the Prophet find common ground—that the faith must stand by its basic tenets.

This incident relates to one of the fixed penalties of the *shari'a*. But how stands the matter with regard to the social consequences that must follow the action of such a conscience from time to time in the course of life?

An illustration of this is provided by the story of the dismissal of Khalid from the command of the Syrian expedition and his replacement by Abu 'Ubaida. Khalid was the general who had never yet been worsted in any engagement, an Arab, proud of himself, of his lineage, and of his victories. Such a man was Khalid who was dismissed from his command; yet he bore no malice, nor was he so much the slave of power as to withdraw from the force— far less did he dream of rebelling. On the contrary, he remained in the army with great determination, and because of his eagerness for the success of Allah's faith and for martyrdom in the way of Allah. He paid no heed to all the other factors in the situation, holding them to be subordinate to that watchfulness which Islam enjoins on the individual conscience and to the keen moral perception laid upon him.

This event has a significance on the other side also; that is, as it affected 'Umar ibn al-Khattab. For his dismissal of Khalid was itself a product of that same keen moral perception. During the caliphate of Abu Bakr he had been offended at Khalid for a number of things that had pricked his conscience and outraged his moral sense. He had been offended at Khalid's ready killing of Malik ibn Nuwaira, and at his marriage to the latter's wife; he was offended again by another similar act, when Khalid married the daughter of Majja'a during the war against Musailima the Liar, on the day following that on which twelve hundred of the chief Companions of the Prophet were killed in the same campaign. 'Umar believed that Khalid had sinned, and it made no difference to him that this was Islam's greatest and most victorious general; it made no difference that the Islamic community stood on the threshold of immense wars in Syria and Iraq; it made no difference that Islam had a supreme need of the genius of the unconquered Khalid. None of these things was able to silence the conscientious conviction of 'Umar that Khalid had sinned, and that therefore he must be removed from the command of the army and ultimately from the army itself. In addition to all that had gone before, Khalid's habit of dealing independently with the missions entrusted to him did not accord well with the strategy of 'Umar and his custom of supervising everything in detail, as a matter of conscience and duty.

But the question may be asked: Why, in view of these sins, did Abu Bakr retain Khalid? Abu Bakr's opinion of Khalid was not as low as 'Umar's; he believed that Khalid had sinned unintentionally and he was not looking out for sins or faults, so he pardoned Khalid freely. Nonetheless he was offended with him, especially on the second occasion, when he wrote to him a letter "sprinkled with blood." Yet, because he believed that Khalid had acted in error rather than maliciously, he pardoned and retained him.

This is surely the true explanation of this incident, an explanation that accords with the moral standards of Islam at this period. It is therefore the more surprising that a man like Dr. Haikal should propose an explanation of the positions of Abu Bakr and 'Umar that does an injustice to the spirit of Islam, though it may well be in conformity with the unscrupulousness of modern politics. In his book, *Al-Siddiq Abu Bakr,* pages 150-152, he says:

The difference of opinion between Abu Bakr and 'Umar in the matter of Malik ibn Nuwaira had reached the level that we have seen. Both men undoubtedly desired to serve the best interests of Islam and of the Muslim community. But that aside, was this difference of opinion due to differing estimates of Khalid's deed? Or did they disagree about the policy that it was necessary to follow at such a critical juncture in the life of Islam, when apostasy and rebellion were rife throughout all Arabia?

My own opinion is that their difference was based on disagreement about the policy that should be followed in such a situation. Such a difference of opinion is in general agreement with the characters of the two men. 'Umar was a pattern of inflexible justice; he held that Khalid had killed a Muslim and had consummated a marriage with the latter's wife before the completion of her legal term. Hence it was not right that he should remain as commander of the army, where he would be able to do the same thing again, and thus bring a corrupting influence into Muslim affairs. This would be bad for Muslim standing in the eyes of the Arabs; and in any case it was not right that Khalid should go unpunished for the wrong that he had done with Laila. And even if it were true that Khalid had simply made an error of judgement in the case of Malik—which 'Umar did not believe—'Umar held that his treatment of Malik's wife still brought him under the ban of the law. 'Umar would not extend pardon to him because he was the "Sword of Allah," or because he was the general to whom victory always came. For if such a pardon was granted, then Khalid and his like would be able to do what was forbidden, the worst possible example of reverence for the Qur'an that could be given to the Muslims. Hence 'Umar ceaselessly urged and begged Abu Bakr to recall Khalid and to reprimand him for his actions.

Abu Bakr on the other hand perceived that the situation was too dangerous for weight to be given to such matters. What was the killing of one man, or even of a number of men, through an error of judgement or even on purpose, when danger encompassed the entire state, when rebellion was aflame from end to end of Arabia, and when this general, now accused of sinning, was one of the strongest forces to save the state from ruin and avert the menace? What did it matter that Khalid had married a woman contrary to Arab custom—even that he had consummated the marriage before her legal term

had elapsed? All this was done in war, and the rules of war permitted Khalid to possess all the women whom he captured. Granted
that it was necessary to apply the law, it was not necessary to
enforce it on eminent and powerful men such as Khalid, especially
since such a proceeding would injure the state and expose it to
danger. The Muslims stood in need of the sword of Khalid, and at
the moment when Abu Bakr sent for him to censure him, they
needed him more than ever before. In Yamama, Musailima was
already in the vicinity of Khalid's camp at al Bitah with forty thousand men of the Banu Hanifa, thus constituting a dangerous threat
to Islam and its adherents; he had already defeated 'Ikrima ibn Abi
Jahl, one of the Muslim generals, and the only remaining hope of
overcoming him seemed to rest on the sword of Khalid. Was Khalid,
then, to be dismissed because of the killing of Malik, or because of
Laila the beautiful who had tempted him? Were the Muslim armies
thus to be exposed to defeat by Musailima, the faith of Allah to be
exposed to the possible results of such a defeat? Khalid was the
instrument and the sword of Allah. Therefore, let the policy of Abu
Bakr be to recall Khalid and satisfy 'Umar by reprimanding him, but
at the same time to order Khalid to march immediately to Yamama
against Musailima.

This is, to my mind, the true reconstruction of the difference of
opinion between Abu Bakr and 'Umar on this matter. Perhaps it was
at that moment, when the false prophet of the Banu Hanifa had
defeated 'Ikrima, that Abu Bakr ordered Khalid to march against
Musailima simply for this reason: that the people of Medina, and
especially such of them as were of 'Umar's opinion, might see that
Khalid was a man condemned; that they might know that in sending
him into the fire of war Abu Bakr was actually punishing him. On
the field Khalid might be surrounded and killed, which would be the
most suitable punishment for his treatment of Umm Tamim and her
husband; or he might gain a victory, which would cleanse his reputation and make him out a victorious leader who had rescued the
Muslim world from a terror beside which his own doings at al-Bitah
were as nothing.

And this is "the true reconstruction" of the matter, according
to Dr. Haikal. Here is a man whose mind and soul are steeped in
the atmosphere of that period of Islamic history, a man whose
mind lives in the shadow of the keen and intensely perceptive

conscience of the men of that age; and yet such a man cannot get his own mind away from explaining events on such a level as this, which is obviously based on an acquaintance with the political expediencies of the present age of materialism, rather than on the spirit and the history of Islam in that age. It is a theory peculiar to the present day that the end justifies the means, a theory that degrades the human conscience to the level of a temporary expediency, a theory that reckons the supreme virtue to be a certain dexterity in the manipulation of affairs. How petty does Abu Bakr appear in this reconstruction which Dr. Haikal calls the true one. If Abu Bakr was much greater and nobler than in this estimate made by an author living in a degenerate age, an author who cannot rise to that sublime level and who is shamefully ignorant of the fundamentals of the *shari'a*.

Dr. Haikal returns to the question in *Al-Faruq 'Umar, Part I,* where he reconstructs the thought of 'Umar, seeking to dismiss Khalid. The degeneracy of the age in which he lives again affects the writer, as does the fact of being the leader of a party which advocates temporary advantages and local gains; such a man can never understand the spirit of Islam at its highest levels. Thus he says (pages 99–100):

> How could 'Umar fearlessly decide on the dismissal of Khalid, when the latter was the commander of the Muslim forces in Syria, especially when these forces were in such a critical situation? They stood at that time face to face with Byzantium, yet without active hostility, for neither the Muslims nor the Byzantines had any excess of strength over the other. Such was the position before Khalid left Iraq to join the Syrian forces, and such the position remained even after his arrival, both sides looking for an opportunity of breaking the stalemate and attacking the enemy. Would not the Caliph be afraid to compromise the situation by striking Khalid off the Muslim strength, and thereby increasing the critical nature of the position? Was it not rather the expedient course to delay until Khalid had extricated the Muslims from their predicament and after that to give what orders he wished?
>
> These were undoubtedly weighty considerations in view of the impending struggle, and, as we shall see, Abu 'Ubaida gave them full

force; but he was afraid of the displeasure and the anger of the Caliph. 'Umar, however, saw the matter from a different angle, and even if he had postponed the matter of Khalid's dismissal until after the battle with the Byzantines, even that would have been against his policy and contrary to his character. The struggle could only have one of two issues: the Muslims would be defeated, or they would be victorious. If they were defeated, the dismissal of Khalid would not then retrieve the defeat; while if they were victorious under the command of Khalid, 'Umar would not be able to effect the dismissal of such a general in the hour of his victory. On the other hand, if the dismissal were carried through now, the difficulty would be resolved. Hence 'Umar was insistent that Khalid should not be left in command, either in Syria or elsewhere. For these reasons 'Umar hastily gave the order for Khalid's dismissal, making the excuse that Khalid had not fulfilled the duties assigned to him by Abu Bakr. Then, when the Muslims proved victorious, no blame could attach to 'Umar, who had done what he was satisfied was right, while Khalid was in the position of not having been wronged by the man who had dismissed him.

Thus would "Haikal Pasha" argue in the twentieth century. It is his own argument which he transfers back to 'Umar at the beginning of Islam, just as he has previously carried out the same process with Abu Bakr. These are the words of a man whose spirit has no affinity with that of Abu Bakr or that of 'Umar; even the fact that he has long lived in the atmosphere of early Islam cannot sever him from the conditions of the twentieth century. All he does is twist and distort facts to give opportunity for an attack on conscience, justice, and religion.

What does Haikal think of 'Umar? Would 'Umar have retained Khalid in his position if the time and the situation had been different? And the more so when he was convinced in his own conscience—as even Haikal admits—that Khalid had sinned in the matter of Malik, sinned against Allah and against the faith. Was 'Umar the man to give weight to such considerations and to bow before them? Was this the 'Umar who crossed mountains without deviating from the straight path, who faced the tempest in faith without bowing to it? Such a course as this was often taken by the

Umayyad and Abbasid kings, in whom it is regarded as the fruit of shrewdness and craftiness; but with 'Umar or with Abu Bakr it is impossible. Such an opinion of these two can be held only by the shallow spirit of this age and by the degeneracy of its standards of judgment.

But we must proceed; for we have spent too much time in pointing out and rebutting this kind of argument. But it was necessary to rectify the profound error that has overtaken those who seek to reconstruct the thought and the morals of the age when the spirit of Islam was at its highest in terms of the thought and the morals of this material age, which is far removed from that fine spirit. This is an error that only publicizes a misunderstanding of the nature of the human conscience and its ability for growth and for sensitivity. We have no desire to clothe these men in garments that are too ample or to portray them as completely devoid of all human weakness. But we do desire to restore to mankind a faith in the human conscience and to portray this period of Muslim life in its true colors, as can be fully comprehended by every individual conscience capable of aspiring to this lofty standard.

And now we may proceed to mention examples of this moral sensitivity in other directions.

This same Caliph, 'Umar, went out one day carrying a skin of water, and his son asked him disapprovingly, "Why are you doing this?" 'Umar replied, "I have been too self-satisfied, and I must humble myself." What moral perception is there! For here is a man who can recognize in the depths of his own soul a pride in his office as Caliph, in his conquests, and in the greatness which he has attained; and unwilling that such pride should continue, he determines to humble himself, and that in the sight of all his subjects. It made no difference to him that he was the Caliph, ruler of a territory which embraced not only Arabia as a whole but also the major parts of the Persian and Byzantine Empires.

So also the Caliph 'Ali used to shiver with cold during the winter; he wore only a summer cloak and would have no other protection, though he had control of the public treasury. He was unable to draw on that treasury because of that same watchfulness of conscience and that same keenness of moral perception.

Similarly with Abu 'Ubaida and his army in Hums, where they were caught by the fatal plague. 'Umar was afraid for the trusted servant of the community, and attempted to get him out of the danger by sending for him in a letter in which he said: "To proceed; I need your presence here concerning an urgent matter that I wish to discuss with you personally; I command you, as soon as you have read this letter, not to lay it down until you have come to me." Abu 'Ubaida read the letter and recognized 'Umar's purpose; he knew that 'Umar only wanted to get him out of the way of the deadly plague, and he said, "May Allah pardon the Commander of the Faithful." Then he wrote to 'Umar, thus: "I know what matter you need me for, but I am with a Muslim army and I have no pleasure apart from them. I have no desire to leave them until Allah completes His decree for me and for them. Therefore release me from your order, Commander of the Faithful, and leave me with my army." When 'Umar read the letter he wept, so that those who stood by asked if Abu 'Ubaida were dead. In a voice choked with tears 'Umar replied, "No; but it is as if he were." And in fact he had died by that point.

What was it but profound faith in the decree of Allah that sustained the courage of Abu 'Ubaida? And with that faith went the moral perception that he could not take to flight alone, leaving the army; for he and they together formed an army fighting in the way of Allah.

Or there was Bilal ibn Rabah, the Messenger's muezzin. After the birth of Islam his brother Abu Ruwaiha besought him to act as his agent in arranging a marriage for him with a Yemenite family. So Bilal said to them: "I am Bilal ibn Rabah, and this is my brother Abu Ruwaiha; he is a man of evil nature and no religion. If you will have him for a marriage arrangement, well and good; but if you do not wish it, then let him be."

Thus he refused to deceive them or to conceal anything about his brother; he could not bear in mind that he was an agent and at the same time forget that he was responsible before Allah for all that he said. But the Yemenites gladly took Abu Ruwaiha in marriage because of such candor of speech; for they had formed a worthy estimate of the agent who thus asked the hand of their daughter for his brother.

Then there was the famous Abu Hanifa, who "sent goods to Hafs ibn 'Abd al-Rahman, his business associate, and informed him that there was a fault in one of the garments and he showed the fault in public. Hafs sold the goods, and, forgetting that the fault had been pointed out, demanded the full price for the imperfect garment. It is said that the price was thirty or thirty-five thousand dirhams. But Abu Hanifa refused to accept the money and sent a message to his partner, making him responsible for finding the customer. The partner could not find the buyer, and Abu Hanifa would only be satisfied with the dissolution of their partnership. And so it had to be. Furthermore he disdained to add this tainted money to his honest money, and so gave it all away in alms."

It is related that Yunus ibn 'Ubaid had in his shop suits of clothes at different prices; one kind was priced at four hundred per suit, and another at two hundred. When Yunus went to prayers he left his nephew to keep the shop, and during his absence a Bedouin came in, looking for a suit at four hundred. The nephew showed him one of those priced at two hundred, which met with his approval; he bought it, and went away with it over his arm. Yunus met him, and, recognizing the suit, asked him, "How much did you pay for this?" "Four hundred dirhams." "It is not worth more than two hundred," said Yunus. "Come back with me so I can give you back the extra money. "But," said the Bedouin, "in our district even this is worth five hundred, and I am satisfied with it." "Never mind that" replied Yunus. "Sincerity in religion is worth more than this world and all that it contains." So he took the Bedouin back to the shop and returned to him two hundred dirhams. He remonstrated with his nephew, saying: "Are you not ashamed? Have you no fear of Allah? You make a hundred percent profit, and you leave honesty to Muslims." "By Allah," protested the nephew, " he would not have taken it had he not been satisfied with it." But Yunus answered him: "Did it not seem satisfactory to him simply because you made it appear so?"

It is related also of Muhammad ibn al-Munkadir that in his absence one of his slaves sold a piece of cloth to a Bedouin for ten dirhams, though it was of a type which was worth only five. All day long Muhammad searched for that Bedouin until at last he found him. "The slave made a mistake," he said, "and charged you ten dirhams for what is only worth five." "O man," said the Bedouin, "I am quite satisfied." But Muhammad retorted, "Even if you are satisfied, I will not be satisfied for you to have anything which does not satisfy me." So he repaid him the five dirhams.[29]

The key to these three stories is in the question of Yunus b.'Ubayd to his nephew, "Are you not ashamed? Have you no fear of Allah?" And indeed the answer is in fact in these two things; shame arising from the conscience, and fear of Allah. That is the result that Islam can have on the human soul when the power of its spirit is acknowledged and when its nobility is widely assimilated.

Beyond these stories that we have quoted there are scores and hundreds of similar instances, drawn from every aspect and sphere of life. We have recorded these few merely to demonstrate the level of purity and exaltation to which Islam seeks to raise the human conscience, a level far above all worldly and material needs, above the love of self and the love of life, the love of wealth and of influence. It seeks to enable the individual conscience to uphold the responsibilities of that constant watchfulness which is enjoined on it, to maintain the duties of that keen moral perception which is laid on the ethical sense. And thus it seeks a guarantee of the achievement of this standard.

Now we may safely proceed to draw attention to some aspects of the historical experience of Islam as they relate to social justice, guided by the brilliantly high standards that characterize Islam.

·:· ·:· ·:· ·:· ·:· ·:· ·:·

The absolute equality of all mankind was the message of Islam, that and an absolute freedom of conscience from all values and considerations that would detract from such equality. We have already discussed the Islamic theory of equality and freedom; we have seen the Qur'anic passages that leave no room for doubt that this theory is profound and fundamental to the construction of Islamic thought on human society. Now we may see how that theory has been applied in practice.

In all parts of the world the slave was regarded as constituting a different class from free men. The same belief was held in Arabia; yet Muhammad married his niece Zainab bint Jahsh, a daughter of the Hashemite clan of Quraish, to his client Zaid. Marriage is a sensitive matter in which the question of human equality arises more than in any other. No man except the Prophet, and no power except that of his religion, could have sufficed to bring about such an impossibility—a thing that is not yet possible in any country outside the Muslim world. In the United States we see today that slavery has indeed been abolished by law, but a negro cannot marry a white woman—any white woman; he is forbidden by law to sit beside a white in public vehicles; he may not live beside a white in an inn or a hotel; he is not allowed to sit beside a white in a college classroom.

When Muhammad instituted a brotherhood between individual Emigrants and Helpers after migrating to Medina, his uncle Hamza and his client Zaid were brothers; Abu Bakr and Kharija ibn Zaid were brothers; Khalid ibn Ruwaiha al-Khath'ami and Bilal ibn Rabah were brothers. This relationship was no mere matter of words, but was a lifelong connection, just as strong as blood relationship. It was a tie of relationship which embraced their persons, their property, and all the other features of their lives.

Further, the Messenger appointed Zaid, his client, as leader of the expedition against Mu'ta, and he later appointed Zaid's son Usama as leader of an expedition against the Byzantine Empire; he gave him command of an army that included a great number of Emigrants and Helpers, among them Abu Bakr and 'Umar, who were the two lieutenants of the Messenger and his closest friends, later to be the first two Caliphs by the common consent of all the Muslims. Also among the members of the army was Sa'd ibn Abi Waqqas, a near relative of Allah's Messenger since he belonged to the family of the Bani Zuhra, who were the Prophet's maternal uncles. Sa'd was one of the first members of Quraish to come over to Islam, which he did under the guidance of Allah at the age of seventeen. He was wealthy and influential, a skilled warrior of great bravery.

When the Messenger died before Usama's expedition set out,

Abu Bakr resolved to despatch the army, and he kept in command
of it the man whom the Messenger had chosen. He went personally to escort Usama out of Medina, the latter riding while Abu
Bakr, the Caliph, walked. Usama was ashamed to ride, he being a
young man, while the successor of Allah's Messenger went afoot,
and he an old man. "O Caliph of the Messenger," he said, "By
Allah, do you ride, else I shall walk?" But the Caliph replied with
an oath, "By Allah, you will not walk, and by Allah, I will not ride.
Would you forbid me to soil my feet with dust for one hour in the
way of Allah?" Later Abu Bakr found that he needed 'Umar at
Medina, for he had been carrying the full weight of the Caliphate
on his own shoulders. But 'Umar was then no more than a common soldier in Usama's army; the latter was the commander, and
therefore his permission must be sought. So the Caliph wrote to
him in these terms: "If you judge it fitting, will you appoint 'Umar
to my service."

This is the level of the spirit of equality to which neither
words nor writing can do full justice.

Then, with the passage of time we find 'Umar himself as
Caliph, appointing 'Ammar ibn Yasir, another former slave, as
governor of Kufa. And while Suhail ibn 'Amr ibn al-Harith ibn
Hashim and Abu Sufyan ibn Harb together with a company of
Quraishite nobles stood waiting at 'Umar's door, Suhaib and Bilal
were admitted before them. These two were clients and poor, but
they were of those who had fought at Badr and were of the number
of the Companions of the Messenger. Abu Sufyan's nostrils dilated
with anger at such treatment, and he gave vent to barbarous
curses, saying, "Never have I seen anything like this. He admits
these slaves and leaves us standing at his door."

'Umar was one day passing near Mecca when he saw servants
sitting, not eating with their masters. His anger was kindled, and
he said reprovingly to the masters: "What is to be done with those
who think themselves better than their servants?" Then he summoned the servants to eat out of the same dish as their masters.

'Umar had appointed Nafi' ibn al-Harith governor of Mecca,
and, meeting him one day at 'Usfan, he asked, "Whom did you

leave as your regent over the people of Mecca?" "I left Ibn Abza." "Who is Ibn Abza?" asked 'Umar, and he was told, "One of my clients." Then said 'Umar, "You left a client as your regent?" "He is a reciter of Allah's Book," responded Nafi'. "He is skilled in the law and a judge." "Of a truth," cried 'Umar, "your Prophet once said that by this Book Allah raises some and puts down others."

'Umar's question was not asked in a spirit of censure; he simply wanted to know where lay the qualifications of Ibn Abza, since he was not acquainted with him. Otherwise he would have spoken openly, for it was he who commanded the six members of the council that was to nominate his successor: "If Salim the client of Abu Hudhaifa had been alive, I should have myself nominated him as my successor." For in his eyes Salim was preferable to any of the six members of the council, though they included 'Uthman, 'Ali, and Sa'd ibn Abi Waqqas.

A certain client once asked a man of Quraish for the hand of his sister in marriage and gave valuable gifts to the woman. Her brother refused to let her marry him, and when 'Umar heard of it he said to the Quraishite, "What prevented your giving her to him? He is an upright man, and he has given your sister fair gifts." The Quraishite replied, "Commander of the Faithful, we have a certain standing, and he is not her equal." "He has standing both in this world and in the next, " said 'Umar, "for in this world he has his money, and in the world to come he has his piety." So the Quraishite promised his sister if she herself were willing; when she was asked she agreed, and so she married the client.

We have already seen how Bilal the client interceded for Abu Ruwaiha, the Bedouin, in a marriage negotiation with a Yemenite family; and we saw how they honored Abu Ruwaiha and received him because of Bilal.

The way was always open for clients to attain to the highest positions of honor in every field. When we hear of 'Abdullah ibn 'Abbas we hear of his client 'Ikrima along with him. So with 'Abdullah ibn 'Umar and his client Nafi', Anas ibn Malik and his client Ibn Sirin, and Abu Huraira and his client 'Abd al-Rahman ibn Hurmuz.

"In Basra there was Hasan al-Basri, while in Mecca there were Mujahid ibn Jabir, 'Ata ibn Abi Rabah, and Tawus ibn Kaisan, all jurists.

"In Egypt the principal jurist consulted in the days of 'Umar ibn 'Abd al-'Aziz was Yazid ibn Abi Habib who was a black client from Dongola."[30]

It is still in this same spirit that the Muslim world regards the working man. He is honored and respected for the labor of his hands not in theory alone but in actual life. There is no trade that can lower the status of the man who exercises it; for work of all kinds is a source of nobility, and no man's trade can disqualify him to acquire learning in it and thereby to gain increased status and regard.

"Abu Hanifa was a silk merchant, just as many of the exponents of jurisprudence after him were merchants or tradesmen.

"The father of Imam Ahmad ibn 'Umar ibn Mihyar, the cobbler, had been a pupil of Muhammad Shaibani and of al-Hasan, both of whom were companions of Abu Hanifa. It was the cobbler who edited the *Book of the Land-Tax* for the Caliph al-Muhtadi; he wrote his great works on the jurisprudence while earning his living by repairing shoes. Similarly al-Karabisi sold *karabis* or cotton cloth, and the famous al-Qaffal used to stretch out his hand and show the marks on the back of it, saying 'These are the marks of my original trade (that of a locksmith).' So Ibn Qutlubugha worked as a tailor; and al-Jassas, the doyen of his age, was so named because he worked with plaster. Thus, too, we have al-Saffar, one who sells brass ware; al-Saidalani, one who sells perfume; al-Halwani, whose father sold sweetmeats; al-Daqqaq (the flour merchant), al-Sabuni (the soap merchant), al-Na'li (the sandal maker), al-Baqqali (the grocer), al-Qaduri (the pot man), and many others. All these cases are illustrations from various periods of history, and they indicate just this: that from the very dawn of Islamic civilization and from its earliest times this community established a principle that the Western world has sought for tens of centuries to establish almost without success, namely, that there are not some trades that are estimable and others that are degrading; rather there are some men who are estimable, and others who are not . . ."[31]

⋆ ⋆ ⋆ ⋆ ⋆ ⋆ ⋆

But this depiction of equality cannot be considered perfect until we have discovered how Islamic society treated its exalted members. For it is not enough to show regard for the humble and promote them to high position; the exalted must also be brought down to the same equitable level. They must be permitted no preeminence save through their work, and through it alone, not through social standing or lineage, influence or wealth.

Abu Yusuf in his book on the land tax says: It is related by 'Abd al-Malik ibn Abi Sulaiman on the authority of 'Ata' as follows. 'Umar once wrote and directed his governors to come to him at the time of the hajj. When they came he stood up in public and said: "O people, I sent out these men as my governors to wield a just authority over you. I did not make them your governors to strip you of your flesh, your blood, and your wealth. So if any man here has been wronged by one of these, let him now stand forth." Only one man got to his feet, and he said: "O Commander of the Faithful, your governor gave me a hundred lashes." 'Umar said to him, "Would you give him a hundred lashes? Come, then, and take your vengeance." Then 'Amr ibn al-'As spoke up: " O Commander of the Faithful, if you start dealing thus with your governors, it will go hard with them; for this will be taken as a precedent after your time." But 'Umar replied, "Shall I not allow this man his retaliation, when I have seen the Messenger of Allah permit retaliation upon himself? Come, you, and claim your vengeance." 'Amr persisted: "Let us then make some accommodation in the matter," and 'Umar said, "As you will." So they compromised to settle the matter for two hundred dinars—two dinars per lash.

'Amr ibn al-'As thus protected someone else, but he could not prevent the same thing happening to his own son for striking the son of the Egyptian. In this case 'Umar permitted the injured man to retaliate, and even said to him, "Strike hard on this son of a nobleman." And even 'Amr himself would have tasted the same experience if the Egyptian had not relented and remitted the penalty.

'Umar was one day sitting making the division of the public funds among the Muslims, with the people jostling around him, when Sa'd ibn Abi Waqqas, whose lineage and courage in the service of Islam we have already noticed, approached him; he fought his way through the people and forced a clear space round 'Umar. The Caliph thereupon set about him with his whip, crying, "If you do not respect the authority of Allah on this earth, I must teach you that the authority of Allah does not respect you."

But it may perhaps be objected that this only refers to one Caliph. So let us look now at how much freedom of speech and conscience the Caliphs and kings were granted by their subjects; for rulers owe their position to that freedom of conscience which Islam bestows and to that absolute equality which it establishes in word and deed.

'Umar once as Caliph said to the people in the course of a sermon: "If you see any evil thing in me, then set it right." Whereupon one of the ordinary members of the Muslim community answered him: "If we had found any evil thing in you we would have set it right with the edge of our swords." And 'Umar's only response was to say: "Praise be to Allah that He has given 'Umar one subject who would set him right with the edge of his sword."

The Muslims once captured a number of Yemenite scarves, of which 'Umar got one as his share of the booty as did his son 'Abdullah, in common with every other Muslim. Now because 'Umar needed a cloak, 'Abdullah gave him his scarf, so that by joining it and his own together 'Umar might make a cloak. When this was done, 'Umar was standing one day delivering the sermon, attired in this cloak; in the course of the sermon he said: "O people, hear and obey." A certain man immediately jumped up and cried, "We need neither hear nor obey you." "Why?" asked 'Umar. "Where did you get that cloak?" asked the man. "All you got was one scarf, and you are a tall man." "Not so fast," replied 'Umar, and shouted, "'Abdullah." No one answered, so he cried again, "'Abdullah ibn 'Umar!" "Here, Commander of the Faithful," answered his son. "I adjure you by Allah," said 'Umar. "This scarf which I wear at my waist—is it yours?" "By Allah it is," replied he. Thereupon the objector said, "The matter is settled. We hear and we obey."

But let us proceed, for still the objection might be raised that this is only the case of 'Umar.

The famous Abu Ja'far al-Mansur[32] built up his position by means which we would today call arbitrary. One day Sufyan al-Thauri came to him and said: "O Commander of the Faithful, how can you justify your expenditure of the wealth of Allah and of the community of Muhammad without their permission? Once 'Umar was making the Pilgrimage and had spent sixteen dinars on himself and his company and said, 'I cannot but think that we have ruined the public treasury.' You know what Mansur ibn 'Ammar told us, for you were there, and were the first to write it down at the time. He told us on the original authority of Ibn Mas'ud that the Messenger of Allah once said: 'A ruler who plunges deep into the public treasury to meet his own desires will tomorrow be in Hell.'" Then Abu Ubaid the secretary—one of the personal attendants in the royal place—cried out: 'Must the Commander of the Faithful hear such stuff as this?' But Sufyan gave him only a reprimand in answer, saying, 'Quiet. Pharaoh and Haman destroyed one another.'" And, so saying, he left, after making a powerful and honest protest, because tyrants, be they never so autocratic, dare not attack those whose heart is pure, who are above material interests and have devoted themselves to Allah.

Or again, al-Wathiq,[33] another of the despotic rulers, was visited one day by a venerable scholar who gave him the greeting of "Peace" as he entered. Al-Wathiq did not return the greeting, but said only, "May Allah give you no peace." Then the old man took him to task: "Evil was the training that your teacher gave you. Allah the Exalted says, 'When you are greeted, return the greeting with a better, or at least in the same terms.' (4:86) Yet you did not return a better greeting; you did not even reply in the same terms."

As Abu Yusuf sat giving judgment, there came before him a case involving an orchard, which concerned a private individual and al-Hadi,[34] the Abbasid ruler. Abu Yusuf perceived that right was on the side of the individual, but that the ruler had witnesses against him. So he said: "The case necessitates that al-Hadi take an oath as to the veracity of his witnesses." Al-Hadi shrank from taking such an oath, for he thought it be a form of humiliation; so he had to give back the orchard. Similarly, Abu Yusuf made al-Rashid[35] take such an oath in a case where he saw it to be necessary. Al-Fadl ibn Rabi' once gave testimony before him, and he rejected the testimony. When the Caliph remonstrated with him, asking, "Why did you reject this testimony?" the judge answered: "I heard him say I am your slave. If such be the case, a slave cannot give testimony; if not, the case is the same."

This flame that Islam kindled in the human conscience has not failed even in the darkest passages of history, and during its lifetime has illuminated various examples of a free conscience and a spirit raised above all worldly values, all temporal powers, and all worldly considerations.

In Egypt Ahmad ibn Tulun[36] paid great respect to Bakkar ibn Qutaiba, the Hanafite judge, and used to come and hear him teach; Bakkar never knew of his arrival until the ruler stood by his side. But when Ibn Tulun desired him to curse al-Muwaffaq, the Abbasid heir apparent, he refused, saying, 'Surely the curse of Allah is already on evildoers.' It was suggested to Ibn Tulun that this remark was actually an attack on him, and he demanded the return of the gifts which he had given Ibn Qutaiba. They were returned to him new and unopened. Then Ibn Tulun imprisoned him, but as the result of an appeal on his behalf, placed him in a rented house where he could sit at a window and teach the people. When Ibn Tulun was attacked by the disease of which he was to die, he repented and asked pardon of Ibn Qutaiba. But the judge said to the messenger: 'Say to him that I am a very old man, and he is ill; so the time is near when we shall meet, and it is Allah who will interpose between us.' So Ibn Tulun died, and Ibn Qutaiba remarked, 'So the poor wretch is dead.'" "Poor wretch" because of the pride which Ibn Qutaiba discerned in him and because of the evil of his character, even though he had acquired power.

So in the time of the Ayyubid dynasty, King Isma'il made an agreement with the Franks during the Crusades and handed over to them Sidon and other fortresses in order to gain their support against Najm al-Din Ayyub. But 'Izz al-Din ibn 'Abd al-Salam took him to task for such an act. This angered Isma'il, and he deposed him from office and imprisoned him. But later he sent him a message, promising him a return to office. This the messenger told him in these words: "All your honors shall be restored to you, and more also, on the sole condition that you humble yourself before the sultan." But the old man answered only: "By Allah, I would not even permit him to kiss my hand. We are complete opposites."

Recent history has also afforded examples of this nobility of character, and we shall look at two instances which the present writer heard at first hand, but which he does not recollect ever to have seen in print. The first was told me by the late Ahmad Shafiq Pasha, the famous historian, concerning the age of Isma'il,[37] and the second, which I have heard from many sources, concerns a period close to it, that of the Khedive Tawfiq.[38]

The first incident relates that when the Sultan 'Abd al-'Aziz[39] visited Egypt in the days of Isma'il, the latter was somewhat anxious about the visit because part of the business of the visit was to secure for himself the title of "Khedive," together with a number of other important matters connected with the administration of Egypt. Part of the program for the visit was a reception for the ulama in the palace; but various customs attached to such solemn receptions, among them that all who entered the Sultan's presence should bow to the ground, using the Turkish form of address three times, and all the rest of those ancient customs, which are so foolish and so contrary to the spirit of Islam. So it became the duty of the palace staff to drill the 'ulama in the procedure of receptions for several days, so that they should not make any blunders in the Sultan's presence.

When the time came, the leading and most eminent 'ulama made their entry; they put aside their religion and paid court to the world; they bowed low in their prostrations before one, who was created like themselves; they greeted him by touching earth to their brows, their mouths, and their breasts; and they retired, keeping their backs to the door and their faces to the Sultan — all just as their ceremonial instructor had bidden them. All but one, the Shaikh Hasan al-'Adawi. He retained his religion and spurned worldly customs; he knew that Allah alone is truly great. So he made his entry with head erect as free men do; he greeted the Sultan with the Islamic formula, "Peace be upon you, Commander of the Faithful"; he talked to him with sincerity as wise 'ulama should, exhorting him to show piety towards Allah, to fear His punishment and to use justice and mercy in dealing with his subjects. And when he had finished, he gave him the greeting of "peace" again, and retired with his head erect as free men do.

The Khedive and the palace staff were horrified, thinking that all their plans would be frustrated, for the Sultan would, of course, be furious; all their efforts would be wasted and all the hopes lost that they had built up. But true and faithful speech is never lost, nor can it fail to touch the heart with force and power; for it is delivered with such force and power. Thus it was in this case; for the Sultan said, "This is the only man among you." And it was he and no other whom the Sultan honored.

The second incident took place in the Dar al-'Ulum between the Khedive Tawfiq and Shaikh Hasan al-Tawil. The latter was a professor in this college, and he always dressed in informal clothes. One day the Principal learned that the Khedive was going to visit the college, so he made his preparations to put the best appearance upon the establishment; and one of his ideas was that the Shaikh al-Tawil should change his clothes and dress in formal attire, so that he might be suitably garbed to meet the dignitaries.

The Shaikh listened to the Principal's request and gave him to understand that he agreed. The next day he appeared in his usual garb, but carrying a handkerchief in which was a bundle of clothes. When the Principal saw him, his face registered his displeasure, and in obvious anger and disappointment he said, "Where are your formal clothes, Professor?" "Here," said the Shaikh, pointing to the handkerchief. So the Principal left him, satisfied that he would change into formal wear when the distinguished visitor arrived and quite content with such a strange proceeding.

Time passed, and at length the pillars of the college shook with the arrival of the long-expected visitor. But now came a tremendous surprise for Principal, Professors, and everyone; for al-Tawil advanced to meet the Khedive with a bundle of clothes in his hand, and with an assured and confident air he said: "I was told that I must have formal clothes, so I brought them. If you want the clothes, here they are; if you want Hasan al-Tawil, here he is."

The Khedive naturally preferred to have Hasan al-Tawil.

Such believing souls as these respect no greatness save that of Islam; hence they know a freedom of mind and conscience from all false values and from all worldly considerations. They have grasped the very essence of Islam and have comprehended its central teaching; they have found their strength in its powerful and lofty spirit, and hence they have no need to seek the pleasure of men. And that is Islam.

❖ ❖ ❖ ❖ ❖ ❖ ❖

In the same connection of human equality, freedom of conscience, and absolute justice we may perhaps also discuss the historical experience of Islam in the administration of conquered territories and of non-Muslim communities in Muslim territory. This is an aspect of equality and justice which transcends individuals to affect whole communities and in which the universally human supersedes Islamic identity.

Any discussion of conquered territories must lead us to discuss the nature, the causes, and the aims of Muslim conquest. This is an immense subject from which we shall select only such few points as are indispensable, such points as have a clear bearing on social justice in its universal application.

The preaching of Islam has always been based on an appeal to the mind, the heart, and the conscience; it has always dispensed with the method of coercion, even with that spiritual coercion used by the earlier religions in the form of wonderful miracles. Islam was the first religion to show respect to the human faculty of perception and intellect and to content itself with an appeal to this faculty, rather than an attempt to overcome it by producing suprarational miracles. And from the very outset it has never made forcible coercion with the sword one of its aims. "There shall be no compulsion in religion." (2:257) "Summon men to the way of your Lord wisely and with fair warnings; bring against them a better argument." (16:126)

It was the Quraish who were the first to put physical force in the way of the new religion by maltreating those whose hearts Allah had turned to Islam; they drove out the few Muslims from their lands, their houses, and their families; they attempted to blockade the Muslims as a body and to destroy them by hunger. There was not a single method of physical violence that they did not use to turn men away from this religion. Thus it became inevitable that Islam should defend itself and repel the oppression. "Permission is given to those who have been opposed by force, because they have been wronged; verily Allah is able to help them." (22:40) "Fight in the way of Allah against those who oppose you by force; but do not open hostilities, for Allah does not love those who do so." (2:186) This is warfare, aimed at guaranteeing freedom of worship and preventing injury to Muslims; it does not aim at compelling anyone to adopt Islam.

Finally, the whole of Arabia was Islamized, and the conquests spread to the lands outside Arabia. Of what nature were these conquests?

As we have seen, Islam reckons itself to be a worldwide religion and a universal religion; therefore, it could not confine itself to the limits of Arabia, but naturally desired to spread over the whole world in every direction. However, it found itself opposed by political forces in the Persian and Roman Empires, which were its neighbors; these stood in the way of Islam and would not allow its propagators to travel through their countries to inform their people of the nature of Islam, this new faith. Therefore, it followed that these political forces had to be destroyed, so that there might be toleration for the true faith among men. Islam aimed only at obtaining a hearing for its message, so that anyone who might want to accept it would be free to do as he wished, while anyone who wanted to reject it could be the master of his own destiny; this was possible only when the political and material forces of the empires had been removed from the path.

The Islamic conquests, then, were not wars of aggression, nor yet were they a system of colonization for economic gain, like the colonizing ventures of later centuries. They were simply a means of getting rid of the material and political opposition that stood between the nations and the new concept that Islam brought with it. They were an "intellectual war" with respect to the peoples and a physical war with respect to the powers that held these peoples, and which denied them access to the new religion through the exercise of power and coercion.

The consequence of the Islamic doctrines, first that Islam is a universal religion, and second, that it must not employ physical or spiritual coercion, is this: Three possibilities are placed before the people of a conquered country, one of which everyone must choose — Islam, the poll tax, or war.

Islam: this is the true way, being the new and perfect philosophy of the universe, life, and mankind. It is like a passage that a non-Muslim may traverse; then, from the first moment of his crossing, he is a brother to all Muslims; he has all that they have, and he must do all that they do; they cannot be superior to him in rank or in lineage, in wealth or in influence. He is one with them, irrespective of race or community or tribe.

Or the poll tax: Individual Muslims must pay with their blood in order to defend the state and also pay the *zakat* to defend society. Individual non-Muslims enjoy the security afforded by the Islamic state, its protection at home and abroad, and all the other benefits that the state extends to its citizens; so in all equity non-Muslims must bear their share of the state's expenses. But since the *zakat* is a form of religious duty for the Muslim, besides being a statutory duty on wealth, Islam has a fine perception for the susceptibilities of those who do not belong to it and is therefore unwilling to force them to fulfill a Muslim religious duty. So it imposes the statutory duty on their wealth in the form of a poll tax, rather than in that of *zakat*. Thus the poll tax is a symbol of submission; that is to say, it is a sign that there is here no opposition to the doctrines of Islam; but it is also a symbol of Islam's universal tolerance, which is the aim of Islam.

Or war: For to refuse both Islam and the payment of the poll tax indicates clear insistence on maintaining the material forces that intervene between Islam and the minds of men. Hence this insistence must be removed by physical force, which is ultimately the only way.

Thus Islam completely established its universal aims in the conquered territories. It gave the conquered peoples absolute equality with the native Arabs if they chose Islam. It gave them their full human rights if they chose to pay the poll tax. And it gave them just and humane treatment if they chose war.

Islam confirmed in their office some of the governors of the conquered territories if they became Muslims. Such a one was Bazan the Persian, whom Abu Bakr confirmed in his office in the Yemen. He also installed Firuz as governor of San'a, and when Qais ibn 'Abd Yaghuth the Arab chief expelled him, Abu Bakr sent him back, thus aiding a Persian Muslim against an Arab Muslim.

Similarly, Muslim governors confirmed lesser officials in the positions that they had previously held in their native countries, now conquered. These might stand by their former religion, without professing Islam; the only qualification necessary was that they should be willing to work honestly for the general welfare.

The tenets of Islam actually allow the conquerors to appropriate everything that formerly belonged to their opponents if these have refused to accept either the poll tax or Islam and if they have fought against the Muslims. Yet 'Umar had assimilated so much of the spirit of Islam that, when Fars was conquered in his time he left the land in the possession of its owners, merely laying on them land tax. Two benefits accrued from this system: The people of the subjugated territories benefitted, for even though they had fought against the Muslims, they still had their livelihood and their work; and subsequent generations of Muslims benefitted, for it meant that they were not excluded from the benefits of the conquest in favor of the one generation that had achieved it; rather, the tax arising from these lands was there for the benefit of coming generations, to the general advantage and to meet public needs for a long time.

This is a significant indication of the manner in which Islam dealt with the conquered territories; it administered them according to humane principles, permitting all that was best for them and allowing them the exercise of all their prerogatives, without limit or condition. Indeed it enjoined upon them by all means to make good use of all their benefits and to exercise their prerogatives. It would not place one color or race or religion or tongue before another; all had the opportunity of exerting their natural zeal for the common good. We have already noticed how clients and natives of the conquered territories acquired prominence in matters pertaining particularly to Islam, such as jurisprudence and law. There was not one of the high positions in public life that was restricted to the Arab conquerors; even the office of governor of a province was within their reach in many periods. In the same way, the taxes gathered in each region were used primarily for the welfare of that region; only what was left over afterwards was sent to the public treasury. The conquered territories were not treated as colonies, where the conquerors lived off the blood and the wealth of the native population.

Also connected with this subject is the freedom that Islam gave to conquered peoples to observe their own religious practices and the protection that it afforded to their synagogues and churches, their sanctuaries, their rabbis, and their monks. And it is to be noted how Islam observed the pacts that it had made, a rarely paralleled phenomenon and one unknown to humanity in its experience of empires ancient or modern. And to this day the tradition of Islam is still to conduct its administration in the same way.

So in every age Islam wears an aspect of outstanding grandeur and high nobility, when it is contrasted with present day Western civilization and its practices in countries that misfortune brings into the toils of colonial administration. Such countries are denied the true prerogatives of Western civilization, such as education, commerce, and economic development, to the end that they may remain as long as possible in the role of milch cattle for the colonizing nations. In addition to this there is entailed the degradation of all human nobility, both individual and collective, the corruption of morals that arises from such evil intentions, the rivalries of party and sect whose seeds are sown and whose growth is encouraged, and all varieties of theft, robbery, and plunder on the part of individuals, societies, and peoples.

As for the freedom of religious belief, of which so much is

often made in this age, the horrors of the Spanish Inquisition hardly bear out such a claim, nor do the horrors perpetrated by the Crusaders in the East. And this kind of religious "freedom" is no more than formal even today; Christian missionaries in the Southern Sudan, are supported by all the power of the government, while Muslims are forbidden to enter the country, even to trade. And Allenby, the English general of the First World War, spoke for every European when he exclaimed as he entered Jerusalem, "Only now have the Crusades come to an end."

Islam has always represented the highest achievement in universal and comprehensive social justice; European civilization has never reached the same level, nor ever will. For it is a civilization founded on pure materialism, a civilization of murder and war, of conquest and of subjugation.

✣ ✣ ✣ ✣ ✣ ✣ ✣

We have already discussed the Islamic theory of benevolence and charity, of that mutual responsibility that makes common cause between the strong and the weak, the rich and the poor, the individual and the community, the ruler and his subjects; in a word, it embraces all men. Now we must turn to some illustrations from the course of history, selected from the great number of such afforded by the long story of Islam.

At the time when he became a Muslim, Abu Bakr had a fortune of forty thousand dirhams, amassed from the profits of his trading, and after becoming a Muslim he still made a great deal through trade. Yet when he accompanied the Prophet on the Emigration to Medina, all that was left of his fortune was five thousand dirhams. The remainder he had spent in two ways: First, in ransoming the slaves who through him became Muslim clients and who had formerly suffered various kinds of afflictions at the hands of unbelievers who owned them; and second, in charity to the poor and the destitute.

So, too, when 'Umar, who was himself a poor man, received a gift of lands at Khaibar, he went to the Messenger and said to him: "I have received a gift of lands at Khaibar, the choicest property I have ever had. What do you advise me to do with the land?" The

Messenger told him: "If you wish you may keep it, but give away the income from it in alms." So 'Umar made the lands a charitable foundation for the poor and for his relatives, for slaves, for use in the way of Allah, and for the weak. There was no sin in his keeping it to live suitably off it and have a good living. Thus, too, he avoided letting his property get a hold upon him and proved the truth of the verse, "You will never be really charitable until you spend what you love." (3:86)

Before 'Uthman became Caliph one of his caravans returned from Syria at a time when the Muslims were hard-pressed by famine by reason of a drought; the caravan was composed of a thousand camels loaded with corn, olives, and raisins. So the merchants of Medina approached him with a request that he would sell them some of the goods, since he knew the straits that the people were in. He assented gladly and asked, "What profit will you give me over my buying price?" They offered double what the goods cost, but 'Uthman said that he had a better offer than that. The merchants protested: "But, Abu 'Amr, there are no merchants in Medina except ourselves, and no one can have approached you before us. Who has made you this offer?" "Allah offers me ten times the price of the goods," said 'Uthman. "Can you go higher than that?" "No, " they confessed. Then he swore by Allah that the caravan and all its contents should be given as alms to the destitute and the poor among the Muslims.

'Ali and his household gave away in alms three loaves of barley bread that they had, to relieve the destitute, the orphan, and the prisoner; they themselves had to sleep hungry, but the recipients were satisfied.

Husain ibn 'Ali was heavily in debt, but though he owned the spring of Abu Naizar, he would not sell it, for the poorer Muslims used to draw their water from it and it was reserved for them. So he decided rather to bear the weight of his debt, although he was a nobleman of noble descent from the best of the clan of Hashim.

In the same way, the Helpers in Medina shared with the Emigrants their property and their houses; they took them as brothers, paid their ransoms, and redeemed their captives, treating them in all things as themselves. As the glorious Qur'an describes them,

"They found no desires in their hearts for the share which had fallen to others; they preferred them above themselves, though among themselves there was poverty." (59:7)

The spirit of Islam continues to be thus active as long as the Islamic world is free from the influence of materialistic Western civilization. This is well shown by this account of the Touareg tribes given by 'Abd al-Rahman 'Azzam in his book, *The Eternal Message*.

I have known Touareg tribes in North Africa who live this happy life of mutual responsibility; none among them lives for himself, but all for the community. The greatest source of pride and glory among them is how much they can do for this community. The first thing that attracted my attention to this system was when a certain man who came from the urban area fled from the French and came to the Touareg at Fazzan, where he settled among them and lived off their bounty. He afterwards went forth, to look for some means of earning money with which to repay the Touareg in full; but his family he left in the protection of this Islamic community. Ill luck, however, pursued him, and he was unable to make any money. He came to us in Misurata, to ask for help, and we helped him to go back to his family. About a year later he came back to see me a second time, and I imagined that in the interval he had been with his family. But he said, "No. Only now can I return to my family." When I asked, "How is that?" he said to me, "After I saw you last time I used all my available money in a business venture, and now I have enough to take back with me to the Touareg community." I asked him, "Are you taking it to your children, or to the community?" and he replied, "To the latter in the first place; for they have sheltered my children during my absence. So I will make myself responsible for the children of anyone whom I find to be away from home. I shall divide what Allah has granted me between my own children and those of my neighbors." Then I asked him, "Does the whole community live in the same way as you with your neighbors?" and he replied: "All of us are equal in good times or in bad; all extra can go to him who wants it. So any member of our community would be ashamed to return empty handed ashamed not in front of his own family, but in front of his neighbors, who have awaited his return just as eagerly as his own household.

This piece of evidence the author follows with a general statement which explains the underlying truth.

Such a communal spirit is not peculiar to this Touareg community or to others similar to it among the desert and wilderness dwellers; nor is this spirit one of the prerequisites of their solidarity. In effect it is no more than the spirit of Islam, which is more clearly apparent among such people who are still isolated from modern materialistic life. I have found this spirit in those Muslim villages and hamlets which are still characteristically Islamic, no matter whether their inhabitants are Arab or otherwise, white or black, eastern or western. In most of these I have found a Muslim community still living a life of virtue and fellowship, of mutual responsibility, and mutual help, inspired by charity. Such people are closer to the righteous society as envisaged by the founder of Islam than the tens of millions who are bewitched by materialistic Western civilization. The latter live for themselves, even though their society may be on the verge of destruction; they prefer the satisfaction of their own desires to charity towards their own families, let alone towards their neighbors.

This mutual responsibility inculcated by the spirit of Islam is not left solely to the discretion of the social or of the individual conscience; a ruler also has his necessary part to play. Thus 'Umar instituted a payment from the public treasury to all who were very young or very old and to all who were sick; this was not a recognized use for the *zakat*, but was an aspect of his perception of social responsibility in the conditions of his time. And in fact this dispensation made the law concerning theft unnecessary during the "Year of Ashes,"[40] when the people were starving, although starvation constitutes almost a compulsion to theft and under such circumstances the relevant penalty is suspended.

Perhaps the following story about 'Umar is most significant for the practical application of the concept of mutual responsibility; it also concerns the right of individual possession and its limits in relation to society.

"They say that some of the slaves of Ibn Hatib ibn Abi Balta'a stole a camel from a man of the Mumaina; 'Umar caught them, and they confessed the crime, so he ordered Kathir ibn al-Salt to cut off their hands. When the latter refused, 'Umar insisted. Then Kathir said to Ibn Hatib: 'I would indeed have cut off their hands but I knew that you made these slaves work hard and that you kept them so hungry that if one of them had eaten anything forbidden by Allah, he would have been pardonable.' Then Ibn Hatib, exclaimed: 'I swear by Allah although I had no part in this deed, yet I will discharge the obligation of the complaint.' So he demanded of the Muzainite, 'How much was your camel worth to you?' 'Four hundred dirhams,' answered the man. But 'Umar said to Ibn Habib, 'Go and pay him eight hundred.' Then he remitted the penalty of the slaves who had committed the theft, on the grounds that their owner had driven them to such an act by keeping them hungry, so that they had to have enough to stave off starvation."

Thus in historical practice there was implemented that far-reaching precedent that was accorded by Islam to the right to live and to the right to possess a competence; this it held to be greater than the right of individual possession. Here also there was a clear and distinct ratification of the principle of mutual responsibility in society, between the "haves" and the "have-nots" within the community.

This conception of social responsibility is made even more famous in the history of Islam by the fact that it passed beyond the limits of the purely Islamic world and was applied to mankind in general.

'Umar once saw an old blind man begging at a door; he asked about him, and learned that he was a Jew. Then said 'Umar to him: "What has brought you to this state?" "The poll tax, penury, and age." 'Umar took him by the hand, and brought him to his own house, where he immediately gave him sufficient to satisfy his needs. Then he sent a message to the keeper of the public treasury: "Look after this man and others such. For, by Allah, we have not given him justice if we have profited from his youth, only to desert him now in his old age. Alms are only for the poor and the destitute; and this man is in destitution and is one of the scripturaries." So he remitted the poll tax to him and to others like him.

Similarly, while on his way to Damascus 'Umar passed a piece of land belonging to some Christian lepers and commanded that a gift be made to them out of the alms money and that food be supplied to them.

Thus 'Umar raised the spirit of Islam to this universal level more than thirteen centuries ago. He made social security a universal right, independent of religion or creed, and not to be precluded by any religious doctrine or belief. Surely this is a supremely high level which mankind is still striving unsuccessfully to achieve.

❖ ❖ ❖ ❖ ❖ ❖ ❖

When we come to discuss political and economic theory from the official point of view of the state, we find that the course of history shows an exemplary period in the life of Islam, a period which regrettably did not last long. The reason for this we shall see in what follows. For we must discover whether the reason for its brevity was some integral part of the nature of the Islamic system of politics and economics or if it was the outcome of chance occurrences of evil, unconnected with the nature of the system.

We shall start with a consideration of political theory, because economic theory follows political in the course of history and is formed by it.

When the death of the Prophet drew near, he appointed Abu Bakr to lead the prayers. 'A'isha protested, because Abu Bakr was a tenderhearted man, and when he stood up to lead the prayers his voice would not be heard for sobs. But the Prophet was angered and recalled the foolish women in the story of Joseph, insisting that Abu Bakr be appointed to lead the prayers.

Does this, then, mean that the Messenger appointed as his successor his former companion in the cave?[41] And if so, did the Muslims clearly understand that fact?

We must reject both of these ideas. If Muhammad had wished to appoint a successor, and if such an appointment had been one of the ordinances of Islam, he would have declared the appointment publicly, as was his custom with all the other ordinances of the faith. And if the Muslims had clearly understood that he had appointed Abu Bakr as his successor, the dispute at the Saqifa would never have taken place between the Emigrants and the

Helpers; for the latter would never have disputed any matter that was governed by a command from Allah's Messenger.

The matter, then, was one for the council of Muslims to decide to the general satisfaction which of the people had the best right to the caliphate. And when at the Saqifa there was a dispute as to whether or not the Caliph should be one of the Emigrants, that matter was not one of the ordinances of Islam, but rather a matter for agreement and accommodation among the Muslim community. The Helpers could have rejected a Caliph and were not liable to censure for so doing; but actually they approved Abu Bakr because of the local hostility between the Aus and the Khazraj, the two main tribes of Helpers, and because both of these parties were unwilling that the caliphate should fall to the other; both preferred that under the circumstances it should go to the Emigrants.

When agreement was reached, it was settled that day that the Caliphate should belong to the Emigrants; but there was nothing in that to necessitate that the caliphate should become the prerequisite of the Quraish. Had it been so, 'Umar, when he named the council to appoint his own successor, would never have said, "If Salim, the client of Abu Hudhaifa, had been still alive, I should myself have nominated him as my successor." For Salim was certainly no Quraishite. The spirit and the principles of Islam alike forbid that the Quraish should have any status above that of ordinary Muslims simply because they are the Quraish or because they have a blood connection with the Prophet.

Abu Bakr certainly appointed 'Umar as his successor, but this involved no compulsion on the Muslims, since they were free to reject the appointment. Therefore, 'Umar became Caliph, not because Abu Bakr had appointed him, but because the people took the oath of allegiance to him. In the same way, 'Umar himself named a council of six, that after his death one of these should be chosen. Yet the Muslims were not compelled to accept one of these six; the only reason was that experience had shown that the six in question were the best fitted for the office, and thus 'Umar's choice was in line with experience. From this fact there arose all the compulsion that there was.

As for the oath of allegiance to 'Ali, there were some who were willing to take it, while others refused to take it; and so for the first time civil war was known in Islam. From that fact there came all the disasters that have encompassed the spirit and the principles of Islam in politics, economics, and in other regards.

This brief review has shown us the fundamental political theory of Islam, namely, that the unfettered choice of all Muslims is the only warrant for authority. This was clearly apparent to the Muslim community when it passed over 'Ali, the nephew and son-in-law of Allah's Messenger, and his nearest kinsman. It may be that 'Ali was deprived of his right when he was passed over, especially after the death of 'Umar; the worst thing that could have happened in the history of Islam, as we see it, was the neglect of 'Ali after the death of 'Umar. Yet this same neglect had a certain value as a practical illustration of Islamic political theory, with its insistence that authority is not subject to the right of inheritance in any way; such an idea is completely foreign to the spirit and principles of Islam. Thus, although the great Imam personally suffered an injustice in this way, yet the emphasis on the preceding fact was from every point of view infinitely more important.

With the coming of Mu'awiya, the caliphate in Islam became a monarchy, or a tyranny, confined to the Umayyad family. This was characteristic, not of Islam, but of the pre-Islamic age, just as the common verdict on the Umayyads is that they had no deep-seated religious beliefs; Islam for them was a cloak which they assumed to cover their preoccupation with material and worldly prosperity.

It will be sufficient at this point to quote as proof of this the account of the oath of allegiance as it was taken to Yazid.[42] From this we may discover the foundation of Umayyad power and find out whether Mu'awiya, who established that power, was true to the spirit of Islam or to some other ideal. Mu'awiya summoned delegates to represent all the provinces at the taking of the oath of allegiance to Yazid. Then Yazid ibn al-Muqaffa' stood up and said: "The Commander of the Faithful is here," and he indicated Mu'awiya. "If he dies, his successor is here," and he indicated Yazid. "And if anyone refuses—here," and he pointed to his sword. Then said Mu'awiya, "Sit down, O best of preachers."

After the oath was taken to Yazid in Syria, Mu'awiya gave to Sa'id ibn al-'As the task of gaining the acceptance of the people of the Hejaz. This he was unable to do, so Mu'awiya went to Mecca with an army and with a full treasury. He called together the principal Muslims and addressed them thus:

"You all know that I have lived among you, and you are aware also of my ties of kindred with you. Yazid is your brother and your nephew. It is my wish that you take the oath to Yazid as the next Caliph; then it will be you who will bestow offices and depose from them, who will collect and apportion money." He was answered by 'Abdullah ibn al-Zubair, who gave him a choice of three things to do: First, he might do as Allah's Messenger had done, and appoint no successor; second, he might do as Abu Bakr had done, and nominate a successor who was not of his immediate family; third, he might do as 'Umar had done, and hand over the whole matter to a council of six individuals, none of whom was a member of his own immediate family. Mu'awiya's anger was kindled, and he asked, "Have you any more to say?" "No." Mu'awiya turned to the remainder of the company:"And you?" "We agree with what Ibn al-Zubair has said," they replied. Then he addressed the meeting in threatening terms: "The one who warns is blameless. I was speaking among you, and one of you was bold to get up and call me a liar to my face. That I will bear and even forgive. But I stand to my words, and I swear by Allah that if any of you speaks one word against the position that I take up, no word of answer will he receive, but first the sword will take his head. And no man can do more than save his life."

Thereupon the commander of Mu'awiya's guard ordered two men to stand over each of the nobles of the Hejaz who opposed him and to each he said: "If your man leaves his guards to speak one word, either for me or against me, then let the guards strike off his head with their swords." Then he mounted the pulpit and proclaimed: "These men are the leaders and the choicest of the Muslims; no matter can be successfully handled without them, nor can any decision be taken without their counsel. They are now satisfied to take the oath to Yazid, and indeed have already taken that oath by the name of Allah." So the people took the oath.

It was on such a basis, completely unrecognized by Islam, that the royal authority of Yazid stood. And what was this Yazid?

He it was of whom 'Abdullah ibn Hanzala said: "We never entered the presence of Yazid without fearing to be struck down by lightning strokes from Heaven. For men were marrying their mothers or their daughters or their sisters, they were drinking wine, and omitting to say the prayers. By Allah, had not other people been with me, I would have called down on him a disaster him Allah."

Even if this represents an exaggeration due to hostility towards Yazid (though there is probably no exaggeration in it), it remains a fact that he was a youth devoted to drinking and pleasure, which he pursued to the limit of folly; it is true that he cared more for the keeping and the rearing of monkeys than he did for ruling and caring for his subjects; he was a man of levity, light-mindedness, and pleasure.

This was the "Caliph" whom Mu'awiya imposed on the people, forcing them to accept him by a means which Islam does not recognize, namely, the force of family and tribal solidarity. This was neither difficult nor strange in the case of Mu'awiya, for he was the son of Abu Sufyan and his mother was Hind, the daughter of 'Utba. Mu'awiya was in all respects a son worthy of such a family, and supremely so in the extent to which his spirit differed from the true nature of Islam. No one can judge Islam by Mu'awiya, or by any of the Umayyads; and Islam can bear no responsibility for him or for any of them.

In order to acquit Islam, its spirit and its principles, from this hereditary system which Mu'awiya introduced into it, we must digress a little to discuss Mu'awiya and the Umayyad clan purely for the purpose of establishing the truth.

Abu Sufyan was the man from whom Islam and the Muslims received such treatment as has filled the pages of history. He did not embrace Islam until its victory was assured, and even then his conversion was a thing of words rather than of faith in heart and conscience; for Islam never penetrated to his heart. Accordingly, he was always watching for the defeat of the Muslims; he expected it at the battle of Hunain[43] and again during the Muslim attack on the Byzantine Empire. He was all this time ostensibly a Muslim himself, but the old loyalties of the pre-Islamic age still had control of his heart. Thus, when he stood one day at 'Umar's door with Suhail ibn 'Amr ibn al-Harith and a number of other nobles and saw 'Umar admit Bilal and Suhaib before them, because these two had been early Muslims, Abu Sufyan was particularly enraged, and in an effort to stir up discontentment he said: "Never have I seen anything like this; he admits these slaves, and leaves us standing at his door." But his companion reproved him in these words: "O people, by Allah I can see what is on your faces. But if you are going to be angry, then let your anger be against yourselves; you were summoned to become Muslims at the same time as others, but the others went over quickly, and you slowly. How will it stand with you on the Day of Resurrection, when others are called and you are left?"

But Abu Sufyan still nourished a rancor against Islam and against the Muslims, and he saw no opportunity of rousing discontent without eagerly availing himself of it. When 'Ali was passed over in favor of Abu Bakr for the caliphate, Abu Sufyan spoke up in these words: "By Allah I foresee here a flame of trouble which will only be quenched in blood. O family of 'Abd Manaf, what has Abu Bakr to do with your affairs? Where are the two weaklings, the humble 'Ali and al-'Abbas?"

> None bear the evil blow of fate save two
> Most humble, cord and peg their tribe to raise;
> Yet this in ignominy silent sits,
> The other dead without a word of praise.

'Ali realized what Abu Sufyan was aiming at, and he forestalled him by saying: "By Allah, your whole object in this is to rouse discord; as indeed you are constantly planning evil against Islam." He is also reported to have said: "O Abu Sufyan, Muslims are those who give honest counsel to one another; but hypocrites are those who deceive one another, who deal treacherously between themselves, even though their homes and their persons are near neighbors."

Abu Sufyan was, of course, dreaming of a monarchy that would be hereditary among the Umayyads ever since 'Uthman became Caliph, and indeed on that day he said: "O Umayyads, take the power now, once for all. For by Him in Whose name Abu Sufyan swears, I have always hoped for this on your behalf—that this power might be yours and your children's by right of inheritance." Authority among the Muslims was never referred to as "kingship" until the time when the Prophet stood reviewing the Muslim army on the day of the conquest of Mecca. On that occasion he said to al-'Abbas, his uncle: "By Allah, Abu'l-Fadl, the royal power of your nephew has today become great." But when al-'Abbas reminded him, "It is rather a prophetic power," he agreed, "You are right."

"You are right." For "kingship" was a word heard only with the ears, rather than a term accepted by the heart. For such a heart as that of the Prophet could accept only the meaning of such a term as kingship and royal authority, not the actuality of it.

Such, then, was the father of Mu'awiya. His mother was Hind, the daughter of 'Utba; she it was who stood at the battle of Uhud and lapped up the blood as she bit into the liver of Hamza like a fierce lioness. Even this shocking deed was not too much to satisfy the hatred of the dead Hamza which had been kindled in her by a blood feud.

She it was, too, who stood firm after her husband had embraced Islam; she still held out against it, even when the success of Islam was assured. Then she cried aloud: "Kill this mischievous rascal in whom there is no good. A ruffian is he who spies upon his people. Will you not, then, fight these fellows to repulse them from your persons and your lands?"

The Umayyads under Islam were exactly the same as they had been before Islam; they alone had refused during the pre-Islamic age to take the Oath of Fudhul.[44] This oath had touched a humane note which the Umayyad nature could not show, for it was phrased thus: "To stand up for the oppressed until he is given his rights, to take from our own possessions and to share our own property to satisfy those rights, to prevent the strong from oppressing the weak, and the native from doing violence to the stranger." The Umayyad nature made it impossible for them to take such an oath; their inherited family characteristics forbade it.

The aunt of 'Umar ibn 'Abd al-'Aziz,[45] herself an Umayyad, perceived that there was in 'Umar a strain not native to the Umayyads when he succeeded to the caliphate and embarked on a course foreign to the nature of that family. He was distinguished for his humane nature; he redressed the wrongs that had been done by the hands of his own kinsman; and he prevented the latter from carrying on their illegal plundering of the public treasury. So when his aunt was brought into his presence, she addressed him thus: "Verily, your kinsmen are complaining about you, and saying that you have taken from them everything except what you give them yourself." "I have taken nothing from them that is their right," he replied, "and nothing which belongs to them." She answered: "I have heard their talk, and I fear that they will inflame evil days against you." Said he: "Allah can guard me from the evil of every day which I fear, save only the Day of Resurrection."

Upon this she realized that 'Umar had in him a strain foreign to the Umayyad nature and one of which she disapproved. When she returned to her own family she told them: "See how things turn out for you as a result of marrying into the family of 'Umar ibn al-Khattab."

Yes indeed; see how things turn out for you. For it was a crime in Umayyad eyes for a ruler to show piety towards Allah, to withhold perquisites and easy riches, to stand for the right, and not to exercise the power of his authority to fill his coffers and to sate his appetites. Yes indeed; this was a crime brought on by an alliance with the family of Ibn al-Khattab; for the great 'Umar was the grandfather of 'Umar II on his mother's side. And it was his influence which disturbed the rooted and inherited mode of Umayyad life.

The erroneous fable still persists that Mu'awiya was a scribe who wrote down the revelations of Allah's Messenger. The truth is that when Abu Sufyan embraced Islam, he besought the Prophet to give Mu'awiya some measure of position in the eyes of the Arabs; thus he would be compensated for the disgrace of being slow to embrace Islam and of being one of those who had no precedence in the new religion. So the Prophet used Mu'awiya for writing letters and contracts and agreements. But none of the Companions ever said that he wrote down any of the Prophet's revelations, as was asserted by Mu'awiya's partisans after he had assumed the throne. But this is what happens in all such cases.

We condemn Mu'awiya not only for instituting a new system of political theory including the idea of hereditary succession, but for forcing the people to accept it. We also condemn him strongly for suppressing all moral elements in his struggle with 'Ali and throughout the course of his reign thereafter; for this was the first time that any such suppression had taken place in the history of Islam. For in Islam politics, like life in general, had always been the expression of those moral feelings that lie deep within life and that are rooted in its very nature. The existence of these feelings was a natural consequence of that constant watchfulness that Islam enjoined upon the individual conscience and of that keen moral perception that it awakens in the souls of its adherents; of this we have seen examples at the beginning of this chapter. The greatest crime of Mu'awiya, therefore, was that he destroyed the spirit of Islam at the very beginning of his reign by a complete suppression of its moral elements.

It was doubly unfortunate that such a calamity should befall Islam so early, when its lofty norms were no more than thirty years old; thus it was given no opportunity of becoming permanently established or of settling the profound traditions that are so difficult to regain once they have been deserted. This was undoubtedly a stroke of ill luck. Yet in actual fact it was not the first misfortune; that was the passing over of 'Ali and the election of 'Uthman, a weak old man, to the caliphate, and the fact that the management of affairs was handed over to Marwan ibn al-Hakam, the Umayyad. If fortune had decreed that 'Ali be elected Caliph after Abu Bakr and 'Umar, then the traditions of Islam would have continued unbroken for a further period, and it would have remained on a steady course for a third term; then there would not have followed the obliteration of the spirit of Islam that did actually take place. If Islamic traditions had been reinforced for an additional period, and its institutions become clearly defined, the task of any-one seeking to subvert the Islamic order would have been more difficult.

In order to appreciate the full significance of this statement we must examine the form of political theory in the different peri-ods; under Abu Bakr and 'Umar, under 'Uthman and Marwan, under the Imam 'Ali, and then under the Umayyads, and later the Abbasid kings, when the spirit of Islam had been extinguished.

When the Muslim community invited Abu Bakr to become the Successor (i.e., Caliph) of Allah's Messenger, his function in his own eyes was simply to ensure the implementation of the observance of the faith and the law of Allah among the Muslims. It did not occur to him that this new position might permit him anything that was not permitted to him when he was a private individual, that it might allow him any new right that he had not previously enjoyed, or that it might absolve him from any one of his former responsibilities—to himself, to his people, or to his God.

After the oath of allegiance had been taken at the Saqifa, he stood up and addressed the people: "Now O people, I have been made your ruler, though I am not the best among you. If I do what is right, support me. If I do what is wrong, set me right. Follow what is true, for it contains faithfulness; avoid what is false, for it holds treachery. The weaker among you shall in my eyes be the stronger, until, if Allah will, I have redressed his wrong; the stronger in my eyes shall be the weaker, until, if Allah will, I have enforced justice upon him. Let the people cease not to fight in the way of Allah, lest Allah abase them; let not evil practices arise among the people, lest Allah bring punishment upon all of them. Obey me as I obey Allah and His Messenger; if I disobey them, then do you disobey me."

Abu Bakr lived at al-Sunh, a suburb in the vicinity of Medina, in a small and humble house; when he became Caliph he changed neither his house nor his mode of living. He used to go on foot from his house at al-Sunh to and from Medina, morning and evening, though sometimes he rode a horse that was his private possession, not supplied out of the public treasury. Finally, when the pressure of his work grew too great, he moved into Medina.

He used to live off his earnings as a merchant; but when he sought to go and attend to his business, the Muslims restrained him, saying: "This office does not go well with business." So he asked them, as one who knew of no other way to earn his daily bread, "Then how shall I live?" Thereupon, after deliberation on the question, they assigned him an allowance from the public treasury to feed himself and his family; this was in the nature of a recompense for having had to give up his business and confine himself to his official duties.

Despite this, when he was at the point of death, he commanded that all that he had received from the public monies should be counted up and repaid out of his property and his lands, in a spirit of abstemiousness and in order to spare the property of the Muslim community. He always held himself personally responsible for the needs of every individual among his flock, because he believed strongly in that constant watchfulness of conscience that Islam lays upon both ruler and ruled and in that keen moral perception that it kindles in the conscience of all and sundry. This he carried to the point of drawing milk for the poor from the flocks and herds of his neighbors at al-Sunh. For when he came to the caliphate he had heard a servant girl say: "The ewes of our household will give no milk for us today." Abu Bakr, hearing it, said: "Nay, by my life, but I will milk them for you." And so he did. Sometimes he would ask the girl: "Girl, do you want the milk frothing or clear?" Sometimes she would say one, and sometimes the other, but whatever she asked, he milked accordingly.

During the caliphate of Abu Bakr, 'Umar took in hand to look after a blind woman of Medina and assumed the responsibility for her affairs; but when one day he came to see her, he found that her needs had been met. 'Umar kept watch for a day and found Abu Bakr supplying her; he was not too busy with the cares of the caliphate to do such things. Then, seeing him, 'Umar cried aloud: "By my life, it was you, then."

This is a sketch of Abu Bakr's habits while he ruled. When

'Umar succeeded him these habits remained unchanged; for 'Umar also believed that his new position brought him no new privileges of any kind, except that it increased his work by making him responsible for the enforcement of the law of Allah.

In his sermon after the oath of allegiance he said. "O people, I am no more than a man like yourselves; and had it not been that I was unwilling to refuse the command of the Successor to Allah's Messenger, I would never have taken the responsibility of ruling you."

In his second sermon he said: "O people, it is your duty, if I show certain evil qualities, to reprove me for them. You must see that I do not exact from you any tax or anything of what Allah has given you, except that which He allows. You must see that when I have control of the money nothing should be spent improperly. You must see that I do not keep you too long in posts of danger, or detain you unreasonably on the frontiers; for when you are away on military service I must be the father of your families."

He also used to say: "The property of Allah has the same standing with me as that of an orphan; if I have no need of it, I will leave it untouched, and if I need it, I will take only what is right."

When he was questioned one day about how much of the public funds he was entitled to, he replied: "I will tell you how much of it I am entitled to. I am entitled to two suits of clothes, one for the winter, and another for the summer, enough to perform the Pilgrimage and to observe its ceremonies, and sufficient to provide food for myself and my household on the level of a man of Quraish who is neither overrich nor overpoor. Beyond that I am an ordinary Muslim, and I share the lot of all Muslims."

In this spirit he lived, but as far as possible he refused to accept even what he was entitled to. One day he was not feeling well, and they prescribed honey for him; now there was a skin of honey in the public treasury, so he mounted the pulpit and announced to the people: "If you permit me to take it, then I shall do so; but if you do not permit me, then I shall not touch it." They gave him permission.

The Muslims perceived what straits he was in, and some of them went to his daughter, Hafsa, the "Mother of the Faithful," and said: "'Umar refuses all things save the most exiguous allowance. But Allah has enlarged our resources, so let him take as much as he wishes out of the treasury; for he has the full permission of the whole Muslim community." But when Hafsa mentioned it to him, his answer was: "Hafsa, my daughter, you have been faithful to your family but unfaithful to your father. My family have a right only to my person and my property; to my religion and to my faith they have no right."

'Umar had a profound understanding of the implications of the equality which existed between himself and each of his flock; thus when the people were starving during the "Year of Ashes," he took a private oath that he would not touch butter or meat until the people were in better circumstances. This oath he kept faithfully until his skin grew dark and he grimaced if he ate an olive. It happened that there came into the market a skin of butter and a skin of milk, and one of 'Umar's servants bought them for forty dirhams. The servant went to 'Umar to tell him what Allah had granted to him; how this skin of butter and skin of milk had come into the market, and how he had bought them for him. But when 'Umar heard the price he said: "It is too dear; go and give them away as alms. I cannot bring myself to eat what is bought extravagantly." He sat silent for a space and then added: "How can the state of my people be of concern to me if what touches them does not affect me?"

Thus he saw to it that he denied himself what was denied to his flock, in order, as he said, to experience what had touched them; also because, from the bottom of his heart he could not see that his status as ruler gave him any rights or privileges that the remainder of the people did not have; and thirdly, because he held that if he did not act with fairness here, he had no claim on the obedience of his subjects. We have already mentioned the story of the two Yemeni scarves, and his acknowledgement that the people were not bound to obey him unless he acted with justice. This is an acknowledgement of one of the main principles of authority in Islam: the unjust ruler has no claim to obedience.

This understanding of Islam was profound within 'Umar, and it governed his actions in all his dealings. He once bargained with a man for a horse and rode it in order to try it out. The beast foundered, and he wished to return it to its owner, but the latter refused to have it. So the two of them took the matter for decision to Shurayh, the judge. He heard both sides of the case and then said: "Commander of the Faithful, either keep what you bought, or else return it as you got it." Said 'Umar: "Could there be a better decision than that?" So he made Shurayh judge over Kufa as a reward for such a fair and honest decision.

Since 'Umar interpreted his authority in this manner, it was impossible that his relations should have privileges greater than those enjoyed by the remainder of 'Umar's subjects. So when his own son 'Abd al-Rahman was at fault in the matter of wine-drinking, there could be no doubt but that he would be punished. This story is well-known, as is that of 'Amr ibn al-'As oppressing the Egyptian, in which case again it was inevitable that 'Umar should permit retaliation against him. In the matter of money all of 'Umar's governors were held accountable for any increase in their possessions following the tenure of an office; for he feared that such an increase might have been made at the expense of the public monies or by the arbitrary exercise of official power. "Where did you get this?" was the law by which he judged his governors individually whenever he had occasion to take them to task. So he compelled restitution in the case of 'Amr ibn al-'As, his governor in Egypt; in the case of Sa'd ibn Abi Waqqas, his governor in Kufa; and so he froze the assets of Abu Huraira, his governor in Bahrain.

'Umar's conception of the nature of political authority was briefly this: obedience and advice in the realm of faith on the part of the subject, and justice and beneficence on the part of the ruler. We have seen how one of his subjects once said to him: "If we had found any evil thing in you, we would have set it right with the edge of our swords." Such a story gives expression to the principle that the subject has a right to correct his ruler. In the same strain 'Umar once said in a sermon to the people: "I do not appoint governors over you to scourge your bodies, or to revile your honor, or to take your wealth. I appoint them to teach you the Book of your Lord and the Sunnah of your Prophet. If any man is oppressed in any way by his governor, I permit it not; let him have the matter brought to my notice, that I may punish the governor for him."

Thus he established the limits that are set to the ruler's power over the people.

It was because of his profound understanding of the responsibilities of a ruler that 'Umar did not wish these to be borne by another member of his own family. Thus he prevented his son 'Abdullah from being prepared for the office, even though he did make him one of the elective council. It was then that 'Umar made his famous remark, still quoted as the truest description of the caliphate: "We have no incentive to undertake your affairs, and I have never estimated them so highly that I would desire to see one of my family concerned with them. If he be good, then he has already made his contribution; if he be evil, then it is enough for the family of 'Umar that one only should be called to account."

❖ ❖ ❖ ❖ ❖ ❖ ❖

This concept of the nature of authority undoubtedly suffered a change under the rule of 'Uthman. It was an evil chance that 'Uthman should come to the caliphate when he was already an old man whose resolution of character was less than what Islam required and whose will was too weak to oppose the craftiness of Marwan and of the Umayyads who stood behind him.

'Uthman held that his office of Imam permitted him free disposal of Muslim funds in gifts and allowances, and his frequent retort to those who found fault with him in this matter was: "Then for what am I the Imam?" Similarly he held that he had the power to promote his immediate family and clan to positions of authority over the people, among them al-Hakam, who had formerly been expelled by Allah's Messenger. It was, he held, his simple right to accord to his own people honor, advancement, and protection.

On the day that al-Harith ibn al-Hakam married 'Uthman's daughter, the latter gave him from the public treasury two hundred thousand dirhams. The next day the treasurer, Zaid ibn Arqam, came to the Caliph with grief written large on his features and with tears sparkling in his eyes. He asked 'Uthman to accept his resignation from his position, and when the Caliph discovered that the reason was his gift to his new son-in-law out of the public funds, he asked in astonishment: "Ibn Arqam, are you weeping because I give gifts to my family?" "No, Commander of the Faithful," returned this man who understood the keen spirit of Islam. "I am weeping when I think of you taking this money which formerly, during the life of Allah's Messenger, I used to spend in the way of Allah. Even if you had given him only a hundred dirhams, by Allah, that had been too much." 'Uthman was enraged at such a man whose conscience could not accept such liberal expense out of public funds on the relation of the Muslim Caliph, and he said: "Leave your keys of office, Ibn Arqam, and we will find some other to take your place."

Examples of such prodigality are numerous in the life of 'Uthman; he gave al-Zubair six hundred thousand one day, and Talha two hundred thousand and he presented Marwan ibn al-Hakam with one-fifth of the land tax of the province of Ifriqiya. When some of the Companions of the Prophet, chief among whom was 'Ali, expostulated with him about this, his answer was: "I have relatives and kinsmen." But they still reproved him, asking: "Did not Abu Bakr and 'Umar also have relatives and kinsmen?" He answered: "Abu Bakr and 'Umar were concerned to deny their relatives; I am concerned to give to mine." So they left him in anger, saying: "By Allah, the practice of Abu Bakr and 'Umar is more beloved of us than your practice." Yes; and better for Islam; and also more true to Islam.

Even apart from money there were also the governorships which 'Uthman scattered profusely among his relatives. Among these was Mu'awiya, whose power 'Uthman expanded considerably, giving him control of Palestine and the district of Hums; he granted to him the single control of four armies, and thus made it the easier for Mu'awiya later to aspire to royal power during the caliphate of 'Ali, by which time he had acquired money and built up armies. Among the relatives whom 'Uthman thus favored were also al-Hakam ibn al-'As, who had been expelled by the Messenger: 'Abdullah ibn Sa'd ibn Abi Sarh, his foster-brother; and many others.

The Companions noticed such a deviation from the Islamic spirit, and they summoned each other to Medina to restore Islam and to rescue the Caliph himself from disaster; for because of his great age and infirmity 'Uthman was unable to protect his own interests against Marwan. It is hard to doubt that 'Uthman had in his heart the spirit of Islam; but it is equally hard to find an excuse for his errors. The mistake from which all the evil emanated was his acceptance of the caliphate when he was already an old man and exhausted, surrounded by the evil influence of Umayyads of an inauspicious nature.

At a public meeting 'Ali was deputed to visit 'Uthman and speak to him. When he entered 'Uthman's presence 'Ali spoke thus: "I bring to you the opinions of the people who have charged me with this message. By Allah, I do not know what to say to you; for I know nothing that you do not know, nor can I tell you anything of which you are unaware. You know what we all know, and we cannot speak to you of anything of which we have a superior understanding. We have no private information to which we can make you party, and we have no facts inaccessible to you. You have seen and heard and companied with the Messenger of Allah, and you even became his son-in-law. Neither Abu Bakr nor 'Umar was better fitted than you to do right; for you were more closely related to the Messenger than were they; by your marriage to two of his daughters you had an advantage that they did not have, while they had nothing that you did not have. By Allah, look well at yourself, for you are not renowned for blindness, neither are you famed for ignorance; the way of Islam is clear and definite, and the characteristics of the faith are plain. You know already, 'Uthman, that the worthiest servant of Allah in His eyes is the just Imam, one who is guided himself by Allah, and who in his turn guides others, who preserves worthy customs and destroys unwanted deviations; by Allah, all this is explicit, and the established customs are well-marked. But the most evil of the people in the sight of Allah is the unjust Imam, who, himself in error, leads others into error, who destroys worthy customs and introduces unwanted deviations. I myself once heard the Messenger say: 'The unjust Imam will be arraigned on the Day of Resurrection; he will have no helper and no advocate, but will be flung into Hell where he will be whirled around like a mill; then he will be plunged into the depths of Hell.'"

Then 'Uthman replied: "By Allah I knew that they would say

just what you have said. In truth, were you in my place, I would never have upbraided you nor betrayed you; I would not have found fault with you nor come to reprove you because you had been generous to your relatives, because you had strengthened a friendship, or because you had given posts of command to such persons as 'Umar had given them to. O 'Ali, I adjure you by Allah, are you aware that al-Mughira ibn Shu'ba is no longer here?" "Yes," said 'Ali. "Are you aware that 'Umar appointed him to a command?" "Yes." "Then," said 'Uthman, "why blame me for giving a command to Ibn 'Amir on account of his being a relative and kinsman?" Said 'Ali: "I will tell you. All 'Umar's governors went in fear of him; if there came to his ears even a hint of a crime committed by them, he visited the utmost severity upon them. But that you do not do. You are soft and compliant to your relatives." "And to yours also," retorted 'Uthman. "By my life," said 'Ali, "They should have no preference from me, simply because of their relationship. Rather would the preference go to others." "Are you aware," asked 'Uthman, "that it was 'Umar who appointed Mu'awiya to the whole of his present command, while I did not more than confirm the appointment?" Said 'Ali, "I adjure you by Allah, do you not know that Mu'awiya was more in awe of 'Umar than was the most terrified of 'Umar's servants? " " Yes," replied 'Uthman. "But," said 'Ali, "now Mu'awiya does as he pleases without out reference to you and without your knowledge. So the people say: 'This is the command of 'Uthman'; and even when you hear about it, you do nothing about Mu'awiya."

Finally the revolt against 'Uthman came to a head; it contained elements both of right and of wrong, of good and of evil. Yet to one who views matters through the eyes of Islam and who seeks to interpret events by the spirit of that faith it must be apparent that the revolt was more akin to the spirit and purposes of Islam than was the position of 'Uthman; or rather, than was the position of Marwan. And behind Marwan stood the Umayyads, who had never at any time been inspired with anything of the spirit of this faith.

The only possible defense of 'Uthman is that it was his evil fortune to come to the caliphate too late; the Umayyad gang surrounded him, while he himself was approaching the age of eighty, with his powers sapped and enfeebled by senility. His position was that described by his friend 'Ali: "If I sit at home and do nothing, 'Uthman says that I have deserted him and his relatives, and that I have denied him his rights. If I satisfy him in this and do proffer advice, Marwan still makes a puppet out of him. Thus he is driven hither and thither as Marwan wishes, despite his great age and his friendship with Allah's Messenger."

Indeed it was a stroke of ill fortune. It was one of the first misfortunes of the infant faith of Islam to fall into the hands of the Umayyad gang by the agency of the third Caliph in his old age. Hence the practical application of Islamic theory was a long time in taking root in the soil of Arab culture. Had 'Uthman come to the caliphate earlier it would have been better, for then his natural strength would not have been failing. Or if he had been Caliph later it would have been better; then 'Ali would have held office after Abu Bakr and 'Umar. In that case the Umayyad seed could not have grown and taken root as it did in Syria and elsewhere; those vast fortunes could not have been amassed as they were under the administration of 'Uthman, as we shall see when we come to discuss economic policy under his rule; and the revolt against 'Uthman would not have shaken the structure of the Islamic community and endangered its connection with the spirit of the faith. Had all this been the case, the aspect of the entire history of Islam would have been changed, and it would have followed an entirely different path.

The vitality of the Islamic spirit and of the Islamic social system merited some result other than that which actually took place. But this consideration will be dealt with in due course. In the meantime we may proceed to notice the development of governmental policy after 'Uthman.

❖ ❖ ❖ ❖ ❖ ❖ ❖

'Uthman went to the mercy of his Lord, leaving behind what was in effect already the Umayyad state thanks to the power he had given the Umayyads, particularly in Syria, and his support of the rooted Umayyad principles, which were so much at variance with those of Islam. These principles comprised the establishment of hereditary kingship, the appropriation of booty and property and profits, a complete absence of any attempt at a spirit of brother-hood or liberty or mutual responsibility, and the encouragement of an onslaught on the spirit of religion itself within the Islamic com-munity. Not the least important factor was the growth—rightly or wrongly—of the feeling among the people that the Caliph could give preference to his own family and could allow them hundreds of thousands of dirhams; that he could dismiss from office the Companions of the Prophet and replace them with enemies of the Prophet; or that he could persecute the likes of Abu Dharr for inveighing against the amassing of riches and against the luxury into which the rich were sinking, and for summoning men to fol-low what the Messenger had taught them about expending their money in alms, and about charity and frugality. The natural out-come of the rise of such ideas, whether right or wrong, was that some were opposed to, while others favored, 'Uthman. The former were those whose minds were imbued with the spirit of Islam; hence they disapproved and condemned. The latter were those who wore Islam as a cloak, those whose hearts had never been touched by accepting it truly, those who were swept away by worldly desires, and who were carried down by the wave. Such were the closing features of the reign of 'Uthman.

When 'Ali succeeded him it was not easy to bring matters back to their true condition. Those who had made their fortunes under 'Uthman, and particularly the Umayyads, knew that 'Ali would not leave them undisturbed, and so they betook themselves and their fortunes to Mu'awiya. If 'Ali had followed 'Umar imme-diately, they would not have been given the opportunity to do so; for Mu'awiya's strength at that time did not permit him to strive after the caliphate or to challenge the religious spirit in men's hearts. Nor yet was Mu'awiya prepared to risk an open breach with the Caliph, as he was later to break with him; for it was only the thirteen years of 'Uthman's rule that had made Mu'awiya what he was; in these years he had built up his economic, military, and political strength in all four regions of Syria.

The real tragedy is that 'Ali was not the third Caliph.

'Ali set himself to restore the Islamic conception of rulership in the minds of governors and people alike. He used to eat barley meal, hand ground by his wife, and he used to seal the meal-bag, with the words, "I like to know what it is entering my stomach." Often he sold his sword to get money to buy food and clothing, and he disliked living in the "White Castle" in Kufa, preferring the lodging houses where the poor lived. He lived in the manner related by al-Nasr ibn al-Mansur on the authority of 'Utba ibn 'Alqama in these words: I once visited 'Ali and found him with sour curds set in front of him. Their sourness and their dryness vexed me, and I said: "O Commander of the Faithful, do you eat this stuff?" He answered me: "Abu Janub, Allah's Messenger used to eat it drier than this and used to wear clothes coarser than these" —and he pointed to his own clothes—"and if I do not accept what he did, then I fear that I will not join him in the hereafter." Or again, there is the story told by Harun ibn 'Antara on the authority of his father: I visited Ali at Khawarnaq during the winter and found him wearing a shabby velvet cloak in which he shivered. I said to him: "Commander of the Faithful, Allah has granted a portion of the public funds to you and your family, yet you treat yourself this way." "By Allah, " he replied, "I will not deprive you of anything, and this is my own cloak which I brought from Medina."

'Ali did not treat himself and his family thus because he was unaware that Islam allowed him more than he took; he knew that Islam did not prescribe asceticism, self-denial, and hardship. He knew that his proper share from the public treasury purely as a private Muslim was at that time several times more than what he was taking and that his allowance as a ruler performing a public service was still more than that. If he had wished, he could have taken the amount that 'Umar had specified to be given to some of his provincial governors; 'Umar had allotted to Ammar ibn Yasir on his appointment to Kufa a sum of six hundred dirhams per month, for himself and his assistants; in addition he had a grant, of which he got his share among his equals, together with half a sheep and half a measure of flour. Similarly, 'Umar had allotted to 'Abdullah ibn Mas'ud a hundred dirhams and four sheep for teaching the people of Kufa and acting as keeper of the public treasury; and to 'Uthman ibn Hanif he had allotted a hundred and fifty dirhams and a quarter of a sheep per day, together with the annual grant, which, in his case, amounted to five thousand dirhams.

'Ali did not treat himself as he did because he was ignorant of all this. It was simply because he realized that a ruler is at once an object of suspicion and an example; he is suspected of squandering the public monies that lie in his power; and to governors and people alike he should be an example of purity and frugality. So 'Ali modeled himself on the discipline of Abu Bakr and 'Umar, rather than on the indulgence of 'Uthman. The reason was that the young faith of Islam and the new social order were more in need of a voluntary degree of extra discipline than of any indulgence that the faith might permit. So only the highest level would befit the successors of the Messenger; the indulgence was not permissible for 'Ali, though he could see that it was legal for others who were naturally inclined towards it. But discipline was needed in one who had to be a pattern and an example to others; for through such discipline he could encourage them to strive in emulation.

Thus 'Ali proceeded to restore the concept of rulership that the Prophet and the two first Caliphs had built up. "He once found his coat of mail in the possession of a Christian, whom he thereupon brought before Shurayh, his judge, in a civil lawsuit, as if he had been a private citizen. His case was: 'This is my coat of mail; I did not sell it, and I did not give it away.' So Shurayh questioned the Christian: 'What have you to say to what the Commander of the Faithful alleges?' When the latter answered, 'This is my own armor, and what a liar the Commander of the Faithful is,' Shurayh turned to 'Ali and asked: 'Have you any proof, Commander of the Faithful?' 'Ali smiled and said, 'Shurayh has found the point. I have no proof.' So Shurayh gave his decision in favor of the Christian, who took the armor away, leaving 'Ali standing looking after him. But he had only gone a few steps when he came back and said: 'I must bear witness that this is of the teachings of the prophets; the Commander of the Faithful takes me to court before his own judge, and the case goes against him. I testify that there is no god but Allah, and I testify that Muhammad is His servant and His Messenger. By Allah the coat of mail is indeed yours, Commander of the Faithful. I used to follow the army, and when you went to Siffin I took it from your dusky-colored camel.' Said 'Ali: 'Since you have become a Muslim, I give it to you."

The course that 'Ali followed was that which he had marked out for himself when, in a sermon following the oath of allegiance being taken to him, he had said: "O people, I am only a man like yourselves, with the same rights and obligations; I will lead you in the path of your Prophet and will enforce upon you what has been enjoined upon me. All lands that 'Uthman assigned and all money that he gave away out of the public funds shall be refunded. Nothing shall invalidate this promise; even if I find such money used as a dowry for women, for the purchase of slaves, or scattered worldwide, it shall be restored. For, in justice there is an ampleness of life, and whoever feels that he is constrained by right, let him remember that he would be more so by tyranny.

"O people, let none say of you on the morrow that the world swallowed them up, they bought estates and opened up water channels, rode horses and chose slave maidens, because I did not restrain them from their pursuits; let none say either that 'Ali b. Abi Talib deprived us of our rights because I have restricted them to their basic rights. Nay, but if any one of the Emigrants or Helpers, the Companions of the Prophet, thinks that he has some excellence over others because of this circumstance, then tomorrow that excellence shall be apparent with Allah, and upon Him shall be the responsibility for the clothing and the allowance of such a man. If any man has accepted Allah and His Messenger, if he has believed in our faith, entered our religion, and accepted our qibla, then he has taken upon himself the privileges and the responsibilities of Islam. You are the servants of Allah, and property is the property of Allah, to be divided equally among you, so that no one has a better claim than any other. But those who show piety towards Allah shall have the best reward."

As was but natural, the place-seekers were dissatisfied with 'Ali; those accustomed to preeminence were displeased by the regulations for complete equality and now rebelled against the regulations for complete justice. Such betook themselves to the other camp where, among the Umayyads, they found their desires could be satisfied and where they could trample on the elements of justice, right, and conscience, alike in life and in authority.

Those who see in Mu'awiya a sagacity they still do not find in 'Ali, and who attribute to these things the ultimate triumph of Mu'awiya, err in their estimate of the conditions as well as in their understanding of 'Ali and of the tasks that confronted him. The first and last task that 'Ali had to face was to restore vitality to the traditions of Islam and its true spirit to the faith, to take away the veil that had been thrown over that spirit by the Umayyads through the age and the weakness of 'Uthman. If 'Ali had copied Mu'awiya in taking no account of any moral instinct, then he would have failed in his purpose, and there would have been no point in his tenure of the caliphate from the point of view of the life of this faith. And what profit could there have been in exchanging one Mu'awiya for another? 'Ali had either to be true to himself or let the caliphate pass from him and with it his life. This is surely the true interpretation of the matter, and the one that he himself had in mind when he said: "Mu'awiya is not more astute than I; but he is prepared to be treacherous and faithless. Had it not been for my dislike of treachery, I could have been the most astute man alive."

❖ ❖ ❖ ❖ ❖ ❖ ❖

So 'Ali went to the mercy of his Lord and was followed by Mu'awiya, the son of Hind and Abu Sufyan.

Whatever faith and gentleness and piety 'Uthman had had, they had acted as a restraint on the Umayyads; but with the removal of this restraint and with the breaking down of this barrier the Umayyads went straight back to the ways they had followed before Islam and after its rise. So Mu'awiya proceeded to promote that family loyalty, which was part of his plan; the first example of it was 'Amr ibn al-'As. The Umayyads were a family united by their desires and their ambitions, but divided by their cupidity and their greed; they were without a trace of morals, religion, or conscience.

It was a calamity that broke the back of Islam.

The territory of Islam was certainly increased during the period that ensued, but the spirit of the faith was undeniably lost; and what is the value of territory if the spirit is lost? Had there not been a hidden strength in the very nature of Islam, together with an abundant source of spiritual power, the Umayyad period would have been instrumental in writing finis to its career. But the spirit of the faith endured, resistant and unyielding, and its latent strength remained capable of the struggle for survival.

We need not speak at length of Mu'awiya, nor need we here record his reign; but we must consider his action in bequeathing the throne to Yazid, in order to discover what kind of a man he was. And we must consider the history of Yazid, in order to discover what a crime was perpetrated when the Umayyads gained control of the Muslim peoples and of Islam.

This we may say: From Umayyad times all restrictions on the public treasury were removed, and it became a legitimate source of plunder for the kings, their courtiers, and their sycophants. The bases of Islamic justice were destroyed, and the treasury became the perquisite of the ruling class, a source of profit for their followers, and a source of income to their hangers-on. The caliphate became a monarchy, and a tyrannical monarchy at that, as the Messenger once said that it would, in a sudden access of profound spiritual insight.

Frequently we hear of immense gifts being made to sycophants and jesters and musicians; one of the Umayyad rulers once gave twelve thousand dinars to Ma'bad the singer, while among the Abbasid Kings Harun al-Rashid presented Isma'il ibn Jami' the singer with four thousand dinars, a costly house and furniture, and rich clothing—all for one song. Thus the wave went on its way, arrested only now and again.

In this connection we must mention the reign of 'Umar ibn 'Abd al-'Aziz, which was a throw-back to the age of the Caliphs, a shining beacon casting light on the path. He began his reign by restoring authority to its original and rightful owners, from whom it had been wrested. He gave power back to the Islamic community, which has the duty of making a free and willing choice of its leaders, unhampered by the might of an army or by the force of inheritance. 'Umar mounted the pulpit and said: "O people, I have been put in this position without my wish or my desire, and also without the Muslims being consulted. I hereby release you from any obligation to take the oath of allegiance to me; you may choose your ruler for yourselves." But the people cried aloud: "We choose you, Commander of the Faithful, and we are content to have you. Command is yours, with the auspiciousness and blessing."

Thus matters were restored to their proper state, for there is no power without common consent, without acclamation or acceptance. Thereupon he addressed the people again, saying: "There have been rulers before me whose respect you have gained by resisting any tyranny on their part; for no obedience can be given to any created man who rebels against his Creator. If a man obeys Allah, it is your duty to obey that man; but when a man rebels against Allah, then he need not be obeyed. So obey me as long as I obey Allah regarding you; but if I rebel against Allah, then you need not obey me."

Accordingly, when he set about his administration he started by making compensation for all exactions; and first of all in his own case. "I must," he said, "start at the beginning with myself." So he made an inventory of his possessions in land and in goods, and discarded much of it; when he looked at a jewelled ring on his finger, he said: "Walid[46] gave me that; but he had no right to it, for it came from his estates in the west"; so he returned it. There was also the income from his estates in al-Yamama, at al-Mukaidas, and Jabal al-Wars in the Yemen, and at Fadak, all of which he renounced and returned to the treasury. But he made an exception of the well at Suwaida, which he had had dug with his own money; the corn produced from the lands it watered brought him an annual income of some hundred and fifty dinars.

When he decided to restore all these possessions, he commanded that people be summoned to the Friday prayers. He mounted the pulpit, said the "Praise be to Allah", and the ascription of glory, and then continued thus: "These people have given us gifts that it was not right for us to take, nor for them to give. This matter is now in my power; and Allah it is Who will call me to account, and I have already restored all these things, making a start with myself and immediate family. Read, Mazahim." Now a basket had already been brought in containing the account books, and Mazahim started to read from each book in turn; 'Umar held the books, and with a pair of scissors that he held in his hand he clipped out each entry until nothing was left.

Then he turned to his wife, Fatima, daughter of 'Abd al-Malik ibn Marwan; she had jewelry which had been the gift of her father, and the like of which had never been seen. 'Umar said to her: "Choose whether you will return your jewelry to the treasury or consent to let me separate from you; for I will not remain in the same house as those jewels." She answered: "Nay, but I choose you, Commander of the Faithful, rather than these; rather than twice these if I had them." So 'Umar commanded accordingly, and the jewels were taken and placed in the public treasury. When 'Umar died he was succeeded by Yazid ibn al-Malik, who said to his sister, Fatima: "If you wish I will restore your jewels to you." "I have no wish for them," said she; "I was happy without them while 'Umar was alive, and shall I now have them again when he is dead? Never, by Allah." When Yazid heard this he divided the jewels among his wives and his children.

But 'Umar was not satisfied with restoring any exactions that he held; they say that he would accept nothing from the treasury and would not take a single dirham from any booty. 'Umar I used to take two dirhams per day from that source, but when someone said to 'Umar II: "Why do you not take what 'Umar I used to take?" he replied: "'Umar ibn al-Khattab had no money, whereas I have enough to satisfy me."

Similarly, he compelled the sons of Marwan to disgorge the possessions that they had acquired unjustly, and these he returned to their proper owners. It is said that there came to him a certain man who belonged to one of the protected peoples, a native of Hums, and complained: "Commander of the Faithful, I require of you the Book of Allah." 'Umar asked him what he meant, and the man said: "al-'Abbas has wrested my land from me." Now, al-'Abbas was sitting there at the time, and 'Umar turned to him, saying: "'Abbas, what have you to say?" al-'Abbas replied that al-Walid had assigned to him the lands in question and had given him letters patent for them. Again 'Umar turned to the complainant: "What have you to say to that?" "Commander of the Faithful," he replied, "I require of you the Book of Allah, Great and Glorious is

He." Then said 'Umar: "Yes. The Book of Allah is more worthy to be followed than any writing by al-Walid. 'Abbas, you will restore his property to him." And al-'Abbas did so.

Al-Walid had a son named Rauh who had grown up in the desert and was almost a Bedouin. A party of Muslims once came to 'Umar with a case against Rauh concerning some shops in Hums. These belonged to them, but Rauh's father, al-Walid, had assigned them to him. 'Umar said to him: "Give them back their shops," but Rauh retorted that they were his by the authority of his father. Said 'Umar: "The authority of al-Walid is not sufficient; the shops are theirs, and the deeds are in their hands; now give them their shops." Then Rauh and one of the men left the court together, and Rauh threatened him; the man promptly returned to 'Umar and told him: "By Allah, Commander of the Faithful, that fellow threatened me." 'Umar said to Ka'b ibn Hamid, who was the commander of his guard: "Go to Rauh, Ka'b, and if he hands over the shops, well and good; if he will not, then bring me his head." Some of those who were friendly to Rauh heard this and told him what 'Umar had commanded. His heart failed him, and when Ka'b came to him with his sword half-drawn and said: "Come, give him his shops." Rauh hastily agreed, and the shops were handed over.

So people would come constantly to 'Umar bringing cases of injustice before him; no case was ever brought to him without being adjusted, whether it was a matter concerning himself or someone else. He took from the sons of Marwan and others the possessions that they had exacted; he restored wrested properties to their owners without demanding definitive proof. He was always content with very little proof; if he recognized from the circumstances that a man had suffered injustice, he adjusted it for him without making him establish a legal proof; for he recognized the exactions that had taken place under previous rulers. They say that he exhausted the treasury in Iraq through this system, so that more money had to be brought from Syria.

Sulaiman ibn Abd al-Malik[47] had allotted to 'Anbasa, another Umayyad, twenty thousand dinars; the order went through all the offices until it was entered at last in the final register, and had only to be paid over. But Sulaiman died before it was paid. Now,

'Anbasa was a friend of 'Umar, and on the following day he decided that he would speak to 'Umar about the allotment, which Sulaiman had promised him. He found the Umayyads waiting at 'Umar's door for an opportunity to talk to him about their own affairs; when they saw 'Anbasa they said: "Let us see how 'Umar treats 'Anbasa before we speak to him." So 'Anbasa went in and found 'Umar. He said to him: "Commander of the Faithful, Sulaiman, the late Caliph, had promised me twenty thousand dinars; the order went through to the final register, and all that remained was for me to collect the money; but Sulaiman died before I could do so. Now you, Commander of the Faithful, are the fittest person to assure this favor for me; for my relations with you are closer than ever were my relations with Sulaiman." "How much was it?" asked 'Umar. "Twenty thousand dinars." "Twenty thousand dinars," said 'Umar, "is enough for four thousand Muslim households. And I am to pay that to one man. By Allah, I can never do that." "Then," said 'Anbasa, "I produced the letter containing the deed of gift from Sulaiman. But 'Umar said to me: 'It is not necessary for you to have the letter with you; possibly you got it from one who was more reckless with money than I, one who would make you such a promise.' So I took the letter and went out, to find the Umayyads still waiting; I told them what had happened, and they said: 'After that there is no hope for us. Go back and ask him if he will permit us to retire to our homes.' So I went back to him, and I said: 'O Commander of the Faithful, there are some of your family at the door, requesting that they may continue to enjoy what they enjoyed before your time.' 'By Allah,' swore 'Umar, 'This money is not mine, and it is impossible for me to grant them that.' I went on: 'Commander of the Faithful, they request, then, that you permit them to return to their homes.' 'They may do as they like,' said 'Umar; 'That I will permit them.' 'Will you permit me to do the same?' I asked, and he said: 'I give you the same permission. But I think it better that you stay; for you are a man of great wealth. Now I will sell you an heirloom of Sulaiman's and perhaps with it you may be able to buy something that will bring you profit in place of that which you did not get.' So I stayed and bought an heirloom of Sulaiman's for a hundred thousand; I took it to Iraq, where I sold it for two hundred thousand. And I also kept the deed of gift; when 'Umar died and Yazid came to the throne I showed him Sulaiman's letter, and he paid me the stipulated sum."

'Umar gathered together the sons of Marwan and addressed them thus: "You have been continually given favors and honors and wealth, until by my reckoning a half or even two-thirds of the resources of this community are in your hands. Restore, then, what you possess of the true property of the people, and do not compel me to take such measures against my will as you will suffer against your will." Not one of them answered him until he commanded them: "Answer me." Then one of them replied: "By Allah, we will not give up the wealth that came to us from our fathers; we will not pauperize our children and dishonor our fathers until our heads are severed from our bodies." Then said 'Umar: "By Allah, were it not that you are protected from me by one to whom I have granted such a right, I would speedily humble your family. But I fear civil war; nonetheless, if Allah spares me, I will restore to every man his rights, if Allah wills."

He did not live to restore to every man his rights, as was his wish, and he was succeeded by others who followed the courses of the Umayyads rather than those of Islam. When the Abbasids grasped the succession, they did so as kings, so that the Muslim world was corrupted and the people lost touch with the duties of the faith, such a divorce and such a wide gulf had the Umayyads succeeded in placing between the people and their religion. The Abbasid kings were no better than the Umayyads, for one and all they represented a tyrannical monarchy.

✣ ✣ ✣ ✣ ✣ ✣ ✣

But since we are not here writing a history of the Islamic state, but rather a history of the Islamic spirit in relation to authority, we shall content ourselves with a sketch of the signs of change and deterioration in this spirit by quoting from three sermons given by these kings; these may be compared with the other three already quoted from the Caliphs; the profound difference will be immediately apparent.

First, the sermon of Mu'awiya to the people of Kufa after the truce. "Men of Kufa, do you think that I fought against you on account of prayers or *zakat* or pilgrimage? I knew that you said the prayers, that you paid the *zakat*, and that you performed the Pilgrimage. I fought you in order to have control and mastery over you; now Allah has granted me that mastery, though you may not like it. Now, therefore, all the money and all the blood that I have had to expend in this war is still to be repaid, and all the promises that I made in the truce are under my feet here."

"All the promises that I made in the truce are under my feet here." Yet Allah has said: "Fulfill your engagements, for every engagement will be asked of you." (17:34) Or again: "If they appeal to you for help in a matter of religion, then you must help them, unless it be against a people with whom the Muslims have a compact." (8:72) Here it is stated that for Muslims to fulfill a compact to a non-Muslim people with whom a treaty exists is preferable even to helping fellow-Muslims in a matter of religion. Yet Mu'awiya was breaking a compact that he had made with Muslims; and his offense becomes the more notorious and shameful because he takes pride in it.

He was an Umayyad, a member of that family whose nature forbade their joining in the oath of Fudhul.

Or again, in a sermon preached at Medina Mu'awiya spoke in these terms: "But to proceed; by Allah, I did not gain the caliphate with any good will on your part, nor did you welcome my coming to office; rather I had to fight you at the sword's point. For myself, I longed for command over you in the caliphate of Abu Bakr, and I wished for the post in the caliphate of 'Umar, but I was forcibly kept from it; I wished it under the rule of 'Uthman, but it was refused me. So now you and I stand in what may prove to be a profitable position, meat and drink to me. And if you do not find that I am the best among you, you may find that I am the best governor for you."

Indeed he did not gain the caliphate by their consent. Yet, as is well known, the caliphate in Islam is an office that can be conferred only by public approval. But Mu'awiya had little in common with Islam.

So also, after the influence of the Umayyads had done its

work of transforming authority until finally in the days of the Abbasids it had become a theory of divine right, al-Mansur, the Abbasid Caliph, could say in a sermon: "O people, I am the Sultan of Allah in His earth; I rule you by His help and support. I am His guard over His property, with which I may do what He wills and what He desires; I can give it away by His permission, for He has made me a lock on it. If He wishes, He can open the lock so that I give you gifts and provision; but if He wishes, He may keep me locked."

At this point political theory has completely parted company with Islam and with Islamic teachings.

❖ ❖ ❖ ❖ ❖ ❖ ❖

Economic theory followed a course conforming to that of political theory, a course dependent upon the rulers' concepts of the nature and course of the political tendency, and according to the rights of ruler and subject. During the life of Muhammad and his two Companions, Abu Bakr and 'Umar, as well as during the caliphate of 'Ali, the ruling theory was characteristically Islamic; property was communal, and neither the ruler nor his relatives had a right to any share greater than that to which they were entitled as individual Muslims; nor could they make gifts from it to any other person, except insofar as such a person might have a right to a gift. Even in the time of 'Uthman, when this practice began to be slightly relaxed, the people still retained their rights. By this time the public funds were more than adequate to meet the claims of the people, and the Caliph conceived that he was permitted to dip his hand into the treasury and bestow gifts on his family or on any others whom he considered worthy. But when the caliphate became a tyrannical monarchy, then all barriers and limits were removed, and the ruler had absolute power to give or to withhold—justifiably in a few cases, but generally the reverse. Thus the public funds became the source of unlimited luxury for rulers and their children, their flatterers and their courtiers. In this final stage rulers completely left the bounds of Islam.

This is a general statement of the case, for which we must

adduce examples from each of the different phases of the course of history.

The sources of public revenue since the time of the Messenger were:

1. The *zakat*, which was obligatory on all Muslims according to well-known categories such as gold and silver, grain and produce, cattle, income from trade, and minerals. The general taxation level was one-twentieth on such things, and the resultant money was expended in the eight recognized ways.

2. The poll tax, which was levied on each individual of the protected peoples who lived under truce. This corresponded to the *zakat* as paid by Muslims, as well as to their obligation to fight, in order that a share of the public responsibilities might be taken by non-Muslims. If a man became a Muslim the poll tax was no longer levied on him, but was then replaced by the *zakat*.

3. The booty. This was what accrued to the state from polytheists who were granted an amnesty without fighting. This belonged entirely to Allah and His Messenger, to the latter's family, to the orphan, the poor, and the wayfarer, according to the Qur'anic precept.

4. The plunder. This was what the state acquired from unbelievers in time of war. Four-fifths of it belonged to those who had done the fighting, and the remainder was disposable on the same terms as the booty mentioned above.

5. The land tax, which was the money paid by those lands that belonged to polytheists who were conquered by the Muslims in war. Or a truce might be granted to the them, and they might then be left in possession of their lands. This, as we shall see, was 'Umar's practice.

In the time of the Messenger the sources of revenue were not extensive. The Emigrants had left their houses and their property, and the Helpers had been generous to them, had shared their own possessions with them, and had treated them as brothers. Besides, the number of the Muslims was limited, so that before the conquests there was only one source of revenue, the *zakat*, and it but slight; and the small numbers made it yet slighter. This revenue was expended in the eight ways detailed in the verse, "The alms money is only for. . . ." (9:60)

But when the conquests started, another source was added, that of plunder. Four-fifths of this went to the fighting men, and of this the Prophet used to give one share to each foot soldier, and two shares—though some say three—to each horseman, so that each would be rewarded in proportion to his effort. Similarly, he used to give one share to a single man and two to a married man; thus he gave expression to the important principle of the care of the family and also to the principle of "to each according to his need." The rest of the plunder he disposed of in the ways that we have mentioned.

The first case of booty occurred in the expedition against the Bani Nadir, and the whole of it was given by the Messenger to the Emigrants, except that shares were also given to two poor members of the Helpers. Soon after this the Qur'an laid down the general Islamic principle, "that it may not be passed around among the rich among you." (59:7)

After this the Muslim revenues commenced to expand along with the growth of Islamic territory, through the successive conquests; thus better circumstances began to spread gradually through the Muslim community, for all shared in the revenues of the treasury in the proportion to which Islam entitled them.

When the Messenger went to his Supreme Friend, there were some who rebelled and withheld the *zakat*. Then Abu Bakr took his famous stand and spoke his immortal words: "By Allah, if they withheld from me even the halter of a camel that they had been paying to Allah's Messenger, I would fight them for it." 'Umar's opinion was different; he was inclined to treat the apostates easily and to delay active hostilities. For Islam was young, its enemies were lying in wait for it, and in every quarter of Arabia the apostates were powerful. His opposition reached the point where he said in exasperation: "How can we fight these people when the Messenger himself said, 'I have been commanded to fight people until they confess that there is no god but Allah, and that Muhammad is Allah's Messenger. Whoever confesses this is safe from me in property and in life, except for his obligations as a Muslim. His reckoning must be with Allah." But Abu Bakr answered him resolutely: "By Allah, I will fight against any distinction being made between the prayers and the *zakat*; for the latter is an obligation on property, and the Messenger said, 'Except for his obligations.'" Then 'Umar commented: "By Allah, then I saw that Allah had strengthened Abu Bakr to fight, and I knew that he was right."

Thus in this famous decision there was finally and historically confirmed one of the principles of economic theory in Islam —fighting in order to establish the right of the community to its property.

Abu Bakr proceeded to distribute the *zakat* monies in the ways sanctioned by the practice of the Messenger; and he did the same with the five parts of the plunder and with the remainder of the revenues. He took for himself only that meagre share that the community bade him take—said to be two dirhams a day, and he distributed their legal share to those who were entitled to it. What remained in the treasury he used to equip the armies for war.

In the time of Abu Bakr there arose a question of precedence, on which he and 'Umar disagreed. Abu Bakr held that equal shares should be given to those who had been the first Muslims and those who had come in later; that there should be equal division between free men and clients, between men and women. 'Umar, along with a group of the Companions, held that the earliest Muslims should have preferential treatment according to their standing. But Abu Bakr replied: "As for what you say about the precedence and the excellence of the first Muslims, how well do I acknowledge it. Yet that is a matter whose reward must rest with Allah alone, glorious is His Praise. But this is a matter of livelihood, in which equality is better than preference."

This equality continued to be observed, and prosperity increased among the Muslims as the revenues grew. But in the time of 'Umar's caliphate he still held to his opinion: "I will not treat one who fought against Allah's Messenger the same as one who fought along with him."

It happened one day that Abu Huraira, his governor in Bahrain, came to 'Umar with a large sum of money. Here is Abu Huraira's account: I came from Bahrain with five hundred thousand dirhams, and in the evening I went to see 'Umar. I said to him: "Commander of the Faithful, take this money." "How much is it?" he asked. "Five hundred thousand dirhams." "Do you realize how much five hundred thousand dirhams is?" said he. "Yes; a hundred thousand and a hundred thousand, five times." "You are dreaming then. Go home, and come back tomorrow." The next morning I went to see him again, and said: "Take this money from me." "How much is it? " "Five hundred thousand dirhams." Then he asked: "Is it derived from legitimate sources? " "Certainly it is." Then said 'Umar: "O people, we have acquired great wealth. If you wish me to weigh it out for you, I will do so. Or if you wish, I will count it out for you. Or if you wish me to measure it out to you, I will do that." Then a certain man suggested: "O Commander of the Faithful, draw up registers for the people, by which they may be paid," a suggestion that 'Umar approved. He allotted to each of the Emigrants five thousand, to each of the Helpers three thousand, and to the wives of the Prophet twelve thousand.

We have quoted this story here as illustrating the belief of 'Umar that some of the people should take precedence over others; we have quoted it also because of its description of the standard of wealth, according to which half a million dirhams appeared to be a dream, only conceivable to a man in his sleep. But that was to change entirely in the period following the great conquests.

Abu Yusuf in his book, *The Land Tax*, says: "I was told the following by a certain Medinan shaikh on the authority of Isma'il ibn Muhammad ibn al-Sa'ib, quoting Zaid who had it from his father. I heard 'Umar say: "By Allah, than Whom there is no other god, there is no one who does not have a right to this money, either to give or to withhold; there is none who has more right to it than any other, with the sole exception of a slave; and in this respect I am but as one of you. But we have our stations in respect of Allah's Book, and we are differentiated by our relation to Allah's Messenger. Islam assesses a man by what he has suffered, by his precedence in the faith, by his wealth, and by his need. And by Allah, if there is any left over, then the very shepherd in the mountains of San'a shall have his share of this money as his right, before his face reddens — that is, by having to ask for it."

Then he allotted to every man who had fought at Badr five thousand dirhams per year. He allotted to every one who had come into Islam at the same time as the men of Badr, those who had been in the emigration to Abyssinia, and those who had fought at Uhud, four thousand dirhams per year. To the sons of the men of Badr he allotted two thousand each, except for Hasan and Husain, the two sons of 'Ali; to each of them he allotted the same as was given to their father, because of their kinship to Allah's Messenger; thus each of them had five thousand dirhams. To every man who emigrated to Medina before the conquest of Mecca he allotted three thousand dirhams, and to everyone who entered Islam at the time of the conquest two thousand. To the young children in the families of Emigrants and Helpers alike he gave the same allotment as that last named. He allotted shares to all the people according to their status, their knowledge of the Qur'an, and their participation in the wars. Finally, he classed all the rest of the people together; to every Muslim who had come to Medina and had stayed there he gave twenty-five dinars; to Yemenites and Qaisites in Syria and Iraq he allotted varying amounts of two thousand, one thousand, nine hundred, five hundred, and three hundred; but none had less than three hundred. 'Umar himself said: "If there were enough money I would allot four thousand dirhams to every man; one thousand for travelling, one thousand for weapons, one thousand for the care of his family, and one thousand for his horse and his mule."

But 'Umar did make exceptions to the principle that he had laid down for the organization of the stipends; to certain men and women he gave larger stipends than were given to others of the same standing and class. Thus to 'Umar ibn Abi Salma he allotted four thousand dirhams; for this 'Umar was the son of Umm Salma, the "Mother of the Faithful." Muhammad ibn 'Abdullah ibn Jahsh took exception to this and said to the Commander of the Faithful: "Why do you give preference to 'Umar over us, when our fathers were in the Emigration and in the fighting?" 'Umar replied: "I gave him preference because of his relation to the Prophet. Anyone who can claim a mother like Umm Salma has only to come to me and I will satisfy him." Similarly, he allotted to Usama ibn Zaid four thousand dirhams; 'Abdullah, his own son protested: "You have given me three thousand, and you have given Usama four thousand, although I have done more fighting than he." 'Umar's answer was: "I have given him a larger stipend because he was dearer to Allah's Messenger than you. And his father was dearer to Allah's Messenger than was your father." He allotted to Asma, the daughter of Amyas and wife of Abu Bakr, one thousand dirhams, to Umm Kulthum, the daughter of 'Uqba, one thousand dirhams, and to Umm 'Abdullah ibn-Mas'ud a like sum. He increased these stipends over those of their equals because of their personal greatness as the wives and mothers of men of outstanding status and excellence.

There are, then, these two opinions on the division of the public monies, that of Abu Bakr, and that of 'Umar. The latter found its support in, "I will not treat anyone who fought against Allah's Messenger the same as one who fought along with him," and in, "Islam assesses a man by what he has suffered . . . etc." This idea can find some justification in Islamic theory, because it does represent a fair balance between effort and reward. But the opinion of Abu Bakr is not without support; "They have handed themselves over to Allah, and to Him alone; He it is who will reward them, and will recompense them on the Day of Resurrection; for this world is no more than a means of livelihood." And we must unhesitatingly choose Abu Bakr's opinion as being closer than the other to the spirit of Islam and as more fitted to express the equality of all Muslims, which is a great principle of this faith. It is also superior inasmuch as it does not give rise to the evil consequences that arise from a discriminatory system—the vast fortunes that are a dividing factor in a people, and the growth of such fortunes year after year merely through their own productivity, a growth that mathematically forms a geometric progression. We must reckon also with the results of the existence of capital sums that 'Umar saw at the end of his life, and which made him swear that if he had time he would again equalize the stipends; these are his famous words: "If I had foreseen the consequences of my action that are now apparent, I would have taken their excessive wealth from the rich and given it to the poor."

But unfortunately the time was past, the days of 'Umar were finished, and the painful events had taken place that were to poison equality within Muslim society; ultimately, thanks to their employment by the Umayyads and their ratification by 'Uthman, they were to lead to civil war.

'Umar then renounced his view that there should be discrimination between Muslims in the matter of stipends when he saw the results of such discrimination; it was then that he came over to Abu Bakr's position. 'Ali's opinion also agreed with that of the first Caliph, and therefore we are inclined to regard his caliphate as a natural continuation of that of his two earliest predecessors, while the age of 'Uthman formed an interregnum. So we may now continue our discussion by dealing first with Ali's caliphate, after which we may retrace our steps to deal with that of 'Uthman.

'Ali supported the principle of equality in stipends, as he indicated in his first sermon when he proclaimed: "Nay, but if any one of the Emigrants or Helpers, the Companions of the Prophet, thinks that he has a claim to special consideration because of his circumstance, then tomorrow that claim shall rest with Allah, and He shall give reward and recompense. If any man has accepted Allah and His Messenger, if he has believed our faith, entered our religion, and accepted our *qibla*, then he has taken upon himself the privileges and the responsibilities of Islam. You are the servants of Allah, and property is the property of Allah, to be divided equally among you, so that no one has a better claim than any other. Those who show piety towards Allah shall have the best reward."

This is the authentic Islamic principle, in conformity with the Islamic spirit of equality; it guarantees the equilibrium of Muslim society, and it permits the growth of fortunes only by means of effort and labor. It forbids such growth of wealth through any kind of preferential treatment; for such gives to one an opportunity denied to others, by means of a superior quantity of wealth.

It was to this principle that 'Umar returned at the end of his life, but unfortunately for Islam his death followed almost immediately. He was unable to put his resolve into effect; yet it was none the less his resolve to take excessive wealth from the rich and give it to the poor. For such excess of wealth had grown up in most cases from the discrimination in stipends which he himself had established. It was also his resolve to equalize the stipends for the future, so that such differentiation should not recur, and so that Islamic society should not again be thrown into the confusion that it was then experiencing.

Then came 'Uthman. He saw no reason to follow either or both of these resolves. He left the excessive wealth in the hands of its owners and took back none of it; he also left the stipends on the preferential footing on which they stood. But this was not all. He enlarged everyone's stipend, and thus even increased the wealth of the rich, although at the same time he did slightly ameliorate the lot of the poor. Again, he granted to those who already had large resources huge loans; he allowed the Quraish to travel the world, using their amassed wealth in trade, so that their wealth was doubled and redoubled. He allowed the wealthy to acquire estates and mansions in Southern Iraq and elsewhere, he made assignments of lands, and thus by the end of his caliphate he had introduced into the Islamic community one of the key elements of feudalism.

Abu Bakr and 'Umar had previously insisted that all the Quraish chiefs should be kept at Medina and that they should not be allowed to travel the conquered territories; care should be taken because, unless surrounded by the Helpers, the eyes of these chiefs would stray to visions of money and power, because of their pre-eminence through their relationship to Allah's Messenger, or because of their sufferings for Islam and their early conversion. In this insistence there was no real contradiction of personal freedom as Islam understands it; for this freedom must always be limited by the welfare and advantage of society. But when 'Uthman came to power he permitted the Quraish to travel the world. Nor was that all; he encouraged and even urged them to lay out their money on mansions and estates in various places; and to that end he gave many of them gifts that ran into hundreds of thousands of dirhams.

All this might have been intended as a charity and a blessing to the Muslims and to their chiefs; but it gave rise to one immense evil that had not been hidden from the insight of Abu Bakr or of 'Umar after him. It produced vast economic and social cleavages in

the Islamic community, and it brought into being an idle aristo-
cratic class whose income was derived from every source except
that of work of any kind. It gave rise also to a spirit of luxury,
which Islam had fought by legislation and exhortation alike, and
against which 'Uthman's two predecessors had struggled in an
effort to wipe it out.

An adequate description of the consequences of this policy is
to be found in passages from *The Great Civil War: 'Uthman* by Dr.
Taha Husain and especially in the following:

> A section of the chief Companions controlled the major part of the
> wealth, both capital and current, of the Hejaz. This they hastened to
> spend in the purchase of land in the provinces; for they knew that
> such land was richer and more fertile than that of the Hejaz. Thus
> Talha ibn 'Abdullah spared no effort to buy out all those who had
> shares in the Khaibar property, either because they had fought along
> with the Prophet and captured the place, or because they had
> received their shares through inheritance. But when 'Uthman gave
> him the chance, Talha sold all his holdings at Khaibar to Hejazis
> who had taken part in the conquest of Iraq at the price of their land
> holdings in that province. Then, having additional money available,
> he bought up also the holdings of other Hejazis in Iraq; and even
> from 'Uthman himself he bought Iraqi land which the latter held
> there, at the price of land which he himself still held in the Hejaz.
> Everyone else did the same, and all who had no desire to move from
> the Hejaz to live on their lands in the provinces sold these lands and
> bought others nearer home.
>
> From this practice there came for the first time the growth of vast
> possessions in Iraq and other provinces. The only people who could
> take advantage of the process were those who, having large re-
> sources, could buy up the small holdings, men like Talha, Zubair,
> and Marwan ibn Hakam; and thus there was in that period great
> economic activity, in buying and selling, in borrowing, bartering,
> and trading. Later this was not confined to Iraq and the Hejaz, but
> came to include all Arabia on the one hand and all the conquered
> provinces on the other. There were vast assignments of land and
> broad estates on the one hand, while on the other hand the workers
> stayed on the land as slaves, as clients, or as free men. Thus there
> came into being in Islam a new social class, the "plutocrats," the

nobility of whose birth[48] was increased by the extent of their financial means, their vast fortunes, and also by the number of their followers.

In the second place there arose from this practice the fact that those who bought land in Arabia in general, and in the Hejaz in particular, wished to exploit that land. Therefore they imported slaves in far larger numbers than heretofore, until in a short time the Hejaz had become one of the most fertile districts of the country, one of the most fruitful and productive, yielding most wealth to its owners. The net result was that luxury and idleness followed in the train of wealth, and in the Hejaz itself, in Mecca, in Medina, and in Ta'if, there grew up a class of idle aristocrats who did nothing; all the work was done by their imported slaves, while they consumed their time in the distractions of sport, amusement, and frivolity.

But at this point there was a reaction based on the spirit of Islam in the minds of many people; the leader and instigator of this reaction was Abu Dharr. This man was the famous Companion whom the Egyptian Fatwa Council has recently judged misguided, claiming for itself a better understanding of religion than his.

Abu Dharr preached against the luxury of the rich, which he held to be unjustifiable in Islam, and against Mu'awiya and the Umayyads in particular, who encouraged such luxury, increased it, and themselves wallowed in it. He inveighed against 'Uthman personally for giving away hundreds and thousands of dirhams from the treasury, and thereby increasing further the wealth and luxury of the rich. He complained that 'Uthman had given to Marwan ibn al-Hakam a fifth of the revenues of Ifriqya to al-Harith ibn al-Hakam two hundred thousand dirhams, and to Zaid ibn Thabit a hundred thousand. The conscience of Abu Dharr was not such as to tamely accept such things, and so in a public address he spoke freely, in such terms as these:

"Things have now come to the position that we see. And, by Allah, none of this is in the Qur'an or in the Sunnah of the Prophet. By Allah, I see right destroyed and wrong preserved, the truthful called a liar, and selfishness in place of piety, O you crowds of rich who oppress the poor." So too he preached against those who amassed gold and silver and who would not spend it in the way of Allah; he warned them that these would be heated red-hot in hellfire and used to brand them on foreheads, sides and backs. "O you who amass wealth, know that there are three who share in your wealth. Fate, which may take away the good or evil of wealth by destruction or death, before you are aware of it; your heir, who watches only for you to lay down your head in order to seize your wealth while blaming you for it; and yourself, the third; and since you cannot but be the weakest of the three, you will not have it long. Is not this the word of Allah, the Great and Glorious: 'You cannot know charity until you spend of that which you love?'

"You have acquired curtains of silk and cushions of brocade, and you make sore trouble to recline on the finest wool; yet the Messenger of Allah used to sleep on a mat. You must have your delicate varieties of food; yet the Messenger used to eat but sparingly of barley bread."

A story is told about Abu Dharr by Malik ibn 'Abdullah al-Ziyadi, thus: He came once seeking audience with 'Uthman ibn 'Affan, and when he was brought in, he had his staff in his hand. Said 'Uthman to Ka'b: "If 'Abd al-Rahman dies and leaves money, what do you think about it?" Ka'b answered: "If thereby he fulfills a lawful obligation, then there is nothing wrong with it." But Abu Dharr lifted his staff and struck Ka'b, saying: "I have heard the Messenger of Allah say, 'If this mountain were of gold for me to spend as if it belonged to me, I should not like to leave behind me six grains of it.' I adjure you by Allah, 'Uthman, do you hear me?" This he repeated three times, and 'Uthman said, "Yes."

This was a type of preaching that Mu'awiya and Marwan could not endure, and the two of them were continually urging 'Uthman, until finally Abu Dharr was sent to Rabadha, banished from the country. Yet he had never opposed Allah or His Messenger, nor had he ever striven to cause corruption in the land, for which crimes alone Islamic law prescribes banishment.

Abu Dharr's protest was one of the reactions of the true spirit of Islam, but it was unpopular with those whose hearts had been corrupted; in the same way such protests are still resented by the modern equivalents of these, the present-day exponents of exploitation. But this protest did represent the watchfulness of a conscience that could not be drugged by desires; it saw all too clearly the drastic growth of wealth that was splitting Islamic society into classes; and along with that it saw also the breakdown of the fundamentals that this faith had sought to establish for all men. It is relevant here to consider some examples of the vast fortunes of that age as given by Mas'udi.[49]

"In the caliphate of 'Uthman the Companions acquired estates and wealth. On the day he was killed 'Uthman held in his coffers a hundred and fifty thousand dinars and a million dirhams. The value of his estates at Wadi al-Qura, at Hunain, and elsewhere was a hundred thousand dinars; he also left a great number of horses and camels. The value of Zubair's estate at his death was fifty thousand dinars; he also left a thousand horses and a thousand female slaves. Talha's income from Iraq was a thousand dinars a day, and from the district of Sirat he had still more. 'Abd al-Rahman ibn 'Auf had in his stables a thousand horses, and he also possessed a thousand camels and ten thousand sheep; at his death a quarter of his estate was valued at eighty-four thousand dinars. Zaid ibn Thabit left gold and silver in ingot form, besides money and estates. Al-Zubair built a mansion at Basra and had palaces also in Cairo, in Kufa, and in Alexandria. Talha also built a mansion at Kufa, and he raised a palace at Medina, using gypsum, baked brick, and teak. Sa'd ibn Abi Waqqas built his palace with cornelian, roofed it, and included a large courtyard, placing on the top of it all crenelated walls. Al-Miqdad built his mansion in Medina of gypsum, both inside and out, while Ya'la ibn Munabbih left fifty thousand dinars, together with property of various kinds to a value of three hundred thousand dirhams."

This was a type of wealth that started in a small form; some Muslims in the time of 'Umar had preferential treatment in the matter of stipends; it was this preferential system that he would later have cancelled, and the evil results of which he sought to rectify, had not the blow fallen just then which struck, not merely at the heart of 'Umar but also at that of Islam. Thus the preferential system continued in force, and even grew in the hands of 'Uthman, extending its range to cover stipends, gifts, and the assignment of lands. Once started, the growth of wealth spread widely and swiftly, through the process of the amalgamation of properties, estates, and profit-making enterprises. It was encouraged by 'Uthman, who permitted the buying of lands in the provinces and the amassing of widespread estates. And the process was increased still more after the suppression of that deep and sincere protest that came from the heart of Abu Dharr. If this protest had achieved its aim, if it had received a favorable hearing from the head of the state, it would sufficiently have set matters to rights; it would have accomplished what 'Umar wished to do at the end of his life, namely, to take from the rich their excessive wealth and to give it to the poor. This he was legally entitled to do by the authority of his office, in order to repel harm from the community. More, this was his bounden duty as a method of ensuring the welfare of society.

But in proportion as wealth was heaped up and amassed on the one side, so on the other side poverty and misery inevitably increased, and with them a sense of grievance and discontent. This was not long in growing to such a height as to give rise to open civil war; this in turn was exploited by the enemies of Islam and was ultimately responsible for the death of 'Uthman and for the end of all security and all peace in the Islamic community. It was this situation that gave the Islamic community over to tyranny and hatred, in a holocaust that was not to be extinguished before it had enveloped the whole spirit of Islam in its smoke. Through it the Muslim community was handed over to the power of a tyrannical monarchy that had no foundation in Islam.

It is not surprising, therefore, that there was considerable anger among the possessors of capital and those who found the preferential system of stipends to their advantage when 'Ali, succeeding 'Uthman, laid down a policy of equality and justice. Nor was it strange that such men should pretend that they advised him to give up this policy simply because they feared that it would cause a rebellion. His only response was to seek inspiration from the spirit of Islam. "Do you, then, advise me to seek success by the oppression of those who are under my rule? If this money had been my own, I would have shared it equally among them; how then can I do otherwise when it belongs to Allah? Surely to dispose of money wrongfully is a form of waste and squandering; it may raise a man in the estimation of this world, but it lowers him in the world to come."

❖ ❖ ❖ ❖ ❖ ❖ ❖

Mu'awiya, who succeeded 'Ali, followed the form of economic theory dictated by his own characteristics; he used public money for bribes and gifts, for buying over supporters for the oath of allegiance to Yazid, and for other similar purposes. He used it also for purposes of statecraft, for his armies and his conquests as circumstances dictated.

The other Umayyad rulers followed his example until the time of 'Umar ibn 'Abd al-'Aziz, who did what we have already seen to return usurped wealth and to check the scattering of public money in a wrongful fashion. Then the Umayyads got no more than anyone else; the court flatterers and sycophants got no share at all, and the poets with their eulogies got no reward from the public treasury.

There is a story about 'Umar and Jarir[50] that relates that when the latter composed a panegyric on him 'Umar said: "O Jarir, are you one of the Emigrants? Tell me, that I may know to give you what is due to such a man. Or are you one of the Helpers, that your reward may be the same as theirs? Or are you a poor Muslim? If so, I shall order the almoner of your tribe to give you what he gives to others of your people." "Commander of the Faithful," answered Jarir, "I am none of these. I am one of the richest and best situated of my people. All I ask from you is what the Caliphs have been accustomed to give me—four thousand dirhams, together with an accompaniment of clothes and pack animals." Then said 'Umar: "Every man must produce his work, but I see nothing on your part which would merit a share of the public money. However, if you wait until my stipend is paid, then I shall set aside enough to support my family for a year; then if there is any left over, it shall be handed over to you." But Jarir refused, saying: "No. Rather let the Commander of the Faithful take all of it, and do what is right, and I shall go away content. That is what I would rather do." So he went; but no sooner had he gone than

'Umar said: "Evil is to be feared from this. Bring him back." When he was brought back 'Umar said to him: "I have forty dinars and two robes, of which one is being washed and I am wearing the other. All this I will share with you, though Allah the Great and Glorious knows that I have more need of these things than you." Then said Jarir: "Allah has returned your gift to you, O Commander of the Faithful, for I am now content." But 'Umar insisted: "Nay, for I have sworn it, and your renunciation of my gift and refusal to cause me hardship have had the same effect on me as praise, so take it and go."

It is not strange, then, when the public monies were conserved and paid out only to those who had a rightful claim to them, that contemporary accounts should represent the people as being so satisfied under 'Umar II that in many districts there were no recipients for alms. The majority of the people were so content with the payment of their other claims that they made no call on the alms money. On this subject we have the testimony of Yahya ibn Sa'd, as follows:

"'Umar sent me to collect the alms in the province of Ifriqya. This accomplished, I started to look for the poor to whom to give the money. But we could find no poor there, nor could we discover anyone who would accept the money. 'Umar had so satisfied the people that I had to use the money to buy slaves and manumit them."

Poverty and need are the fruits solely of vast and concentrated wealth, and the poor in every age are the victims of the rich. And the rich are produced generally by stipends and assignments, by partiality, by injustice, and by exploitation.

✢ ✢ ✢ ✢ ✢ ✢ ✢

Thus in the times of the Umayyads, and later in the days of the Abbasids, the public treasury was open to the ruler, as it had been his personal possession. And that too despite the fact that there were two treasuries, one public and the other private. In the first of these it was laid down that the revenues and expenditures should be from and on behalf of society; in the second the revenues and expenditures were to be the private affair of the ruler. Yet we find occasions when the public monies were taken straight to the private treasury and other occasions on which the ruler's private expenses were met directly from the public treasury.

Pensions and all expenses connected with the office of the caliphate were taken from the public treasury. We have a statement dating back to the beginning of the fourth (tenth C.E.) century, which details the sources of income which were available to the private treasury.

1. The private resources of the Caliphs, which were passed on from father to son in the treasury. It is said that al-Rashid left the greatest amount of money, totalling forty-eight million dinars. Al-Mu'tadid (A.H. 279-289/892-902 C.E.), after paying all his expenses, increased the contents of the private treasury by a million dinars every year of his caliphate, until he had acquired nine million in his coffers. He desired to make this up to ten million dinars, and then to melt it down to form one ingot; he intimated that when he had achieved this, he would remit to the people one-third of the land tax payable for that year. His intention was to leave the ingot in public view, so that all corners of the world might learn that he had ten million dinars which he did not need. But fate prevented the fulfillment of his desires. He was succeeded by al-Muktafi (A. H. 289-295/902-907 C.E.), who raised the treasure to fourteen millions.

2. Income from the land tax and the public estates in the provinces of Fars and Kirman, after local expenses had been deducted. The value of this reached an annual level of twenty-three million dirhams between A.H. 299 and 320 (911 and 932 C.E.). Of this total only four million went directly to the public treasury; the remaining nineteen million went straight to the private treasury. From this we must deduct the constant expenditures necessitated by these lands; thus in A.H. 303 (915 C.E.) the Caliph spent seven million dirhams in pacifying those regions.

3. Income from Syria and Egypt. The poll tax from the protected peoples was one example of what went directly to the Caliph's treasury, as pertaining to the Commander of the Faithful, rather than to the public treasury. This theoretically was what the Caliph deserved.

4. Income arising from the seizure of the wealth of ministers, officials, or governors who had been dismissed, or from the proceeds

of the sale of their lands; or income deriving from the estates of men deceased. The Caliph was in the habit of inheriting the possessions of his servants, and those of the clients of his family who died without an heir. Since such men were generally eminent personalities and in a good financial position, this produced a comfortable income of considerable proportions flowing constantly into the Caliph's treasury.

5. There went directly to the private treasury a portion of the estate taxes and the land taxes from Lower Iraq and Ahwaz and from the eastern and western provinces.

6. The surplus that each successive Caliph amassed. Each of the two last Caliphs of the third century (ninth C.E.), al-Mu'tadid and al-Muktafi, had had an annual surplus of a million dinars; the purpose of al-Muqtadir was to have a similar surplus, so that after twenty-five years he would have twenty-five million dinars, or approximately half of what al-Rashid left.[51]

From all this it is apparent how greatly there trespassed on the public funds of the Muslims those kings who were called Caliphs. It is also apparent what a gulf lay between this form of economics and the principles of Islam. It is clear to what an extent wealth and luxury increased on the one hand, and on the other misery and destitution. It is obvious how far these results led the Islamic community away from the true path of Islam and how contrary were these things to Islamic principles.

✛ ✛ ✛ ✛ ✛ ✛ ✛

Yet in spite of all this, the historical experience of Islam can prove a number of the fundamental principles of economic theory and can provide confirmation of most of the theories and principles of Islam. And this despite the reverse that it suffered in the course of time at the hands of the Umayyads to the great misfortune of all mankind.

The historical experience of Islam can prove these points.

1. That the poor have a better right to the public monies than those who were the earlier converts to Islam. We find in the *Musnad* of Ahmad ibn Hanbal: Adi ibn Hatim related this story. I came to 'Umar ibn al-Khattab along with a number of my people,

but he allotted to another man of Tayy the sum of two thousand dirhams and he turned away from me. I went up to him, but he turned away from me again. So I said to him: "Commander of the Faithful, do you know me?" He smiled broadly and said: "Yes, by Allah, I know you. You were a Believer when these were unbelievers, you came into us when they turned their backs, you fulfilled all your obligations when they defaulted. The first tax money that came in to cheer the hearts of Allah's Messenger and his Companions was that of Tayy, which you brought to the Messenger." Then he started to apologize, saying: "I have allotted to people who have been ruined by destitution, to people who are the noblest of their tribes, only as much as will meet their needs."

And this, be it noted, refers to 'Umar who gave preferential treatment to those who had been early converts when he was making up the stipends; therefore it is surely valuable and significant evidence. Neediness is the first justification for making a claim on Islamic society. This is a deep-seated principle that indicates the horror in which Islam holds need and destitution and which demonstrates the Islamic insistence that these things should be removed first of all, before attention can be given to any other matter.

2. That Islam is opposed to excessive wealth on the one hand, and to privation on the other. In an effort to put an end to any such state of affairs it will grant to the head of the state a freedom of action which is in proportion to the conditions that obtain. The historical experience of Islam draws this principle from the account of Allah's Messenger distributing the whole of the Banu Nadir booty to the poorer Emigrants as their private property and to the two poor Helpers, in an attempt to restore a measure of equilibrium to the Muslim community at the first possible opportunity. And the Qur'an adds its ratification to this historical precedent: "In order that it may not be passed around among the rich among you." (59:7)

This precedent is intensely significant. The head of the state always has the right to give the poor a share in the public money; thereby he restores a measure of equilibrium to the Islamic community and reasserts the desire of Islam that there shall be no great gulf between the classes to destroy that general equilibrium.

3. The principle of pro rata taxation, according to the amount of one's means, much or little. When the poll tax was imposed on protected peoples, it was imposed on the following scale:

a. The rich had to pay forty-eight dirhams per head per year.

b. Those of average means had to pay twenty-four dirhams.

c. The poor who were yet earning had to pay twelve dirhams.

No poll tax was taken from the destitute who were in receipt of alms, from those who were incapacitated for work, from the blind, the crippled, the insane, or the deformed. This obtained throughout all countries. Poll tax was not imposed on anyone save free and sane men; there was no tax on women or children.

When the Muslim community was overtaken by the "Year of Ashes" in consequence of a drought, 'Umar did not send out his collectors to take in the *zakat*; he left the people alone until the year of drought had passed. Then, when conditions were normal and prosperity had returned, he sent out his governors to collect a double due from the rich; one part for the "Year of Ashes" and the other for the current year. Others he excused from payment altogether. Then he commanded that these others be given one-half of what had been collected, while his governors brought the second half to him.

4. The principle that there must be no sequestration of the staple commodities in order to pay the taxes, and that taxes must not be exacted by force. 'Ali once said to one of his governors: "When you collect their taxes you must not force them to sell an article of clothing, in winter or in summer, the food that they must eat, or the beasts that they must use for work. You must not strike anyone even once over a dirham, nor must you whip or bastinado anyone in search of a dirham; and you must not sell anyone's goods to pay his taxes. For our business with them is simply to admit their excuses."

5. The principles of "to each according to his needs" and "each to enjoy the fruits of his labor." Thus the Prophet allotted to a single man one share and to a married man two shares of the plunder. In this allotment it is indicated that need as well as effort put out by the married man is just the same as that put out by the single man, but the former has double the need of the latter; therefore his

share should be double. Thus need alone is a satisfactory justification of possession according to Islam; hence the emphasis of Islam on social security.

6. The principle of universal social security for all who are disabled and for all who are in need. Thus 'Umar allotted a hundred dirhams to every newborn child; when the boy grew up he was given two hundred, and when he came to manhood the allowance was further augmented. A foundling was allotted a hundred, and his guardian received a monthly provision allowance specifically for him; his nursing and expenses were chargeable upon the treasury; then, when he grew up, he was treated as the equal of the other children. This humane treatment by 'Umar inspired a similar humanity throughout Islam, so that a foundling is always regarded as guiltless and does not have to bear the weight of his parents' sin. We have already noticed what allowance 'Umar made for the blind Jew and the Christian lepers. This is the essential humanity of Islam represented in the person of 'Umar towards all people and not merely to Muslims. It means social security against the misfortunes of need, disability, and privation.

7. The principle of "Where did you get this?" A governor has no means of preventing society calling him to account for the money that he has acquired and making him prove whether it is his money or theirs. The application of this principle guarantees that the governor will think twice before misappropriating public monies. Such a principle was adopted by 'Umar in the case of all his governors, and by 'Ali in the case of some.

8. The principle of universal liability to pay the *zakat*. This has never been dropped even in times of intense oppression or corruption of the Islamic spirit. No one has ever objected to it, either in theory or in practice since the Wars of Apostasy at the beginning of Abu Bakr's caliphate. But in our present age, when Western civilization has become paramount, this last living principle of Islam has fallen into desuetude.

9. The principle of universal mutual responsibility. This makes the people of every town generally responsible for any of their number who die of starvation. This is a criminal responsibility for which the blood money is payable; for the townspeople are

regarded as having killed any man who dies of starvation while living in their midst. This principle means that it is the established right of any man who is hungry or thirsty to use force on anyone who has food or water, if the needy man fears that he is in danger of death. If the result is the death of the man who has the food or water, then no blood money and no punishment attach to the other.

10. The principle that usury is forbidden and the granting of respite to the debtor in case of hardship. Usury was always forbidden until material Western civilization made it legal and French law brought it to us, making it one of the general principles of economic life. The sole and inevitable result was the checking of the moral element in life and the destruction of the spirit of cooperation and charity in men's hearts. But it was this spirit that Islam took as the basis of society and as the foundation for men's cooperation with each other.

All of this takes no account of the traditions of charity, equality, and mutual responsibility within society—outside of purely legal considerations. Evidence of the spirit of Islam in Muslim societies has been provided in the recent past, even in our fathers' times, not to mention our grandfathers', everywhere in the countryside throughout of the Muslim world; a remnant of this spirit is still in evidence after material Western civilization has made havoc of the Islamic world, for it has been sufficiently abundant to dispense with laws and with compulsion. The numerous endowments and the various charitable foundations, which today are diverted from their true purposes and plundered by sundry persons under a variety of excuses and pretexts, testify to the forces of benevolence and charity, responsibility and social security that existed in the hearts of succeeding generations before they were corrupted by this rigid material civilization that hardens the heart and the feelings.

The desire to ensure the needs of the weak even embraced the animal realm, for some of the charitable foundations were devoted to the care of ailing animals, to provide homes for them, and to ensure to them a safeguard against homelessness and starvation.

❖ ❖ ❖ ❖ ❖ ❖ ❖

This is Islam, in spite of the thwarting of its first practical steps by the victory of a family whose hearts were unfamiliar with its spirit, but who looked forward to a time when they would be able to overcome Islam itself. They kept dreaming of an hereditary tyrannical monarchy until at length they achieved it, and they led it along a path not sanctioned by Islam.

8 THE PRESENT STATE AND THE PROSPECTS OF ISLAM

Our mission is to call for a renewal of Islamic life, a life governed by the spirit and the law of Islam, which alone can produce that form of Islam that we need today, and which is in conformity with the genuine Islamic tradition. We have already examined the theoretical bases of society as they are outlined in the Qur'an and the Traditions, and we have looked briefly at Muslim society as it evolved in the course of history. It now remains for us to ask: Is it possible today to renew something similar to that form of Islamic life for the present and for the future?

It is not sufficient that Islam should have been a living force in the past; it is not enough that it should have produced a sound and well-constructed society in the time of the Prophet and in the age of the caliphate. Since that distant time there have been immense changes in life, intellectual, economic, political, and social; there have even been material changes in the earth, and in its powers relative to man. All these things must be carefully considered before an answer can be given to our question.

There is also a further consideration that cannot be overlooked in any discussion that is directed to a practical and particular end, rather than to a theoretical and general; we must discover why it was that the spread of the Islamic spirit came to a halt in matters of political and economic theory only a short time after the age of the Prophet. Was this the longest possible span of life which the inner spirit and resources of Islam could command?

Before dealing with these two considerations we must emphasize the two following truths:

1. That Islamic society today is not Islamic in any sense of the word. We have already quoted a verse from the Qur'an that cannot in any way be honestly applied today: "Whoever does not judge by what Allah has revealed is an unbeliever." (5:48) In our modern society we do not judge by what Allah has revealed; the basis of our economic life is usury; our laws permit rather than punish oppression; the *zakat* is not obligatory and is not spent in the requisite ways. We permit the extravagance and the luxury that Islam prohibits; we allow the starvation and the destitution of which the Messenger once said: "Whenever people anywhere allow a man to go hungry, they are outside the protection of Allah, the Blessed and the Exalted." The Imam Ibn Hazm[52] also delivered a *fatwa* on the same subject, to the effect that if a man dies in starvation in any town, the people of that town are regarded as having killed him, and the blood money may be demanded of them. Let us pass over this rule, which some people may dispute for no good reason. The Qur'anic text itself is undeniably applicable to such things; it refers to the existence in our modern society of such laws as those that permit usury, adultery, and refusal to pay the *zakat*, which thereby prove themselves to be in opposition to the divine laws laid down in the Qur'an.

2. So long as Muslim society adhered to Islam it manifested no weakness and no tendency to abdicate its control of life. It was when it fell away from Islam that these things took place. Emphasis on this fact will compensate for the idle aspersions that Westerners have cast on our faith, and which they have evidenced from history. These aspersions have been taken up by some in the East, who were either gullible or mercenary, and have been the cause of the sullying of hundreds of pages by such men, under the claim of being liberal thinkers and accurate scholars. This is nonsense and can only serve as a pretext for the false, the gullible, or the mercenary mind.

We may now return to treat of the two considerations whose discussion we deferred until we had noted the above points. We may start by answering the second question: Why did the spread of the Islamic spirit come to a halt a short space after the time of the Prophet?

Here again we must emphasize two historical facts:

1. This halt was only partial, never complete; it never came to a complete stop on a particular day. It took place only in a limited sphere, that of politics. The tolerant caliphate became a tyrannical monarchy; the public funds were made accessible to the monarch, his relatives, his courtiers, and his flatterers, while they became inaccessible to those who had a true claim on them by the laws of Allah and His Messenger. But the remainder of the teachings of Islam remained in force; the charity and benevolence, the mutual help and responsibility, the tolerance and freedom of conscience and human equality, the payment of the *zakat* and the alms, and all the other positive and negative virtues of Islam—all these continued in force to a greater or a lesser extent in many Muslim societies. The *shari'a* even continued in force as the system of civil law until the nineteenth century, when we introduced French law, thus giving the coup de grace to another tie that bound us to the beliefs of Islam.

2. The change that overtook the system and the development of politics—a partial change, as we have just said—was the product of an unfortunate mischance, as we have already contended. The mischance was that control should fall into the hands of the Umayyads, first in an indirect way in the reign of 'Uthman, and latterly quite openly in the reign of Mu'awiya. If we are to be fair to Islam we cannot hold it responsible for the Umayyads; for it was injured far more by this clan of the Quraish than by the fiercest of its enemies.

I am certain that, if the life of 'Umar had lasted several years longer, or if 'Ali had been the third Caliph, or even if 'Uthman had become Caliph when he was twenty years younger, then the course of Islamic history would have been very considerably changed. For the policy that 'Umar enunciated was: (a) to take excessive wealth from the rich and give it to the poor; and (b) to equalize the stipends assigned to the people, as had been the practice under Abu Bakr. If 'Umar had done this, there could have been no opposition to a policy so consistent with Islam. 'Umar's conscience was above all question, as was his zeal for the faith; the reverence in which he was held for his fidelity to the faith was similarly above

the attacks of jealousy and doubt. So if this program had been carried out by 'Umar, it would have restored economic and social balance to the Islamic world, and the civil war would have been
averted at its very beginning, or, at the least, would have been
postponed for a long time.

Or, if 'Ali had succeeded 'Umar, he would have guided the
people in 'Umar's policy, whatever might have been the position of
the Quraish, who had more temerity in dealing with 'Ali than they
had in dealing with 'Umar. In that case the matter would not then
have come to the stage of rebellion or civil war. The Umayyads had
not yet raised their heads in rebellion, for their nobles had no high
standing in Islam because of their early conversion or renown in
the early wars; they were only among the reluctant converts who
embraced Islam at the conquest of Mecca, when the success of the
new faith was already assured. They were merely governors in the
army or the provinces, without the special authority and power
they gained in thirteen years under the reign of 'Uthman.

But it will be asked: How were the Umayyads able to effect
such a speedy revolution during a period of great vitality in Islam?
Does not this indicate that the Islamic system is unsteady by
nature or at least unsuited to permanency? Does it not indicate
that by nature Islam provides no adequate safeguards against such
revolution?

We must here take account of the condition of the Islamic
state in that age, and we must reckon not only with factors of
apparent power, but also with those of hidden agitation.

The truth is that at that stage Islam was indeed vital, and it is
a strange thing that the Umayyads did with it what they did. But it
is also true that the astonishing speed of the conquests, to which
history can produce no parallel, added to Islamic society a huge
territory, teeming with various races and skills, mentalities and languages, systems, traditions, and heritages. However strong the
spirit of Islam may have been, and however powerful in extending
its hold over all these heritages, an element of time was essential
before all this new material could be homogenized, before a change
could be wrought in the old moral ideas, the rooted traditions, the
cherished social systems and customs. Thus the Umayyad attack

on the spirit of Islam just at this juncture took place at a unique point of time; if it had been stayed for a space, it could never have accomplished all that it did.

We have seen that the bulk of Muʻawiyaʼs support lay in Syria, a conquered country, rather than in Arabia itself. Those of his supporters who did hail from the Peninsula, such as ʻAmr ibn al-ʻAs, were of a nature akin to Muʻawiya himself, men who trampled down the moral element in their reckonings, who justified the means by the end, and who justified the end simply on the grounds that they desired it.

As for the suggestion that the Islamic system does not provide by nature adequate safeguards against disruption, for one thing we must bear in mind that this system was assailed by disruption before it had properly struck roots; and for another thing we must remember that in practice no system has any real such safeguards. Where, for example, are the safeguards of democracy in Europe? This is a strongly entrenched system, which has achieved a definite form, and which has had time to establish itself and to spread its influence over a long period into every quarter of life. Yet where were its safeguards at the time of the Nazi coup dʼetat, or the Fascist, or the Spanish? Or again, take the freedom of opinion in the United States, whose people fled from Europe to form a free society—where are its safeguards? Today a few newspaper and radio companies hold a monopoly on both information and opinion and forbid any contrary opinions to find their way to the eyes, the ears, or the thoughts of the people.

The truth is that any suspicion that the Islamic system does not afford safeguards against its own overthrow is due to ignorance of what is practically feasible in any system. It betrays also an ignorance of the true facts of Islamic history; we have the evidence of the great rebellion against ʻUthman; we have the rebellion of the Hejaz against Yazid; we have the evidence of the Qarmatian rebellion,[53] and of many others, all of which were directed against exploitation, arbitrary power, and class distinctions. The spirit of Islam has continually struggled against all such things, in spite of the grievous injuries that it has suffered throughout thirteen hundred years.

The spread of the spirit of Islam, then, was not halted because that spirit was unable to establish itself, nor because it was found inadequate to cope with the demands of life. As we shall shortly see, this spirit has been continuously operative in many of the aspects of life and society. The halt in its spread was the product of an unfortunate mischance at a unique point of time. And as soon as chance brought to Islam a Caliph who retained something of the true spirit of the caliphate in the person of 'Umar II, the spread of Islam became again apparent and the government again truly Islamic. But then the times were not propitious for such a truly Muslim Caliph to restore what had been destroyed or to establish the roots of Islamic traditions in the political system.

But nonetheless the attempt of 'Umar II does give us a clear indication that the inner power of Islam was really strong and capable of application in very different times. For his attempt followed several periods of oppressive and evil rule by the Umayyads, and it indicated clearly that a renaissance of Islamic government was possible and not out of the question. What 'Umar did in earlier times can be done today by the Muslim masses.

But we must repeat our contention that even when the spread of the Islamic spirit came to a halt in the realm of politics —though even here it was only a partial halt—it still continued to operate in other aspects of both social and individual life. It continued to realize many of its ideals and to achieve many of its aims; indeed even to the present day it is still effective in such spheres as are not strongly under the influence of official government policies.

As the Frenchman, Gouilly, says in *Islam and the Great Powers*:

> The number of Muslims in Madagascar is not less than three-quarters of a million. Most European authorities explain the spread of Islam in the Dark Continent by the fact that it is a unifying religion that ensures for the negro an equality and justice for which he longs; it emancipates him finally from the bondage of priesthood and superstition, and therefore from the nightmare of evil spirits.

Or H.A.R. Gibb in *Whither Islam?*:

Islam still has it in its power to render a conspicuous service to mankind. There is no other society which can show such a record of having united various races in one unity based on equality. The great Islamic community in Africa, India and Indonesia, the small community in China, and the still smaller community in Japan, all show that Islam has still the power completely to reconcile such divergent elements as these of race and class. If ever the opposition of the great states of the East and West is to be replaced by understanding, this can only be done through the medium of Islam.

The conduct of the Muslims during the Crusades showed the full inspiration of the strong spirit of Islam as it rose superior to lowliness, treachery, and ruthlessness. It showed a belief in the unity of mankind and the relationship of humanity beyond all differences of faith and above all temporal and ephemeral enmities. Saladin was not the only one whom the history of the Crusades has recorded as being of the true and lofty Islamic spirit; rather would this description apply to all the Muslim armies that took part in these long and bitter wars. And this remained true despite the atrocities of the Crusaders. These may be exemplified in the fall of Jerusalem on the fifteenth of July, 1099 C.E. (A.H. 492), during the first Crusade. The Muslims sought refuge and sanctuary in the Aqsa Mosque, but the Crusaders followed them inside and dispatched them with their swords, so that blood flowed through the sacred precincts in a flood. In this act the Crusaders violated a solemn treaty that their leader had made with some of the Arabs. This was only one example of the barbarity of the Crusaders, which included the raping of women, mutilation of the living, and torture of the old women and the children.

Yet even after that, when fate turned against the barbarians, their treatment at the hands of the Muslims was imbued with the Islamic spirit, which was strong enough to check the desire for vengeance in Muslim hearts and to keep them within the bounds of humanity and religion.

Again, within our own times, the recent war against the Jewish settlers in Palestine has revealed the penetration of the Islamic spirit. For even after the long interval during which Muslims have been divorced from the spirit and traditions of their faith, these have proved effective in keeping the Arab forces from taking vengeance for the most horrible and inhuman crimes committed by the Zionists in Palestine. They have been effective in keeping Muslim armies true to the lofty traditions that their religion has maintained for fourteen centuries, and that in the midst of a constant record of inhumanity.

While we are discussing the inner vitality of Islam, we must not overlook the succession of disasters and calamities, both internal and external, which Islam has withstood throughout its long history. To this day it is still a powerful element in human history and commands the attention even of some Occidentals as a means of saving humanity from its present dilemma, as we have already seen in the quotations from Gouilly and Gibb. And this despite the fact that such men are unable fully to comprehend the Islamic spirit, but confine themselves rather to a review of its practical benefit as it now exists than to an appreciation of its profound spiritual content. For it is difficult for Occidentals who have been brought up in the shadow of a deeply rooted materialistic civilization—and such we shall later see that it is—to appreciate this subtle spiritual element.

We have already indicated the first internal disaster that overtook Islam, namely, its subjugation by the Umayyads. This took place at a time when Islam was still like a fresh young plant: its practical traditions had not taken root; its moral and legislative dimensions had not been transformed into firm foundations for society, a concrete and generally observed reality.

We must now examine quickly the more important blows that befell Islam and mark their influence through the following centuries.

The first of these is to be found in the rise of the Abbasid state, with its reliance on elements newly converted to Islam. The attitude of these peoples to their new religion was never wholehearted because of the national loyalties whose roots remained strong within them. As time went on, the Abbasid state deserted these elements on which it had been founded, and which were now beginning to acquire a tincture of Islam for others whose hearts were closed to Islam, Turks, Circassians, Dailamites and such like. So this dynasty continued to find its support in elements that were opposed to the spirit of Islam and to which it gave a favored position because it relied on them. There was nothing to withstand these elements—and hence to withstand the power of the dynasty—except the spirit of Islam, with all the inner force and vitality that it could muster.

Then followed the destructive raids of the Mongols, bursting with savage ferocity on the Islamic world. Without delay Islam turned aside the force of the onslaught, swallowed it up, and assimilated it. Yet this was not accomplished without causing in the spirit of Islam itself a profound upheaval in which the practices and traditions of this religion were forcibly modified. Nonetheless, in spite of the destruction of the state by the Mongol onslaught, the Islamic community continued, powerful and loyal to its ideals and constant in the fundamentals of its religion, no matter how far it may have wandered from them in a few purely official aspects.

We must also bear in mind here that the Roman Empire, the building and growth of which had occupied almost a thousand years, was cut off and fell to pieces in a single century as a result of the incursions of the Huns and Goths; nothing was left of it except a few scattered traces. But the Islamic state remained in occupation of a wide territory, although its building had occupied little more than half a century, and though it had had to contend with a number of internal struggles between ruling families, as well as the external attacks of the Mongols and others. Such factors demonstrate the intense vitality of Islam in that it was able to meet these circumstances.

As we trace the development further, in the West we find the disaster in Andalusia, and in the East the disaster of the Crusades. In the first of these Islam was worsted, in the second it was victorious. But from that time to this it has had to contend with ferocious enemies of the same spirit as the Crusaders, enemies both open and hidden.

But the final disaster to befall Islam took place only in the present age, when Europe conquered the world, and when the dark shadow of colonization spread over the whole Islamic world, East and West alike. Europe mustered all its forces to extinguish the spirit of Islam, it revived the inheritance of the Crusaders' hatred, and it employed all the materialistic and cultural powers at its disposal. Added to this was the internal collapse of the Islamic community, and its gradual removal over a long period from the teachings and injunctions of its religious faith.

When we speak of the hatred of Islam, born of the Crusading spirit, which is latent in the European mind, we must not let ourselves be deceived by appearances, nor by their pretended respect for freedom of religion. They say, indeed, that Europe is not as unshakably Christian today as it was at the time of the Crusades and that there is nothing today to warrant hostility to Islam, as there was in those days. But this is entirely false and inaccurate. General Allenby was no more than typical of the mind of all Europe, when, entering Jerusalem during the First World War, he said: "Only now have the Crusades come to an end." Similarly, the governor-general of the Sudan was no more than typical of the European mind when he placed all governmental power at the disposal of missionaries in the southern Sudan, while forbidding any Muslim trader even to pass through the country. It happened once that a certain official was stationed for a rather long time in the south, and so asked for a transfer to the North; it was not granted. He then bethought himself to try lifting up his voice in the Muslim call to prayer; that single act sufficed to ensure his transfer the following day.

And England is, of all the European countries, the most tolerant and patient and skillful in dealing with questions of religion.

People sometimes wonder how this obstinate spirit of resistance to Islam can persist so strongly and to such a pitch in a Europe that has discarded Christianity, and where the exhortations of preacher and monk no longer fill European ears as they did in the age of the Crusades. But this fact ceases to be surprising when we take account of two facts:

1. "The enmity that the Crusaders stirred up was not confined to the clangor of arms, but was, before all else and above all else, cultural enmity. The European mind was poisoned by the slurs

which the Crusaders' leaders cast on Islam as they spoke of it to their ignorant Western compatriots. It was in that age that there grew up in Europe the ridiculous idea that Islam was a religion of unbridled passion and violent sensuality, that it consisted merely of formal observances, and that it had no teaching of purity or of regeneration of heart. And this idea has remained as it started. It was in this age also that the Messenger, Muhammad, was contemptuously known as 'My Dog.' (*Mahound*).

"Thus was the seed of hatred sown. The ignorant mass of Crusaders had dependents in many places throughout Europe; and the process was hastened by the Spanish Christians in their war to deliver their country from 'the yoke of the idolators.' But the downfall of Muslim Spain was to require many centuries before it was completed; when this protracted struggle and the constraint that it involved grew too great, a hostility to Islam started to take root in Europe, and ultimately became permanent. Finally, it took the form of a complete extirpation of Islam throughout Spain, after a persecution that reached a pitch of ferocity and bitterness hitherto unknown. The cries of joy, which all over Europe greeted this event, were uttered in full knowledge of the consequences that would arise; for the result was that science and learning were blotted out, and in their place came the ignorance and the barbarity of the Middle Ages.

"But before the echoes of these happenings in Spain had died away, there took place a third event of immense significance, which was to hasten the breaking of the ties between the Western world and Islam. This was the fall of Constantinople to the Turks. Europe had always looked to Byzantium as a relic of the glory of ancient Greece and Rome and had regarded it as the fortress of Europe against Asiatic barbarism. Hence, with the fall of Constantinople the gate was thrown wide open to the flood of Islam. In the centuries that followed, and which were filled with wars, the hostility of Europe to Islam was no longer a question of merely cultural importance; it was now a question of political import also. And this fact further increased the violence of that hostility.

"Despite all this, Europe derived great profit from this conflict. The Renaissance or rebirth of European arts and sciences in the widest sense arose particularly from an Islamic and Arab source; in most cases it can be traced back to material contacts between the East and the West. Europe profited more than did the Muslim world, but it did not acknowledge the gift by lessening its loathing of Islam. Or, more correctly, the reverse is true, that loathing increased with the passage of time until it was second nature. At this point loathing swamped all understanding whenever the word 'Muslim' was mentioned; it entered into all their thoughts until it came to form a permanent part of the thinking of every European, man or woman. And still stranger than this is the fact that this feeling continued to flourish even after all the movements of cultural exchange. Then followed the age of the Reformation, during which Europe was divided into various sects, each continually employed in arming itself against every other; yet hostility to Islam was the common feature of all of them. This inturn was followed by an age when religious feeling started to subside, but the hostility to Islam continued unabated. One of the clearest proofs of this is that the French philosopher and poet, Voltaire, was one of the bitterest critics of Christianity and of the Church in the eighteenth century; yet he was at the same time violently hostile to Islam and to its Messenger. A few score years later came the age in which Western scholars commenced to study foreign cultures and to regard them with a measure of sympathy. Yet in all matters connected with Islam the traditional dislike began to creep in under a form of partisan spirit which was not conducive to academic study. Thus the gulf that history had dug between Europe and the Islamic world remained still unbridged. Dislike of Islam thus became a fundamental part of European thinking; and the fact that the first Orientalists of the modern age were Christian missionaries who were working in Muslim territory meant that the picture that they formed of the teachings and the history of Islam was distorted; for it was founded on an axiomatic conception that Europeans were superior to 'idolators.' And despite the fact that Oriental studies have now been liberated from missionary influence, this intellectual bias has persisted, although any mistaken view can no longer claim the excuse of ill-informed religious zeal. Hence the attacks made by Orientalists upon Islam betray an inherited instinct and a peculiarity of nature; they are based on an impression created by the Crusades and shaped by all the mental influences of these on the early Europeans.

"But it will immediately be asked: How does it happen that an ancient antipathy such as this, which was originally religious in its basis, and which in the period of its birth owed its inception to spiritual domination by the Christian Church, can persist in Europe in an age when religious convictions are no more than a matter of antiquarian interest?

"There is nothing surprising in these complexities; for it is well known to psychology that men may lose all the religious beliefs that they held in their youth and at the same time retain some of the superstitions that formerly centered upon the very religious beliefs that they have now discarded. It is these superstitions that defy rational explanation in the lives of such men. This is the state that obtains in Europe regarding Islam. Despite the fact that the religious convictions that gave rise to European hostility to Islam have now lost their power and been replaced by a more materialistic form of life, yet the ancient antipathy itself still remains as a vital element within the European mind. So far as the strength of this antipathy is concerned, it undoubtedly varies from one individual to another, but that it exists is indisputable. The spirit of the Crusades, though perhaps in a milder form, still hangs over Europe; and that civilization in its dealings with the Islamic world still occupies a position that bears clear traces of that genocidal force."[54]

2. European imperial interests can never forget that the spirit of Islam is like a rock blocking the spread of imperialism. This rock must either be destroyed or pushed aside. No weight need be attached to the contention of gullible or mercenary writers that religion is of no concern to Europe, that it does not view religion as a source of power, and that the only thing about the Muslim world that Europe fears is its material power. Fundamentally, religion is a spiritual power that is always effective for the renewal of material powers. Besides, Islam is essentially different from Christianity; it commands the fostering of material powers, it enjoins resistance and struggle in war, and it warns the weaklings who tamely submit

that theirs will be an evil fate in this world and in the next. "Prepare for them as much as you can in the way of forces and cavalry, with which you may overcome Allah's enemies and your own." (8:62) "Do not take unbelievers for your friends in preference to Believers." (4:143) "So let those fight in the way of Allah who would exchange the life of this world for that of the next." (4:76) "Do not grow weary or grieve for you shall be the uppermost, if you are true Believers." (3:133)

So Islam is at once a spiritual power and an incentive to material power; it is at once a form of opposition in itself, and an incentive to a still more forcible opposition. Therefore European imperialism cannot but be hostile to such a religion. The only difference lies in the fact that the form of that hostility varies according to the imperialistic methods of each nation and according to local conditions. Thus, for example, France declared open war on Islam in the western Arab world, under the name of "protecting the Berbers," or some such phrase. Its representatives in Damascus openly declare in broad daylight that they are the descendants of the Crusaders. But England took a more devious and tortuous road to the same end in Egypt, that of education. Her aim was to encourage the growth of a general frame of mind that would despise the bases of Islamic life, and even of Eastern life; when this was accomplished there would be a generation of teachers educated into this frame of mind, ready to go out into the schools and educational offices to imbue the coming generations with the same ideas. These would set a fashion in manners and customs that would ultimately lead to the permanent establishment of the desired frame of mind and would banish all elements of an Islamic education from the policies of the Education Ministry. Thus England could dispense with direct confrontation as a means of opposition to religious convictions. This task it left to a large party, influential in molding the Egyptian mentality. In the Southern Sudan, again, there was no call for such guile; the position there was simply that which we have already described in speaking of the Christian missionaries and the Muslim merchants.

Thus each imperialist state has proceeded by one means or another to oppose and to throttle Islam since the last century, and even before that. And that they still proceed to do essentially the same thing in concert is obvious from the position taken up by the Western nations on the question of Indonesia and Holland; on that of Kashmir, India, and Pakistan; and on that of Hyderabad, India and the Nizam. Finally, the same thing is supremely evident in the position on Palestine.

There are those who hold that it is the financial influence of the Jews in the United States and elsewhere that has governed the policy of the West. There are those who say that it is English ambition and Anglo-Saxon guile that are responsible for the present position. And there are those who believe that it is the antipathy between the Eastern and Western blocs that is responsible. All these opinions overlook one vital element in the question, which must be added to all other elements, the Crusader spirit that runs in the blood of all Occidentals. It is this that colors all their thinking, which is responsible for their imperialistic fear of the spirit of Islam and for their efforts to crush the strength of Islam. For the instincts and the interests of all Occidentals are bound up together in the crushing of that strength. This is the common factor that links together communist Russia and capitalist America.

We do not forget the role of international Zionism in plotting against Islam and in the pooling against it of the forces of the Crusade imperialists and the communist materialists alike. This is nothing other than a continuation of the role played by the Jews since the migration of the Prophet to Medina and the rise of the Islamic state.

The truly remarkable thing is that the spirit of Islam has survived all these attacks that have been launched against it from the earliest period of its life right up to the present. It has persisted in spite of sudden assaults and the effect that these have had on its life; it has lasted out, in spite of the modern conquest by Western civilization with its material and cultural weapons, which have turned some Muslims into instruments for breaking down and destroying Islam at the direction of imperialistic powers.

Despite all these things, the spirit of Islam has remained essentially sound and its inner force has left clear imprints on the course of human life in the broadest sense. Islam has left its marks on the forms and objectives of world politics throughout fourteen centuries to the present day. There is no political or military development in the world but owes something to Islam; and this has been true even in those ages when the Muslim world has been weak and divided, when it has seen its spiritual, social, and economic life disturbed.

But the period of obscurity and weakness is now at an end, and the tide of Islam has commenced to rise. In East and West alike the Arab world is gaining unity, and two great Islamic blocs have made an appearance in Pakistan and Indonesia. These are portents that cannot be overlooked, significant of the underlying vitality of Islam. They are significant also of the massive resources of Islam, sufficient to bring about a complete renewal of Islamic life. This estimate is not based merely on wishful thinking or on optimism; rather it is based on actual concrete facts which are apparent to the sight.

Although I have my absolute faith in the possibility of a renewal of Islamic life within the Muslim world and believe in the soundness of Islam as a worldwide, rather than a local system for the future, I have no desire to take refuge in vain speculation or to pretend that the task will be easy.

By no means! There will be various and vast difficulties; there will also be great tasks that must be accomplished before the complete renewal of Islamic life can take place with any facility within Muslim society. The assessment of these vast obstacles and the inspiration to undertake the tasks involved is something that is necessitated by any true understanding of the immensity of the goal at which we are aiming and of the weight of responsibility awaiting any man who aims at that goal. It is something that is necessitated also by an understanding of the importance of public opinion in such vast undertakings.

It is not enough for any one man to issue a ringing call for hope to become actuality, and expectation reality. The obstacles and the consequences must be assessed, and the man who exhorts others must equally offer to them the same vast effort that he demands of them.

In the very nature of the case, the wide divergence between existing political theory and the spirit of Islam, which has arisen over a long period and has hence become deep-seated, will make it a matter of some difficulty to return to a theory that is truly based on that spirit. For the machinery of the state and of society, the foundations of life in all its aspects, the psychological and intellectual background are all so built up on specific bases that they are difficult to change without the application of vast energy over a long time. And the longer the time, the greater the difficulty and the greater the need for yet vaster and longer enduring effort.

The time factor is linked up with another consideration in the present age. We do not live by ourselves in this world, nor can we live in isolation from it. Thus our interests and our needs are interwoven with this present world, which is governed by a certain form of civilization involving an outlook completely contradictory to that of Islam. This we shall see later. In one respect this fact will slow down our progress along the path of renewing the true Islamic form of life, and in another respect it will lay additional responsibilities upon us.

The importance of this last consideration is enhanced by the fact that this Western world with which our interests are interwoven is at the present moment stronger than we; we do not have today the control over it, or the strength equal to its strength, that we had in the first age of Islam. At the same time, it is hostile to us, and in particular hostile to our religion. Therefore, it will not permit us to produce a new Islamic system or to renew a truly Islamic form of life, however great the effort we put forth. This result we could hope for only if we had control of the Western world, if our strength were comparable to its, or if it were honest with us and with our religion to which we seek to return.

But all this does not mean that return to the Islamic system is impossible. All that it means is that this is a great and difficult task, requiring extraordinary effort. Above all it demands courage to believe in it, boldness to face the inevitable obstacles, patience to endure the hard work demanded, and faith to believe that this is necessary for Islamic society and for mankind as a whole. It demands the fostering of a constructive and positive mentality, whose task will be not simply to elevate the existing state of things, but rather to produce a new and perfect state.

This is our task. We have already seen the foundations on which the system must be built; thus we can now balance the advantages that we shall enjoy if we return to it against the labors and sacrifices that we must make in order to realize it. When our faith in these advantages reaches the point at which they outweigh the sacrifices, then let us settle the matter, make up our minds, and leave the result with Allah.

Perhaps one valuable aspect of the present situation might be here pointed out. The great Western civilization has led the world into two global wars within a quarter of a century; after the second of these it has led it to a complete division into two blocs, an Eastern and a Western, and to the constant threat of a third war. It has brought about disturbances in every quarter, it has produced starvation and destitution and adversity throughout three-quarters of the world. It should be pointed out also that the world order today is in that state of insecurity and instability where it must look for new foundations and search for some spiritual means of restoring to man his faith in the principles of humanity.

We must not, however, read more than is legitimate into this readiness of the Western world to accept the foundations of our Islamic civilization; this is another matter, although be it noted that such a man as Bernard Shaw says that the West has already started to turn in this direction and even prophesies that it will come to it eventually, in these words:

> I forecast that the religion of Muhammad will be accepted in Europe in the near future, for it has already started to gain some acceptance. The priests of the Middle Ages insisted on portraying Islam in the darkest colors, either out of ignorance, or from criminal bigotry. They went to extremes in their hatred of Muhammad and his religion; indeed they held him to be the anti-Christ. For myself I find it preferable to call Muhammad the savior of mankind, and I believe that if such a man were given authority over the modern world, he would succeed in

solving its problems and giving it peace and happiness. And how great is the world's need of these things.

There were some impartial thinkers in the nineteenth century who discovered how much value there is in the religion of Muhammad, among them Carlyle, Goethe, and Gibbon. From this fact there has arisen a salutary change in the attitude of Europe towards Islam; thus Europe has seen a great advance in the past years of the twentieth century, and has even started to respect the faith of Muhammad. It may be that in the century that lies ahead Europe will make further progress, and will acknowledge the contribution of this faith towards a solution of its problems. Many among my own nation and among all European nations already belong to the religion of Muhammad, a fact which enables us to say that the conversion of Europe to Islam has already begun.[55]

But so far as we can see Shaw's prophecy is still no more than a prophecy—if, indeed, it is not intended to drug the senses of Muslims and to make them content to wait idly for Europe to embrace their faith. But however this may be, it is at the least premature to wait for this to happen for two principal reasons:

1. There is this deep-seated and inherited hostility to Islam in the European nature itself. This is at present augmented by the opposition of the imperialistic interests of West and East to the very existence of our faith as being an obstacle in their path.

2. The European mentality is rooted in material foundations, and the influence of intellectual and spiritual interests is very weak; such has been the case from the time of Roman civilization to the present day. This matter requires detailed consideration and a full treatment, the benefit of which goes beyond our current concern. So let us here make an extended study of this important question: Is it possible for Islamic and Western civilization to work together in partnership? And if so, then what are the limits of that partnership?

We have already asserted at the beginning of this book that Europe was never at any time truly Christian, because by its very nature its peoples had to fight over their meagre territories. Thus the tolerant principles of Christianity could gain no footing in such a stubborn ground. In addition to this, Christianity is essentially an asceticism, a refusal to take an interest in a practical, worldly life. To these two factors we must now add a third, to which we have already made a passing reference. This factor was the existence of the Roman Empire and its position athwart the path of Christianity, together with the permanent influence of that empire on the bases of European civilization even today, and that despite the infusion of Christianity, which the Roman Empire received in its last days.

We may quote here some passages from *Islam at the Crossroads*, which we find completely satisfactory:

> The doctrine on which the Roman Empire was founded was to destroy by force, or to exploit other peoples for the sole benefit of the mother country. In order to indulge this privileged body the Romans saw nothing wrong in their violence and nothing humiliating in their oppression. The famous Roman justice was a justice for Romans only. It is apparent that such a tendency as this was possible only on the basis of a materialistic view of life and civilization—though it may be a view promoted and shaped by a philosophical taste. In any case it was far removed from any appreciation of spiritual values. The Romans did not really understand religion; their traditional gods were only imitations of the Greek superstitions which, as being mere shades, were never believed to have any connection with social affairs, and which were never permitted to interfere in any way with the real business of life. Their duty was to speak in metre through the agency of their attendant priests, when questions were asked of them; but no one ever expected them to enunciate laws for the guidance of mankind.
>
> Such was the soil in which modern Western civilization grew up, though during the period of its growth it undoubtedly came under many other influences. Thus in the very nature of the case it changed and thereby modified the cultural legacy which it had received from Rome in more than one way. Nevertheless the fact remains that all that is truly authentic in the modern

West, whether of life or nature, owes its origin to Roman
civilization. Hence since the intellectual and social environment
of ancient Rome was always self-seeking rather than religious—and that not *ex hypothesi*, but in actual fact—so the
same environment persists in the modern West. The European
mind has no proof for the complete falsity of religion, nor will it
even admit the need for such a proof. For modern European
thinking in general leaves the absolute outside its scheme of
practical considerations—although it does tolerate religion, and
even at times may assert that it is a social convention. Western
civilization does not irrevocably disown God, but it can see no
place and no significance for Him in its present intellectual
system. It has made a virtue out of a philosophical inability on
the part of man, that is to say, out of his inability to take a
comprehensive view of the whole field of life. Hence it is that
modern Europe tends to attach the greatest practical importance to the values deriving from the experimental sciences, or
at least from those sciences from which may be expected some
perceptible influence of human social relationships. And because the question of the existence of God does not fall into
either of these categories, the European mind tends to drop the
concept of God out of the sphere of practical considerations.

A question emerges here: How is this tendency to be reconciled with Christian thought? Is not Christianity a faith
founded on the Absolute, as is Islam? And is it not ostensibly
the spiritual foundation of Western civilization? There is no
doubt that all these things are true. But there could not be any
greater mistake than to imagine that Western civilization is the
outcome of Christianity. The true philosophical basis of the
Western system is to be sought in the ancient Roman view of
life as a matter of advantage, quite independent of absolute
values. It is a view which can be summarized thus: Because we
have no specific knowledge, either in the way of practical
experience, or in that of proof, about the origins of human life,
or about its destiny after physical death; therefore it is best for
us to confine our powers to those material and intellectual fields
which are accessible to us, rather than let ourselves be tied

down to metaphysical and moral questions arising from claims
which can have no scientific proofs. Such an argument as this,
which is characteristic of modern Western civilization, will
certainly not find acceptance in Christian thought, as it will not
in Islam or in any other religion, simply because it is essentially
irreligious. Thus to try to establish a causal relationship between Christianity and modern Western civilization, is a gross
historical error. Christianity may indeed have played a very
small part in the material and scientific progress in which the
West excels today, but the truth is that this progress has been
the product of Europe's prolonged struggle against the Christian Church, and against its supervision of life. In the view of
the majority Christianity today is a purely formal affair, as was
the case with the Roman deities, which were neither permitted
nor expected to exert any real influence on society. No doubt
there are in the West numerous individuals who are still prepared to judge and to think on a religious basis, prepared to
fight a last ditch action to reconcile their beliefs with the spirit
of their civilization; but they cannot be more than isolated
cases. The average European, whether he is the is a democrat
or a fascist, a capitalist or a bolshevik, a worker or an intellectual, knows only one necessary religion — the worship of material progress; the only belief that he holds is that there is but one
goal in life — the making of that life easier and easier. It is, as the
definition has it in significant terms, "an escape from the
tyranny of nature." The shrines of such a culture are huge
factories and cinemas, chemical laboratories and dance - halls
and power stations. The priests of such a worship are bankers
and engineers, cinema stars and industrialists and aviators. The
inevitable result of this state of affairs is that man strives to gain
power and pleasure; this brings into being quarrelsome societies, all armed to the teeth and intent on mutual destruction
whenever their conflicting interests come into active opposition.
On the cultural side the upshot has been the evolution of a
humanism with a moral philosophy confined to purely prag-
matic questions, in which the highest criterion of good or evil is
whether or not any given thing represents material progress.

The sum and substance of all this is that the present-day European conscience is not ready to accept the spirit of Islam or to seek in it a solution of human problems. But even so, it is not impossible that even this may take place after a number of other changes and developments in the West, and after the Islamic world itself has entered upon a clearly defined and independent renewal of Islamic life. In this the West may find philosophical realities and practical truths that will attract its attention and balance its thinking. But it is my personal belief that many generations must elapse before the West will be able to appreciate the spirit of Islam in any real sense.

Again, the substance of this argument is that the mode of the Muslim doctrine that work must serve moral ends cannot be reconciled with the modern Western doctrine that morals must serve some material advantage. We must reckon with this fact, and hence we must work to establish a sound form of Islamic life; this cannot be achieved by the importation of elements borrowed from abroad, since such elements will not fit into the texture of our authentic beliefs.

The Muslims concede defeat in the first round whenever they seek to renew their own life by borrowing Western ways of thought, life, and custom. Such an experiment can only result in the suffocation of that very form of life that it seeks to revive; for from the very first step the Muslim world will be departing from its own true and natural path. This path involves a belief based on Islam that the moral element is fundamental to the structure of life; it regards work as a means to moral ends, and it will not make material advantage the highest aim of morals.

We have already seen in an earlier chapter of this book that Islam satisfies all the highest aims of life, among them the moral consciousness. We have also seen that Islam's supreme virtue is that it preserves the unity of life and that it makes no distinction between means and ends. It will not lend its authority to any idea that there is an opposition between material and spiritual in the substance of life or in the nature of the universe or of mankind; rather it emphasizes that the whole of life is a unity that must make an orderly progress towards the highest objectives.

Islam, then, enunciates for men a complete theory of life. This theory is always liable to growth by development or by adaptation; it is not open to modification or to adulteration, either in its fundamentals or in its general aims. Therefore, in order that this complete theory may bear its full natural fruits, it is necessary to make a complete application of it. Otherwise, even the slightest change in its fundamentals or its aims will produce a disorder, because it will no longer be in conformity with the Islamic conception of life.

Continual growth based on this universal theory by development or by adaptation is a natural product of the nature of Islam; it is encouraged by Islam, the institutions of which are adapted to recognize it. Analogy, interpretation, and the wide powers entrusted to the head of the state—all these are living methods of ensuring growth through development and adaptation, in order to keep pace with life and to meet its needs as they emerge. But there is one thing that must be kept in mind: these developments must not contradict the principles of the fundamental Islamic theory, nor must they be allowed to serve any alien aim; they must not betray the spirit of Islam or give allegiance to any other spirit in preference to it.

The criterion by which we may accept or reject any development is first to compare it with the basic theory and the general spirit of Islam. Anything that is in agreement with this theory and this spirit we may accept, and anything that is contrary to these we must reject. Thus we may profit by all the fruits of human labor within the bounds of our basic philosophy of the universe, man, and life; we need raise no barriers between ourselves and human endeavor, nor need we stand in isolation from the continuous advance of humanity. Above all we must be firmly convinced, with complete faith and enthusiasm, that we have a scheme of life greater than any possessed by the followers of any religion or school or civilization that has yet been born, because it is the product of God, the creator of life.

✦ ✦ ✦ ✦ ✦ ✦ ✦

However, this is only a general statement; it requires a detailed discussion of the practical methods of attaining this great objective. It requires also a detailed discussion of the specific question of social justice, which is the primary interest of this book. May the blessing of Allah be with us, then, as we start this discussion.

❖ ❖ ❖ ❖ ❖ ❖ ❖

No renaissance of Islamic life can be effected purely by law or statute, or by the establishment of a social system on the basis of the Islamic philosophy. Such a step is only one of the two pillars on which Islam must always stand in its construction of life. The other is the production of a state of mind imbued with the Islamic theory of life, to act as an inner motivation for establishing this form of life and to give coherence to all the social, religious, and civil legislation. Social justice is an integral part of this Islamic life; it cannot be realized unless this form of life is first realized, and it cannot have any guaranteed permanence unless this form of life is built up on solid foundations. It is in this similar to all other social systems; it must have the support of public belief and confidence in its merits. Failing this, it will lose its spiritual foundations, and its establishment will depend on the force of religious and social legislation; this is a force that obtains only so long as evasion is impossible.

Hence Islamic legislation relies on obedience and conviction; it depends on religious belief. Thus we must always keep in mind the necessity for a renaissance of our religious faith; we must cleanse it of all accretions, such as alterations and arbitrary interpretations and ambiguities; only thus can it be a support for the necessary social legislation that will establish a sound form of Islamic life. This form of life will depend upon legislation and exhortation, those twin fundamental methods of Islam towards the achievement of all aims.

We must, then, establish our Islamic theory in individuals and societies at the same time that we set up the Islamic legislation to regulate life. And the natural method of establishing that philosophy is culture.

But how can we possibly induce Islamic theory by a culture, educational methods, and modes of thought that are essentially Western and essentially inimical to the Islamic philosophy itself; first, because they stand on a materialistic basis, which is contrary to the Islamic theory of life; and second, because opposition to Islam is a fundamental part of their nature, no matter whether such opposition is manifest or concealed in various forms?

As we have already maintained, we shall proclaim our defeat in the first round whenever we adopt a Western theory of life as the means of reviving our Islamic theory. So, primarily, we must rid ourselves of the ways of Western thought and choose the ways of native Islamic thought in order to ensure pure results, rather than hybrid.

The import of these words is not that we should adopt a position of isolationism in regard to thought, education, and science; all these are a common heritage of all the peoples of the world, in which we already have a fundamental part. We continue to take our rightful part in the furthering of these things, even if it appears that we are far distant from exerting any influence. For, mutual influence among all the nations of the earth is a permanent reality.

Isolation from the human caravan, then, is not our aim; rather, what we seek is to build up a characteristically Islamic theory of life and to renew that form of life now, when it is apparent even to some of the more enlightened Occidentals that the philosophy of materialistic Western civilization is a danger to the continued existence of man. It breeds in human nature a ceaseless anxiety, a perpetual rivalry, a continuous strife, and a degeneration of all human qualities. And this in spite of all the triumphs of science that could have tended to human happiness and peace and content had it not been that the bases of the Western philosophy of life were purely materialistic and hence unsuitable to guide men along the path to perfection.

As long as our aim is the building up of this Islamic theory along these lines, we must make a distinction between things that we may profitably accept and those that we may profitably reject out of what the Westerners possess. Only thus may we complete the building of an Islamic society out of sound materials that will produce a structure that will not be endangered by either cooperation or opposition alike, either borrowing or giving. To put it differently, we must ensure to the theory of life that we establish a safeguard in the form of a period of fostering—fostering, that is, in our own minds rather than in its own essence. For the Islamic idea in itself is a strong and definite thing that does not stand in awe of any alien idea. Rather, it is we who need to be fostered and nurtured, as we are living on a strange diet; hence we must be on our guard while we are engaged in the establishment of our new system.

In the case of the pure sciences and their applied results of all kinds, we must not hesitate to utilize all things in the sphere of material life; our use of them should be unhampered and unconditional, unhesitating and unimpeded.

But when it comes to philosophy, which is the intellectual interpretation of the universe and life; to literature, which is the emotional interpretation of these things; to history, which is a factual interpretation; and to legislation, which is an interpretation of the relationships between individuals and societies, we must be cautious in making use of them.

It will do us no harm to make use of the pure sciences in all the details of life; but on the other hand, it will do us harm to adopt alien interpretations of life as a whole, for such interpretations are based on a philosophy that is not ours. It tends to establish a conception of the universe and of life that is at variance with the Islamic conception of these things; ultimately it would lead us along a path that is not that of Islam. It is this path that has produced the present ailments of mankind, and which is responsible for their present troubles.

It is sometimes objected that even if this be so, the pure sciences themselves cannot be regarded as completely harmless, because essentially they cannot be divorced from the method of Western thought. The experimental method rests on the basis of a definite philosophy that is neither rational nor spiritual; if this had never established itself in favor, science would never have followed the course that latterly it has taken. In the same way, science can never remain in isolation from philosophy, nor can it be content to be influenced by philosophy without in turn influencing it. For philosophy benefits from the experimental results of science and is influenced by it in aim and method. Therefore, the adoption of pure science involves the adoption of the philosophy that is influenced by that science, and which in turn exerts an influence on it. All this is over and above the fact that the applied results of science must influence all material life, methods of gaining a living, and the division of wealth. All this will in due time produce new forms of society based on a new philosophy, or at least based on a theory of life that must be influenced by these developments in the course of life.

All this is very true. But what must be must be. There is no possibility of living in isolation from science and its products, though the harm that it does may be greater than the good. There is no such thing in this life as an unmixed blessing or an unalloyed evil. Islam does not oppose science or the utilization of science; there is nothing contrary to the spirit of Islam in culling the fruits of science from all the sources of the world. But if in acknowledging the universal influences of philosophy and culture, history and law, together with all their consequences in the way of educational methods and modes of thought and logic, we set all of this in its proper place on a spiritual Islamic foundation, we will be safeguarded from any effect the results and material consequences of science might have on our universal philosophy of life and conduct.

When we mention educational methods we might well bear in mind here that these are indivisible and inseparable from the general philosophy of the community. Thus when we borrow Western methods of education, systems of training, and curricula, we borrow also a general scheme of philosophy and a mode of thought that underlies these methods and systems and curricula, whether we like it or not.

There is a belief that these are questions of pure "pedagogy," and therefore universal and identical throughout all countries. This is a naive and shortsighted belief, encouraged by the delusion of the psychologists, who giving an undue weight to their own subject and wish to connect it to philosophy, despite the separation that occurred between the two in the last century.

That claim is one thing, but the actual fact is quite another. Psychology may one day become a pure science to be studied in the laboratory. But the channeling of its results and the uses to which these are put, such as educational techniques and

curricula—all these things are still influenced by the general philosophy of life, still accept the dictation of that philosophy, and still
form an integral part of it. More, the very fact that psychology is
ruled by the laboratory is one of the influences exerted by experimental philosophy or by the experimental method. It is this same
method that in latter years has governed all materialistic Western
thought. The only type of independence that psychology can expect from the philosophy that is its mentor is that superficial independence that cannot influence the final result. The same applies to
methods of education.

For an example of this we may look to the American curriculum, their methods of education and instruction. These are more
akin to vocational training than to any system of thorough and systematic study; they have as their objective the promotion of technical skill instead of theoretical principles. The reason for this
tendency is to be sought in the philosophy of Pragmatism, founded
by Charles Pierce in 1878, which was advanced by William James
and applied by John Dewey, the contemporary educational philosopher. This school of thought represents a reversal of the accepted terms of thought and study; abstract ideas and theoretical
principles are abandoned, as is the study of things according to
their essence and nature. According to Pragmatism all study
should be confined to the practical effects and results of objects.

> According to Charles Pierce and according to Pragmatism
> the idea is no more than a secondary product of some act or
> activity; it is not in itself a reality. For example, I may have the
> 'idea' of the horn of an automobile passing in the street; this
> 'idea' gains no meaning by my study of its nature, its origin,
> and the method of its production. There is no point in asking
> whether it is a reality or a figment of the imagination; produced
> by the ear and the nervous system, or produced by the horn. It
> means only that the automobile is turning to right or to left, and
> that a path must be cleared for the vehicle and its driver. It
> means only: 'I am about to change the direction of my vehicle
> and to proceed in a different direction.' Hence Pragmatism
> argues that the idea is secondary to the act, or the product of

certain conditioning circumstances. This is the first step along the path of Pragmatism in which all the remaining steps must follow."[56]

It has been the rise of this theory or this method of thought which has produced the educational techniques of America. It has been responsible for a teaching curriculum and a system that will encourage the mind to take this view of things and to rationalize life along this line. More, it is this that has given American life its most characteristic mark, which has directed it towards technical production and which has to a large extent diverted it from academic and theoretical education.

Accordingly, we must reckon with this general philosophy of life; if we borrow educational techniques, teaching systems, and curricula, this philosophy underlies all of them. This philosophy shapes and forms them, assisted by the results of pure psychology. Such an influence is inevitable, though this same science of psychology in its methods and in its results is itself influenced by that very philosophy.

❖ ❖ ❖ ❖ ❖ ❖ ❖

From the theoretical point of view, then, our method of establishing an independent Islamic scheme of thought is to proceed readily but cautiously in the matter of borrowing such a philosophy along with its concomitants, such as educational techniques, teaching systems and curricula, literature, history, and law. But we shall deal now with all these subjects together.

❖ ❖ ❖ ❖ ❖ ❖ ❖

So far as the study of philosophy is concerned, we have already indicated the universal theory of Islam on the universe, life, and mankind. This is essentially different from the nature of other universal philosophies that have obtained in the West from the days of the Greeks to the present. This is not the place to discuss this difference, and it will suffice to recognize merely that there does exist a radical divergence.[57]

The Azhar in particular has had a mission in this regard, a

mission it has not fulfilled: to research the overall concept of Islam, to present it forcefully and coherently in the language and style of the age, and to compare it with other schools of philosophy. But instead of undertaking this task, the Azhar has continued to teach what it erroneously calls Islamic philosophy, taken from the books of Ibn Sina and Ibn Rushd. These are reflections of Greek philosophy, which has no connection whatsoever with the overall concept and philosophy of Islam. The responsibility resting on the shoulders of the Azhar was neglected as if to acknowledge a spiritual and intellectual defeat on behalf of Islam!

If, then, we are to establish a sound Islamic theory of the universe, life, and mankind, it is essential that Western philosophies and their moral corollaries should not be studied at all in our secondary schools, and that they should be studied in the university only after at least two years in the department of philosophy. And by the very nature of the case they should not be studied in the Azhar colleges until the very end of the course. In every center of study such Western philosophies should be preceded by a course in pure Islamic thought, as distinct from the so-called "Islamic philosophy," in order to emphasize the true Islamic viewpoint.

Thus, the minds and thoughts of the students will assimilate the firm bases of the spirit of Islam, together with its ideas on the universe, life and mankind, good and evil, work and reward, and all the other philosophic aspects of pure Islamic belief. This having been assured, we may in the later years proceed to give to students specializing in philosophy some account of the other philosophies; these would include Greek philosophy and its Islamic reflections and modern European and American philosophy; these should be compared in every case with Islamic philosophy. In this way we can ensure that the student mind and conscience will not be too much influenced; we can ensure also a minimum influence on student ideas and thoughts, because by then they will be equipped for critical appreciation. They will have the requisite knowledge to reject all that does not agree with the fundamental modes of thought of a Muslim people. Under these circumstances their new knowledge will not harm, but will rather benefit students; for it will be purely intellectual knowledge, largely independent of any influence on their conscience or on their conception and under-standing of life and its requirements.

We have already given one example of pragmatism in its view of things. But in this example there was no indication of the dangers inherent in that philosophy or in its method; so we must now follow out this philosophy in its further results, in order to note the dangerous influences of its intellectual system on any nation that follows such a mode of thought.

"Most people believe in God. This is an idea that logically may be either false or true. Intellectual theory says: If God really exists, then His existence must be logically demonstrable. Pragmatism on the other hand attacks the problem from a different angle and approaches it differently. In its view the truth of the idea of God does not depend on logical necessity; it depends solely on the profit of this idea to our present life, in our daily activity, and in our experiences. If the idea tends to produce a profit in life, then it is sound and therefore true. Hence God does exist. Apart from this test, pragmatism claims, in the first place we cannot judge this idea; and in the second place we cannot trust our own judgment."[58]

The Islamic line of thought differs to a greater or lesser extent from that of pure intellectual theory, insofar as it does not entrust the whole question to human logic alone, but relies also upon revelation. But it is in complete opposition to pragmatism; for when we follow out its logic to a conclusion we find that the idea of God must disappear if the outward benefits of material life are not forthcoming. When this happens the idea of God loses its existence because it cannot control its instruments and set the machinery in motion.

The next step is to conclude that material profit becomes the sole criterion, not only of the acceptance or the rejection of things, but also of their existence or non-existence. This implies a state of affairs in which man loses all nobility, where he is neither more nor less than an instrument.

Policies in this world cannot be divorced from such philosophies. Thus perhaps we are not far from the truth when we say that the policy of the United States on the Palestine question and its stand in the United Nations on the question of Egypt were merely the results of its intellectual background of pragmatism — in conjunction, of course, with other factors. The idea of right and justice has little effective place in materialistic American life; and hence it has little chance of permanent acknowledgment in international policies. This idea is perhaps the most satisfactory comment on these puzzling policies.

What we do not want is to establish such an intellectual background as this in our Islamic society. We must therefore be cautious about the study of Western philosophy until we have first established in the developing minds of youth a firm, strong, and clear pattern of thought that is founded on the universal Islamic theory. Similarly we must be cautious about borrowing educational techniques, curricula, and systems of teaching; for all of these are ruled by the general field of philosophy in their native lands; they subserve the aims that philosophy assigns to them, whether directly or indirectly.

❖ ❖ ❖ ❖ ❖ ❖ ❖

Literature, again, is the emotional interpretation of life. It issues from the same wellspring whence flow in any culture all the philosophies, the religious beliefs, the experiments, and the influences.

Literature is the most important factor in the establishment of a moral philosophy of life and in the production of any specific influence on the human mind. Hence we must exercise care in the choice of Western literature that we make available to our youth, alike in their Arabic and their foreign studies.

It is not necessary to take this as meaning that our youth are to be prohibited from reading European literature; what we have in mind here is simply a process of choice and selection. For in this literature there are elements the spirit of which is at one with the spirit of Islam. By this we do not mean that such books encourage goodness and reprobate wickedness; for literature is no preacher to exhort and to direct. Rather we mean that such books have a view of life that is spiritual in tone, rather than materialistic, and that they acknowledge the spiritual values of life. This type of literature agrees in spirit with the general teachings of our Islamic theory; it can therefore do no harm to the moral consciousness of our youth, nor can it upset their emotional and mental development at a vulnerable stage. This vulnerable stage lasts at least until the third year of university work, if not until the time of graduation. There is no harm, but rather great benefit, in having specialized study include all types of the literatures of the world, without restraint or exception. But the prime aim of a process of choice and selection at a certain age is to safeguard the period of adolescence from being defiled and led astray.

History is a branch of literature; but it is one that has its own characteristics, and which therefore has also its own significance. For history is an interpretation of the events of life, which is necessarily influenced by a given philosophy and concept of life. Its interpretation of events may therefore lead to a philosophy of life completely opposed to Islamic theory.

Beyond this, historians, who are for the most part Europeans, have made the history of Europe the focal point of world history. In view of the nature of man this is excusable, and we have borne it with patience as a characteristically Western and European delusion. Yet if our youth are to study history in this spirit and by this method, then they will finish with two false beliefs:

1. That spiritual factors have no influence on the course of events in time, or at least that any such influence is very weak.

2. That Europe is the mistress of historical events and that the influence of the East and of Islam is exiguous.

Both these ideas have harmful and dangerous results; they establish a false general idea of life, of the world, and of events, and they endanger our pride in Islam, which is so necessary in face of the sweeping pride of Europe.

In order to guard our youth from this evil we must take the two following steps:

1. We must begin by establishing general world history, as Islam views it, as the interpretation of events and happenings. We must not be concerned solely with the European point of view in this present dangerous fashion. In such a history we must give Europe its rightful place and no more, and we must emphasize the part played in world history by the East in general, and by Islam in particular.

2. We must change the present curriculum of history teaching in our schools and colleges. We must start by teaching primarily the history of Islam throughout the Muslim world, and by expounding it from the Islamic point of view. It is not enough to teach our children the history of Islam as written by Western authors, or as expounded by Western philosophies. When their minds are filled with the history of their own country, then we can give them world history, as written by ourselves, to form the next stage of study. And when they have completed that, then we can give them at the level of specialization the remainder of the developments of history.

✧ ✧ ✧ ✧ ✧ ✧ ✧

The study of law is similarly influenced by the Western point of view, by Western philosophy, Western history, Western law, and Western society. For law is a reflection of society or is produced by it; and society is the offspring of all these factors.

Thus, in order to build up a sound Islamic doctrine, we must teach Islamic law in a broad general way before beginning to teach any other legal system. The teaching of Islamic law must be firmly in the control of Muslim professors, and the Western point of view must not be allowed to obtrude, except at the stage of specialization. And similarly, the study of law in general must not be opened up till that same later stage.

It is one of the requirements of Islamic life that Islamic law shall occupy a paramount position; and that very fact will make necessary such a study of Islamic law as we have indicated. The great necessity that faces our professors of Islamic law in this field is to follow the authoritative path traced out by the Imams and their students at the time of the first growth of Islamic law.

✧ ✧ ✧ ✧ ✧ ✧ ✧

When we have achieved our goal of proper intellectual orientation, we are still confronted by that of the specific legal enactments that will ensure a sound form of Islamic life and which will guarantee social justice to all. In this question it is not possible to take a stand purely on the form of the original Islamic life; rather we must utilize all possible and permissible means that fall within the general principles and the broad foundations of Islam. Nor must we be afraid to use also all the discoveries that man has made in the way of social legislation and systems, so long as the principles of these do not run counter to the principles of Islam, and so long as they are not opposed to its theory of life and mankind. We must include these in our legislation so long as they conduce to the true welfare of society, or so long as they ward off any impending evil. In the two principles of "public interest" and "blocking of means" we have two clear Islamic principles that give wide powers to the temporal ruler to ensure the general welfare at all times and in all places.

Before we go on to deal with the application of these two principles it might be well to quote a short passage in explanation of them.[59]

Public Interest. "Any welfare measure that has no specific detailed authority to support it is known as a measure of public interest. The question of whether or not it is a source of jurisprudence is a matter of dispute among the jurisconsults. Al-Qarafi has argued that all the jurisconsults have used it or have admitted it as a proof at one time or another, even though in lecturing most of them deny it the status of a source. He says in regard to this point: 'Other people loudly deny the validity of public interest. But when the case is closely examined, they are found to refer to the word in its absolute sense. They do not trouble to take any account of the evidence offered by the reference of the term in its synonyms and contexts; they hold that it means merely 'convenience,' and that such is the sole meaning of the phrase 'public interest.'

"No matter whether this claim is true or false, it is certain that the validity of any measure of welfare that lacks a specific validating authority is a matter on which the 'ulama may well disagree. And even if public interest is not one of the accepted sources of jurisprudence, at least it has the status of custom, as al-Qarafi indicates.

"The opinions of the ulama on this matter can be divided into four main views, as follows:

"1. The Shafi'ites and those who share their opinions do not believe in any form of public interest whose validity is unsupported by legal evidence; for they only admit legal precedents and the treatment of these by analogy, based on the existence of a solid connection between the root and its derivatives, that is to say, between a case governed by a precedent and another analogous to it. If we follow al-Qarafi we must admit that it is strange that they should deny public interest while they admit analogy.

"2. The Hanafites and others of similar opinions maintain the principles of preference and analogy, but their interpretation of preference is sometimes almost indistinguishable from public interest. A fair estimate would say that in their system they make a greater use of interest than do the Shafi'ites. But even so, the extent to which they do use it is negligible, and hence we cannot say that this is one of the principles of their system; not, at least, on any grounds of the use which they make of it in itself.

"3. There are those who attach an excessive importance to public interest, even to the point of making it stronger than precedent in their dealings with cases; they regard it as a form of precedent, or rather, as a form of consensus. Thus where the 'ulama are agreed on a point turning on precedent, but some aspect of that point runs counter to public interest, then the validity of the latter is the stronger. This applies also to specific cases, as al-Tusi has maintained.

"4. There are those who hold a middle course, which is the soundest of all. Here validity is granted to public interest, but it is not derived from precedent, which is held to be entirely different. To this view most of the Malikite rite adhere.

"Malik held that public interest was an independent principle of the system of jurisprudence, but that it was a derived, rather than an original principle; and that, for the following reasons:

"1. The Companions of Allah's Messenger found that questions arose after his death that had not been apparent during his lifetime. Thus they collected the noble Qur'an in book form. This had not been done in the time of the Messenger, but now such a collection was in the public interest; for they feared that the Qur'an might be forgotten because of the deaths of those who had memorized it. 'Umar saw such men dying in numbers during the

Wars of Apostasy, and, fearing that through their death the Qur'an might pass from memory, he advised Abu Bakr to have it collected in book form. To this the Companions gladly assented.

"2. After the death of Allah's Messenger his Companions agreed that the punishment for wine-drinking should be eighty lashes. Their reason for this was the public interest or general inference; for they saw that drinking tended to produce lying and the slandering of chaste women because of the wild talk in which drinkers indulged.

"3. The rightly guided Caliphs agreed upon imposing conscription on craftsmen, although the root principle was that the exercise of their craft was a matter of good faith. But it was found that unless they were conscripted they would neglect the care of the people's belongings and wealth. There was great need for craftsmen, and therefore it was in the public interest to conscript them, that they might perform the duties that they had. Thus 'Ali, when he prescribed the conscription, said: 'The people's interests cannot be served otherwise.'

"4. 'Umar ibn al-Khattab used to claim half of the wealth of those governors whom he suspected of having increased their resources by extortion. This also was a form of public interest, because to his mind it was in the interests of the governors to prevent them capitalizing on their power to amass money and heap up illegal plunder.

"5. It is told of 'Ali that he poured out on the ground milk that had been adulterated with water, as a lesson to the man who had done it. This act also was akin to public interest, to show that people were not to adulterate goods.

"6. There is a tradition that 'Umar put a whole community to death for the murder of one man, for which they had been jointly responsible. This he did because the public interest demanded it. There was no precedent for the case, but the public interest demanded that the case be considered as one of premeditated murder of an innocent individual. To let the murder pass unavenged would have been to deny the basic principle of 'an eye for an eye'; while to choose one out of the many who had had a hand in the business would have made the whole matter ridiculous. For the man chosen would know that in his case it was not a case of retaliation. Or if it were said that this was an anonymous murder, a killing without a killer, on the grounds that every single individual could not be said to be the murderer, then the guilty party was the community itself. The whole of a community can commit a murder in exactly the same way as an individual criminal. And murder can be charged against a community just as it can against a single person, and the members of the community stand in the same relation to the act of murder as does an individual. Hence the community furthers the public interest when it prevents bloodshed and guards communal life.

"Another general aspect of public interest is the power that is granted to the Imam to levy upon the rich whatever impost he thinks that the circumstances warrant. This he can do when the public treasury is empty or when the army has extraordinary needs, while there are no funds to meet those needs. Toll may be levied until the treasury is replenished, or until the needs are sufficiently met. Further, the Imam has the duty of instituting this levy at times of bountiful harvest and plentiful crops, so that the rich will not be overburdened by the fact that it is they alone who pay it. The public interest here lies in the fact that if a just Imam did not do this, his power would be in vain, and wealthy establishments would provide an incentive to unrest and to attacks by envious persons. It is sometimes said that the Imam, instead of enforcing the provisions of the levy, borrows money for the public treasury. To this al-Shatibi retorted that: 'Borrowing in time of need is allowed only when the treasury has the prospect of more revenue. Otherwise, or alternatively, when the revenue is too small to be sufficient, then recourse must be had to the principle of a levy.'

Means. "A means is that which leads to an end, and to 'block the means' is to remove it. The sense of the phrase is that anything that conduces to a forbidden end is itself forbidden, while anything conducive to a desirable end is itself desirable. Thus, for example, adultery is forbidden, and therefore to admire the charms of a strange woman is also forbidden, as being a means towards adultery. On the other side, attendance at prayers is compulsory, and therefore an effort to attend prayers is also compulsory, as is leaving one's business to make that effort. To make the Pilgrimage is compulsory; therefore an effort to visit the sacred House and to perform the other rites of pilgrimage is also compulsory.

"The fundamental reason for the validity of 'blocking the means' is a realization of the repercussions and final results of all actions. If they are conducive to those public interests that constitute the aims and objectives of the dealings of man with man, then they are as desirable as those aims themselves. But if they are not equally desirable, or if their results might be evil, then they are forbidden just as that evil is forbidden, even though the means may be somewhat less objectionable.

"In considering the results of actions the matter of interest is not the purpose or the objective of the agent; rather it is the result and outcome of his action. The individual will be rewarded or punished for his intention in the next world; but in this world it is according to its result and outcome that an action is good or bad, desirable or undesirable. For, this world must take its stand on the welfare of mankind, on judgment and justice, and these things require a scrutiny of results and outcomes rather than of estimable aims and worthy intentions. A man who out of a sincere love for the worship of Allah reviles idols has gained the approval of Allah by the formulation of his purpose; and yet He has forbidden such reviling in cases where it would result in the rage of the idolaters, who would then revile Allah Most High Himself. So His exalted words run: 'And do not revile those who invoke deities other than Allah, lest in response they revile Allah without knowledge.' (6:108) In this noble prohibition regard is had to the actual consequences, rather than to the commendable religious aim. Hence it appears that in cases that tend towards crime or evil, the veto is directed not towards the aim itself, which is sincere, but towards the consequences that will arise; thus an act may be forbidden because of its consequences, even though Allah may be aware that the intention underlying it is sincere.

"Sometimes, also, a man may seek an evil end through a legal act, in which case he is guilty in his own conscience and in the sight of Allah. But no man may take measures against him, nor may any legal penalties be invoked upon him. Such is the case of a man who cuts the price of his goods in order to injure a business rival. This is undoubtedly a legal act; yet it is a means towards a crime, that of injuring another. This crime is the man's object, but in spite of that his action cannot be punished by the power of the law, nor does it fall under any penalty that the law of the land can impose. His action, from the point of view of intention, is a means to evil, but externally it is a means to public and private benefit. Undoubtedly the seller benefits by selling, by the circulation of his goods, and by the goodwill which he gains; equally certainly the public benefits by the cut in price, by which a general lowering of prices is encouraged.

"The principle of blocking the means has regard not then to individual aims and intentions, as we have seen, but to the encouragement of public welfare and to the prevention of public evil. Thus it must take account of the consequences along with the intention, or even of the consequences alone.

"The principle of 'means' is firmly established in the Qur'an and the Sunna. In the former there is the verse: 'And do not revile those who invoke gods other than Allah, lest in response they revile Allah without knowledge.' Of this it is related that the idolaters said that they were content to have their gods reviled if they in turn could revile Muhammad's God. Thus again: 'O you who believe, do not say *Ra'ina*; say *Unzurna* and hearken.' (2:104) This was because the Muslims used the former word with good intention, but the Jews took it as implying a derogatory sense to the Prophet.[60]

"In the Sunna there are many stories of the Prophet and many decisions of his Companions; among them is that of his refusal to kill the hypocrites, lest the unbelievers should have a pretext for saying that Muhammad killed his companions.

"There is also the story that the Prophet forbade a man who had loaned money to accept a gift from the debtor, unless the gift was counted as part repayment of the loan. The reason was simply that the gift was a means of postponing payment and was therefore a form of interest. For, the lender would get his money back and extra also in the form of the gift. We have also the account of the Prophet's having forbidden that men's hands should be cut off in time of war; the purpose was to stop this practice leading to an illegal treatment of fighting men that would inevitably ensue. Similarly, laws should not be intermitted in time of war, lest freedom become license; the two are closely related. And there is the account of the earliest Believers, both Emigrants and Helpers, having on their deathbeds appointed their divorced wives as their heirs; this they did because there was a suspicion of a plot to debar such wives from inheriting. It was not even certain that such a plot existed, but divorce was a 'means' that might have produced injustices.

"Again the Prophet forbade monopolies, saying: 'Only sinners hold monopolies.' For a monopoly is a means to oppress the people in all things that are considered to be essential. But there is no law against a monopoly in any article that cannot injure the people by being withheld, such as cosmetics and the like; for these things do not come under the heading of necessities.

"The Prophet also forbade any man who had given alms in kind to buy them back, even though he might see them displayed for sale in the market. Thus he sought to check the means to recover what had been given to Allah, even by purchase. Thus anyone who gives alms in kind is forbidden to repossess them by purchase and is yet more stringently forbidden to repossess them by any other means. To permit repossession by purchase might be a means of cheating the poor; the rich out of his wealth would give alms in kind to the poor and might then buy them back from him at less than their value. The poor man, on the other hand, would see some profit to himself, and thus his conscience would not oppose the sale.

"Thus there are many indications of this principle, deriving from the Messenger and his Companions. Ibn Qayyim has collected some ninety such examples from actual occurrences, in all of which the principle of blocking the means is clearly illustrated.

"Means are counted to be half of the legal principles of Islam."

These two principles, that of public interest and that of blocking the means, both run back to a common root, that of ensuring the welfare of society. They are integrally connected with the established laws of Islam and with its general purposes. It is these two principles that can guide us towards the legislation necessary to ensure a sound form of Islamic life and to include in its scope a comprehensive social justice.

This discussion must suffice us in a general work dealing with social justice in Islam. It is desirable next to mention some of the things that Islam is able to ensure in this sphere for the present and the future. We must also deal with the legislation necessary to produce these things, so that it may be used as a pattern for analogous treatment in other cases. We cannot deal with all possible developments but these may be safely left to the dictation of circumstances, times, and conditions.

+ + + + + + +

1. **Legislating the Zakat**. This tax is a compulsory duty in Islam, levied on all possessions according to a sliding scale of one-tenth, one-twentieth, and one-fortieth. In all cases it represents a very small fraction, and hence it is but natural that the question should arise: How could such a small sum raise the level of Muslim society? To answer this question we must consider the following facts:

a. The low level at which the taxable minimum is fixed makes the greater part of the community liable to paying it. The exemption value for the *zakat* is fixed at approximately twelve Egyptian pounds, which means that practically all the population has to pay the tax; thus the income from it can be relatively great particularly bearing in mind that it is levied on capital, not on profit.

b. Disbursements from the *zakat* confined to specifically limited classes of people. For their livelihood the great majority must rely on work, which has always been reckoned by Islam to be the primary source of a living.

c. Most important of all, the livelihood of society never depended solely upon this source of income. There were also the vast sums acquired as booty during the war days, which lasted for more than half a century. In this booty all the fighting men shared, and most of them were of the poorer classes. They received four-fifths of the booty, while the other fifth was turned into a charitable foundation for the benefit of all classes of necessitous persons, relatives, orphans, the destitute, and the wayfarer. And when 'Umar resolved not to take the booty away from the conquered countries, but to leave it for the benefit of the native peoples, he instituted the land tax in its place; then this latter was so abundant that it provided for all the poor.

Today this last primary source of revenue is no longer available, and the *zakat* in itself is not sufficient. Therefore, we must consider alternative sources to take the place of booty and plunder, in order to provide an ample living for the generality of men.

But before we consider new sources we must first exhaust the *zakat* as a source in itself. It is a compulsory duty, and it must be paid if the community is justifiably to be described as Islamic, for the *zakat* fulfills a spiritual function as well as a financial one. Again we must consider the sources of the *zakat* as including all types of property, some of which are not at present included because they were not familiar in the early days of Islam.

That is to say, we must bear in mind those forms of wealth that are liable to the *zakat* but which are not mentioned in the Qur'an except summarily in the verse: "O you who have believed, expend of the goods which you have acquired, and of that which We have provided for you from the earth. And do not aim at acquiring something bad, in order to give it away, even though you would not receive yourselves except with closed eyes." (2:269–70) The fact that the *zakat* was prescribed as a duty only upon such types of property as were familiar in the time of the Prophet does not prevent its being prescribed today as a duty on all that is known as property or wealth and on all that produces an income. It makes no difference that such things may not be of the kind on which the tax was originally imposed.

Similarly, we can modify the outlets for the tax money, just as 'Umar modified them when he stopped payments designed to support recent converts. It need not be given in cash or kind to those who are eligible for it. Factories and workshops might be established on their behalf, or they might be given shares in various enterprises to serve as a source of income. This would distance the *zakat* from any kind of temporary or haphazard charity; for these things are not in accord with the needs of modern life.

But in any case such detailed considerations have no place in this book. The scope of our thinking here is the broad field of the promotion of social justice and equity, as the Muslim world gives its attention to a renaissance of the true Islamic life.

2. **Legislating the Mutual Responsibility of Society**. The Prophet said: "Any household that suffers a man to remain hungry among them is outside the protection of Allah, the Blessed and the Exalted." In this brief sentence he emphasized the principle of mutual responsibility in society, a principle for which we provided many proofs at the beginning of this book. This principle was authoritatively imposed on both the individual and the social conscience. Today the law must again enforce it as an essential root of Islam.

This means that the ruler can enforce that which 'Umar intended to enforce: "If I had known earlier what I now know, I would have taken the excess of their wealth from the rich and given it to the poor." Thus he can impose taxes, the only limit of which is the establishment of equilibrium in the social sphere, the removal of crime and oppression from the community in general, and the ample provision of food and drink, clothing and housing, medical treatment and education for every single individual in the country. It does not matter how much tax is placed upon capital so long as the latter is not thereby made incapable of work and of reasonable increase; this condition must be observed because the steady turning of the wheels of labor brings other benefits that cannot be overlooked.

Thus the ruler can put into the hands of the poor with perfect justification a stretch of public land that they may use without paying any basic rent, or at a nominal rent, that they may from it obtain a means of life. For, this constitutes a source of livelihood and is the only means of work within their power. By this act he will fulfill the Messenger's words: "That one of you permit his brother the use of his land as a gift, is better than exacting for it an agreed rent."

The ruler may also with justification fix the wage of the factory or the farm worker at a stipulated proportion of the production or of the harvest. The lowest limit of this wage must be a competence to cover food, drink, clothing, and medicine and medical care at a reasonable level. The standard is to be taken as that of a moderate living, determined by the proportion of the inhabitants of the country to its general wealth.

3. **Legislating General Taxation.** Every individual in the muslim community has the duty of taking a share in the general expenses of the state according to his ability. We have already noticed the opinion of the Imam Malik on what may be done when the treasury is empty or when the needs of the army are increased; the ruler has the power according to need to levy an impost on the wealth of the rich. Similar to the needs of the army are the other needs of the state, such as improvements in public works, cultivating of waste lands, the education of the people, and the medical treatment of the sick. All these things are communal duties that must be met and satisfied just as much as the needs of the army; they must be preserved as strongly as frontiers and defense posts must be guarded. This is particularly true today when wars make demands on all the resources and services of the belligerent nations. In modern war everyone may be said to be in the army, and thus should be capable of taking responsibility in time of peace.

4. **Legislating the Nationalization of Public Resources.** Monopolies on the necessities of life are forbidden by Islam. A monopoly on food is forbidden, for example, since Islam has always asserted the communal ownership of water, pasturage, and fire, as being the primary needs of life. But the needs of life are not unchangeable, varying as they do from age to age. Consequently, the preservation of this general Islamic principle demands what is known today as the nationalization of natural resources. It is essential not to have in the hands of private individuals or companies resources such as mines, oil wells, water, light, heat, electricity, coal, and oil, or the resources of public transport and public food supplying, and other such things. For, private ownership gives the power of monopoly, imposes upon the general public the will of the monopolists, and permits them to indulge in that disgraceful exploitation that we witness today.

The head of Muslim state must enforce the *shari'ah* by making all these things state-owned, and fixing prices and costs so that they will be within the reach of the poorest, they may be bought or rented at equitable rates without excessive prices. By these means Islamic aims for preventing hoarding can be realized.

5. **Legislating Matters Related to the Public Interest and the Blocking of Means**. Everything that tends to advance the public welfare or to repel harm is a duty laid upon the ruler: everything that tends to an obligatory end is obligatory, and everything that tends towards a prohibited end is itself prohibited. The application of these established principles of Islam lays on the ruler today several duties.

a. The taking of excessive wealth out of the hands of bloated capitalists. The fact that such excessive wealth is in their possession tends towards a number of crimes. In the first place, it tends to produce that luxury which is forbidden by Islam. Luxury is a relative matter, which can be defined only in terms of the general condition in each age and country. The permanent rule is that luxury shall not increase beyond the mean struck by the national wealth in proportion to the population. One result of luxury is the iniquitous rise in prices that springs from the fact that one section of the populace has an unlimited power to buy, while the goods available for sale are not equal to the demand. Another result is the rise of social vices, springing from the fact that some people possess more money than they need; to dispose of this they look for illegal outlets and seek sensual and corrupt pleasures; through these their morals and their standards are degraded, and on the other hand, their victims are the needy men and women who always exist in an unbalanced society.

b. The removal of extreme poverty, because of its results in the way of crime and evil. These results include a great number of social evils, which can only exist in surroundings of privation and destitution, theft, infamy, and moral degradation, a general atmosphere of corruption, and so on.

This is over and above the vast differences that are set between those who have and those who have not, the hatreds and the social disturbances that the ruler must prevent before they occur by removing their causes.

If it be asked how this extreme poverty is to be removed, it is by the ample provision of work for every able-bodied man, and by the provision of an adequate wage, by social security for all who are disabled, and by speedy relief. This is the method in general outline; the specific applications are easy once the general aim is established.

c. The struggle against disease and ignorance. Because of their evil effect on the individual and the community these weaken the general strength of the community and afford a footing to its enemies. This condition is forbidden, as is any factor that leads to it. Nothing can oppose disease and ignorance successfully except a rise in living standards and in general wealth; projects of charity and such other things are only palliatives to soothe the sore, not to heal it. The real treatment is that every individual should be possessed of private means for medical and educational purposes. Or alternatively, that medical care and education should be provided free to every individual in the country on a common basis and to a common level. The rich must not be able, by money, to get more than the poor in schools or hospitals.

6. **Legislating Governing Legacies**. "When there are present at the division of the estate relatives, orphans, and poor people, give them a provision out of it and speak them fair." (4:9) Thus runs the Qur'anic precept. It clearly means that out of every estate there must be a share for relatives, orphans, and the poor. The law has the power of disposal according to the nature of the case; it may change the beneficiaries, or it may leave them unchanged. So 'Umar did in the case of paying out money to support recent converts. The law also has the power to fix the proportions given to each category of beneficiary in accordance with communal need. And we must remember that the meaning of being "present" can legitimately be extended to cover virtual presence, that is to say, existence. In every community there are orphans and poor, and there is no necessity for them to be present in person when an estate is being divided; they are already present in time and space. So, by the power of the law all duties must be enforced that are not enforced by the power of conscience.

7. **Legislating Matters Relating to Mutual Help and Usury**. Islam rooted out usury and fought it in all its forms and appear-

ances; hence it is impossible for any form of Islamic life to exist on an economic basis that includes the institutions involved in usury. We have already discussed the causes that made Islam unable to countenance usury, but they may be summed up by saying that it is the negation of the spirit of mutual help and friendliness. If usury obtains, then it is to the benefit of the capitalist who can thus increase his wealth without working and without the risk of loss.

The national economy must be set on a basis of mutual help rather than of usury. All the objections that might be made have been summarily refuted by Maulana Muhammad 'Ali in his book, *Islam and the New World Order*, from which we may quote the following passage:

> It is objected that to forbid interest on money will hinder business and commercial transactions and will hinder the accomplishment of important private projects. Let us suppose this to be true, for the sake of argument, but on the other side we have the far greater advantage that to proscribe interest will prevent world wars, which can only end in misery, and which are kindled and inflamed only by loans and debts governed by interest. And if we examine the facts of the case, we shall find that, from the very first, trade followed its natural course and spread more and more widely as important private projects were maintained and as ever wider limits were brought within the Islamic sphere. So that the Islamic states were among the greatest competitors in the advance of world civilization.
>
> This prohibition of usury cannot, indeed, be reconciled with the conditions of the new world that materialistic Western civilization is bringing into being. The ideal social system which Islam has in mind is that practical system that was successfully applied in practice by Islam at its inception centuries ago. As for the capital sums, without which business cannot be carried on, there was little difference between the gains that they made under the Islamic system and those that they made by ordinary lending; for the Islamic system was in effect one of partnership between capital and labor. Such a partnership is not impossible, for the Islamic system holds that capital and labor should share

together in all profit and loss; whereas the result of paying a steady rate of interest is that capital makes a continual profit, even when labor has to work at a loss.

It is sometimes objected that the partnership of capital and labor in both profits and losses is not practicable, because it means that regular accounts have to be kept. This, however, is one of the necessities of trade, because in any event trading records have to be available for the assessing of taxes that have to be paid. All the share-issuing companies that take part in trading on a large scale have to keep accounts. And indeed this partnership system is more to the public advantage than that of giving all the dividends to capital; for it is the latter system that increases the evils of capitalism, and which is the source of the oppression of the workers. And the loans that are floated by governments or companies to carry out major projects such as railroads or canals or such things have done no more than prove this point.

But since the system of state banking depends on the principle of mutual help, which is approved by the Islamic social system, it must be of great benefit to mankind.

This is a general statement, the particular details of which are too lengthy for a book dealing with general ideas. At the same time there can be no harm in giving an example as a guide to the mode of implementation that we have in mind.

Suppose that the state decrees the abolition of interest on funds in banks, companies, public enterprises, and private loans, what will happen then?

What will happen will be that capitalists will find themselves unable to increase their wealth except by two general methods. First, they may put it to some profitable use themselves in manufacture or trade or agriculture. Or second, they may put it to a profitable and helpful use by investing it in share-issuing companies, where the share values may rise or fall. Both these methods are sanctioned by Islam, and neither of them will work the slightest injury to economic life.

It is sometimes feared that the rich will refrain from depositing their money in the banks, which generally finance the large public projects. This is an imaginary danger that gains currency among us because we are familiar only with European methods of using money. There is a primary natural impulse to make money increase; this can be accomplished only by putting it to use in some way or another and so this natural impulse is a guarantee that money will not be kept out of circulation. But when we desire to take in hand some large project to undertake some major form of production, we have the power to create legislation covering various kinds of industry; this legislation enacts that no new enterprise may be set up except on the basis of capital over such and such a sum. On that, capital sums flow in to take up shares and to become liable to profit and loss on the market. Thus there is no more need for banks, except for the issuing of currency. If other banks wish to make a profit, then they must buy shares with their own and their depositors' funds—the latter only with permission—in some profit-seeking enterprise, where the shares are liable to fluctuation on the open market. But the banks' guaranteed rate of interest is undoubtedly usury. This system will not stop the flow of capital, either domestic or foreign; for the greater proportion of capital wealth is not deposited in banks, but is put out to profit in enterprises.

As for insurance companies, it may be that they become Islamic institutions, inasmuch as the funds that are deposited with them are liable to profit and loss, to fall or rise. Funds deposited in these companies are put to work in profit-seeking enterprises, subject to fluctuation. Every time a beneficiary receives more than he has paid in, the amount of the company's loss is deducted from the remainder of the depositors in proportion to the funds which they have invested. Thus insurance companies' members form a cooperative society; in effect they pay out of their own pockets to support any unfortunate one of their number when need arises. They have a form of security from which they can benefit in time of hardship or need. This can be applied also to savings banks and similar institutions, all of which can be transformed into cooperative societies, which use their funds in profit-seeking enterprises, always liable to fluctuation. Such institutions have no fixed rate of interest, and hence our economic system here can be free from the taint of usury; hence also all capital is compelled to work as the only method of achieving profit and increase.

8. **Legislation Prohibiting Gambling**. Gambling is a vile practice, both in act and in spirit, for it represents an effort to make money without working. In addition, it produces enmity and hatred among its adherents and gives rise to laxity and insecurity in the fabric of society. There are many forms of gambling, of which lotteries are but one. It is not any spirit of charity that prompts people to buy lottery tickets, nor is it any desire to assist hospitals and charitable institutions. It is merely the desire to gain more money without working. This is at once practically and spiritually vile, as we have said; it hinders and pollutes the feelings of mercy. There is no need to mention the obscene and lascivious gatherings that are called charity balls; they are merely the outcome of luxury and the corrupting result of luxury-loving natures with their aversion to virtue and their love of vice, with their avarice except when money is lavished on sensual pleasures and coarse enjoyment.

We must halt the practice of gambling altogether, with its green tables, its tempting lottery tickets, and its naked bosoms and abominable parties. Islamic life has need of none of these things, and Islam will never admit that relations between man and man should ever stand on such a basis or that charity should spring from such impure desires.

9. **Laws Prohibiting Prostitution**. Prostitution is the product of spiritual degradation and material destitution, sometimes together and sometimes separately. Islam prohibits illegal sexual intercourse in all its forms, and the most degraded of these is prostitution. Prostitution is the hallmark of an unbalanced community, for the two factors that produce prostitution are excessive wealth and humiliating necessity. It was once said: "A wellborn woman cannot feed from her own breasts because she is hungry; but she may do so if she is in danger of death." We must not expose people on the one hand to the trials of need, and on the other to the temptations of wealth and other things, and then expect them to be models of self-control and virtue. The principle of blocking

the means demands that the law give attention to check this thing at its root. The laws prohibiting prostitution are categorical and unalterable.

10. **Legislation Prohibiting Alcohol**. The nature of this legislation needs no discussion. Alcohol is undeniably forbidden, and the Islamic community can never countenance its use. It is closely related to prostitution in most cases and is especially allied to it socially; similarly, it is related to luxury and to the idleness that arises from luxury. For, luxury produces a spiritual weakness and a need for inhibiting thought and vital activity by means of some intoxicant. Whereas the life, the work, and the watchfulness that Islam prescribes can never be reconciled with alcohol or with any other drug. Islam does not accept any form of cowardly escape from reality or distortion of life.

÷ ÷ ÷ ÷ ÷ ÷ ÷

Islam forms a flexible social system, capable of directing human life at all times and in all circumstances, while preserving its general spirit and principles. Its duty is to ensure a form of life that will be virtuous, sound, productive, and strong; to ensure a comprehensive social justice based on all the foundations of human nature and aiming at giving every man his due. But it must never stand in the way of fruitful individual activity nor must it permit that activity to become a harmful egotism.

The Islamic theory of life is the most perfect that the world has known because it brings together the material and the spiritual elements of life, making out of them a unity directed towards the highest standards and aimed at patterns that can be actually achieved and be perceived by the imagination.

But the perplexed and disturbed world, fearful and anxious, can only be brought to security and justice when it submits to this perfect system, whenever Allah wills.

9 THE PARTING OF THE WAYS

I n what direction are we now going? We must pause for a
moment and ask ourselves this question, in order to direct our
lives in the direction we wish. The world today, after two wars
in close succession, is divided into two main blocs: That of communism in the East, and that of capitalism in the West. That is what
appears on the surface; it is what everyone says and what everyone
thinks. But it is our belief that this division is merely superficial,
rather than real; it is a division based on interests rather than on
principles; it is a fight for goods and markets rather than for beliefs
and ideals. The nature of European and American philosophy does
not differ essentially from that of Russian; both depend on the supremacy of a materialistic doctrine of life. But while Russia has already become Communist, Europe and America are as yet merely
going the same way and will ultimately arrive at the same position,
barring the occurrence of any unforeseen happenings.

There is but one thing beyond the materialistic philosophy
that the West holds, which makes morals a matter of advantage
and advocates grabbing markets and benefits. There is only one
thing beyond this philosophy, which banishes the spiritual element
from life, which denies the existence of faith independent of the
laboratory and experiment, which despises the loftiest abstract
objectives, and which rejects the existence of any reality in things,
save only their usefulness—even to the point where it can conceive
a philosophy such as pragmatism. There can be only one thing
beyond such a philosophy, and that is communism, which will
come about in the West when economic circumstances change.

No essential difference is to be found between the American and the Russian philosophies, though some differences do exist in the economic and social circumstances. What keeps the ordinary American from becoming a communist is not a philosophy of life that rejects any materialistic explanation of the universe, of life, and of history; rather it is the fact that he now has the opportunity of becoming rich and the fact that a worker's wages are high. But when American capitalism reaches the end of its tether, when the restraints of monopolies are tightened, when the ordinary man sees that he has no longer the opportunity of himself becoming a capitalist, when wages drop because of the tightening of monopoly control or for any other reason, then the American worker is going to turn right over to communism. For, he will not have the support of any stronger philosophy of life than the materialistic, nor will he have the support of any spiritual faith or moral objective.

We need not be deceived by the apparently hard and bitter struggle between the Eastern and Western camps. Neither of them have anything but a materialistic philosophy of life and in their thinking they are closely akin. There is no difference between their principles or their philosophies; their only difference lies in their worldly methods and in their profitable markets. We are their markets!

The real struggle is between Islam on the one hand and the combined camps of East and West on the other. Islam is the true power that opposes the strength of the materialistic philosophy professed by Europe, America, and Russia alike. It is Islam that stands for a universal and articulated theory of the universe, life, and mankind, and which sets up the idea of the mutual responsibility of society in place of the idea of hostility and struggle. It is Islam that gives to life a spiritual doctrine to link it with the Creator in the heavens, and to govern its direction on earth; and it is Islam that is not content to allow life to be limited to the achievement of purely material aims, even though material and productive activity is one of the Islamic modes of worship.

The truth is that all spiritual religions—and Christianity most of all—are opposed equally to European and American materialism and to Russian communist materialism; for both of these are of the same nature and are equally at odds with any spiritual philosophy of life. But Christianity, so far as we can see, cannot be reckoned as a real force in opposition to the philosophies of the new materialism; it is an individualist, isolationist, negative faith. It has no power to make life grow under its influence in any permanent or positive way. Christianity has shot its bolt so far as human life is concerned; it has lost its power to keep pace with practical life in succeeding generations, for it came into being only for a limited and temporary period, between Judaism and Islam. When it was embraced by Europe owing to specific historical circumstances, and when it proved incompetent to keep pace with life as it developed then, Christianity confined itself to worship and to matters of the individual conscience, ceasing to have any control over the practical affairs of life; for it had not the power to persevere, to develop, or to grow.

Christianity is unable, except by intrigue, to compete with the social and economic systems that are ever developing, because it has no essential philosophy of actual, practical life. On the other hand, Islam is a perfectly practicable social system in itself; it has beliefs, laws, and a social and economic system that is under the control of both conscience and law, and which is open to growth through development and application.

It offers to mankind a perfectly comprehensive theory of the universe, life, and mankind, as we have shown, a theory that satisfies man's intellectual needs. It offers to men a clear, broad, and deep faith, which satisfies the conscience. It offers to society legal and economic bases that have been proved both practicable and systematic.

Islam bases its social system on the foundation of a spiritual theory of life that rejects all materialistic interpretations; it bases its morals on the foundation of the spiritual and moral element, and it rejects the philosophy of immediate advantage. Thus it is very strongly opposed to the materialistic theories that obtain in both the Eastern and the Western camp. It raises life to a higher level than such petty standards as those that claim observance in Europe, America, and Russia.

❖ ❖ ❖ ❖ ❖ ❖ ❖

From this brief conspectus it will be apparent that in the Islamic world we need to review our entire situation, for we possess a universal theory of life far higher than any held in Europe or America or Russia. We can offer to mankind this theory whose aims are a complete mutual help among all men and a true mutual responsibility in society. This theory professes as an aim the raising of the value of life to a level compatible with a world that has emanated from Allah. So our true place is not at the tail of the caravan, but where we may grasp the leading rein.

But it will not be easy for us to take our rightful place; we can reach it only by making great and ineluctable sacrifices, for our own sake and for the sake of all mankind. Heavy burdens will fall on capitalists and the affluent, who are accustomed to enjoying plenty, but these burdens are inevitable. We may go the Islamic way, or we may go the communist way; one of these two we must inevitably follow in the end. Or there are also Europe and America to whose social systems we adhere in preference to our own Islamic social system. But finally these systems also run out into communism, over a short or a long period, because their doctrines are by nature the same as those of communism, their philosophy of life is the same, and any differences are superficial rather than real.

The capitalists and the profiteers realize what communism means, and they shrink from its very name as a superstitious man shrinks from genii and demons. Let them understand, then, that neither they nor humanity as a whole can have any defense against communism except Islam; the true, real Islam, the principles of which we have outlined here, in giving examples of its social system and its demands on life and property.

We are indeed at the crossroads. We may join the march at the tail of the Western caravan, which calls itself democracy; if we do so we shall eventually join up with the Eastern caravan, which is known to the West as communism. Or we may return to Islam and make it fully effective in the field of our own life, spiritual, intellectual, social, and economic. We may draw our strength from it, and we may promote its growth through development and legislation within the limits of its universal and comprehensive theory of life, and we may fulfill its demands on life and property.

And certainly if we do not do this today, we shall not do it tomorrow. The world is broken by two consecutive wars, disturbed in faith and shaken in conscience, perplexed among varying ideologies and philosophies. It is today more than ever in need of us to offer to it our faith and our social system, our practical and spiritual theory of life. But we cannot offer these things to the world at large until first we have applied them in our own life, so that the world may see their truth demonstrated in practice, may understand that this is not merely an imaginative and theoretical scheme.

Conditions today are favorable because of the birth of two great new Islamic blocs in Indonesia and Pakistan, and because of the awakening of the Arab world, both in East and West. The ultimate issue is with Allah; our duty is to trust in Him, and to have faith.

NOTES BY HAMID ALGAR

1. Gospel of St. Matthew, 5:38–41.

2. Ibid., 5:21–37 (with omissions).

3. Ibid., 5:40.

4. I.e., the *qibla,* the Ka'ba in Mecca as House of God and point of orientation in prayer.

5. The point of this anecdote is presumably that one of the brothers toiled for a living, enabling the other to devote himself to worship, and that this choice made the former more pious than the latter.

6. Ibn Sina (d. 429/1037) and Ibn Rushd (d. 595/1198): In accordance with his general rejection of most of the Islamic intellectual heritage, Sayyid Qutb exaggerates the dependence of these two figures on Greek philosophy in order to deny the Islamicity of their thought. It is, however, undeniable that both—particularly the former—produced insights that were clearly inspired by Qur'anic precepts and became incorporated into Islamic intellectual tradition.

7. A well-authenticated *hadith.*

8. *Hadith.*

9. *Hadith.*

10. In support of his argument, Sayyid Qutb here refers to Anna Freud and Dorothy Burlingham, *Children Without Families.*

11. *Hadith.*

12. *Hadith.*

13. *Hadith.*

14. *Hadith.*

15. *Hadith.*

16. *Hadith.*

17. Muhammad Husayn Haikal (1888–1956): Egyptian politician and journalist whose works on Islam, written mostly in the 1930s, were marked by a strong rationalist and apologist tendency, as well as the determination to discover in the Qur'an the beliefs and concepts of the contemporary West.

18. Taha Husayn (1889–1971): Egyptian novelist and literary critic, inclined like Haikal to regard the West as the paragon of all virtue.

19. *Hadith.*

20. *Hadith.*

21. A reference to the digging of a trench around the city of Medina in order to ward off an attack by the Quraish and their allies in 5/627; this measure was proposed by Salman al-Farisi, the Persian Companion of the prophet.

22. The revelation in question is 8:67: "It is not fitting for a Prophet that he should have prisoners of war until he has thoroughly subdued the land."

23. *Hadith.*

24. Banu Nadir: a Jewish tribe expelled from the environs of Medina in 4/626 because of their plotting with the Meccan enemies of Islam.

25. Here Sayyid Qutb cites Muhammad Abu Zahra, *al-Malikiya fi 'l-Fiqh al-Islami.*

26. Wars of Apostasy: The wars waged by Abu Bakr, the first Caliph, against those Arab tribes who refused after the death of the Prophet to continue paying the *zakat.*

27. "The blocking of means": for a detailed discussion of this concept, see pp. 299–301 below.

28. Note by Sayyid Qutb: We have already seen that Europe was not at any time truly Christian. The destruction and division to which the author here alludes arose, not from the nature of Christianity, but from the reaction of the peoples of Europe against Christianity.

29. Cited from 'Abd al-Rahman 'Azzam, *The Eternal Message.*

30. Taken from a work by 'Abd al-Halim al-Jundi.

31. Also taken from the same work.

32. Abu Ja'far al-Mansur: second of the Abbasid Caliphs, he reigned from 136/754 to 158/775.

33. al-Wathiq: ninth of the Abbasid Caliphs, he reigned from 227/842 to 232/847.

34. al-Hadi: fourth of the Abbasid Caliphs, he reigned from 169/785 to 170/786.

35. al-Rashid (more fully, Harun al-Rashid): fifth of the Abbasid Caliphs, he reigned from 170/786 to 193/809. It was during his reign that the Abbasid Caliphate reached its apogee of territorial expansion and prosperity.

36. Ahmad ibn Tulun: governor of Egypt from 254/868 to 270/883, he was effectively independent of the Caliphate, and established a local dynasty that was named after him.

37. Isma'il: fifth ruler of the dynasty established in Egypt by Muhammad 'Ali Pasha, an Albanian military commander sent by the Ottomans to Egypt to recapture it from the French. He ruled from 1863 to 1879.

38. Tawfiq: sixth member of the same dynasty, he ruled form 1879 to 1892.

39. Sultan 'Abd al-'Aziz: Ottoman sultan from 1861 to 1876, he was the nominal overlord of the rulers of Egypt, and thus empowered to grant or withhold the legitimizing title of "Khedive."

40. Year of the Ashes: the year 18/639, when a combination of famine and pestilence reduced the Muslim community to penury.

41. "Companion in the cave": a reference to the fact that Abu Bakr took refuge in a cave together with the Prophet in the course of their migration from Mecca to Medina, an episode alluded to in Qur'an, 9:40.

42. Yazid: second of the Umayyad Caliphs, he reigned from 60/680 to 64/683. Chief among his crimes was the martyring of Imam Husayn, the grandson of the Prophet.

43. Hunain: the first battle fought by the Muslims after the liberation of Mecca in 9/630; it was waged against the Hawazin.

44. Oath of Fudhul: an oath taken by some of the men of Mecca in pre-Islamic times to defend the rights of strangers in the city who lacked the protection afforded by tribal affiliations.

45. 'Umar ibn 'Abd al-'Aziz: Umayyad Caliph from 99/717 to 101/720, he was distinguished from other members of that dynasty by the honesty he brought to the exercise of the caliphal office; this, together with his coincidence of name with the second Caliph, 'Umar ibn al-Khattab, sometimes results in his being referred to as 'Umar II.

46. Walid: fifth Umayyad Caliph, he reigned from 86/705 to 96/715.

47. Sulayman ibn 'Abd al-Malik: Umayyad Caliph from 96/715 to 99/717, he was the immediate predecessor of 'Umar ibn 'Abd al-'Aziz.

48. Note by Sayyid Qutb: We have already said that the spirit of Islam destroyed the influence of this kind of aristocracy. Until the time of 'Uthman this older kind had not revived, so that there was only an aristocracy based on early conversions and on sufferings for the faith; and this was a milder form of aristocracy.

49. al-Mas'udi (d. 345/956): one of the principal Arab historians and geographers.

50. Jarir (d. 114/733): a poet equally celebrated for his panegyrics and his diatribes.

51. Cited from Adam Mez, *The Renaissance of Islam*.

52. Ibn Hazm (d. 456/1064): scholar of both law and literature.

53. Qarmatians: an Isma'ili sect, insurrectionally active from the late 3rd/9th to the mid 4th/10th century.

54. Cited from Muhammad Asad, *Islam at the Crossroads*.

55. Note by Sayyid Qutb: Cited from Haikal's *Hayat Muhammad*, where he in turn cites the magazine *Nur al-Islam*, no. 40, 1353/1934, p.5720.

56. Jacob Fahm, *Pragmatism or the Philosophy of Means*.

57. Note by Sayyid Qutb: The present author hopes in the near future to produce for the Arab reader a complete study on "The Islamic Doctrine of the Universe, Life and Mankind."

58. Cited from Fahm, op. cit.

59. Cited from Muhammad Abu Zahra, *al-Imam Malik*.

60. The word *Ra'ina* was used by the Muslims in the sense, "please look at us, attend to our needs," but evidently had some insulting meaning in Jewish usage; hence they were instructed to use instead the unambiguous word *Unzurna*.

BIBILIOGRAPHY OF WORKS
ON SAYYID QUTB

WORKS IN ARABIC

al-'Azm, Yusuf. *Ra'id al-Fikr al-Islami, al Shahid Sayyid Qutb*. Beirut, 1980.

al-Balihi, Ibrahim b. 'Abd al-Rahman. *Sayyid Qutb wa Turathuhu 'l-Adabi wa 'l-Fikri*. Riyad, 1972.

Barakat, Muhammad Taufiq. *Sayyid Qutb: Khulasat Hayatihi wa Minhajuhu fi 'l-Harakah*. Beirut, 1977.

al-Diyyab, Muhammad Hafiz. *Sayyd Qutb: al-Khitab wa 'l-Idi'uluzhiya*. Beirut, 1988.

Fadlullah, Mahdi. *Ma'a Sayyid Qutb fi Fikrihi 'l-Siyasi wa 'l-Dini*. Beirut, 1984.

Hamuda, 'Adil. *Sayyid Qutb min al-Qaryah ila 'l-Mashnaqa*. Cairo, 1987.

al-Khabbas, 'Abdullah. *Sayyid Qutb, al-Adib al-Naqid*. Amman, 1983.

al-Khalidi, Salah 'Abd al-Fattah. *Sayyid Qutb, al-Shahid al-Hayy*. Amman, 1981.

Qutb, Muhammad. *Sayyid Qutb, al-Shahid al-Azali*. Cairo, 1974.

WORKS IN ENGLISH AND FRENCH

Algar, Hamid. "Social Justice in the Ideology and Legislation of the Islamic Revolution of Iran." In *Social Legislation in the Contemporary Middle East*. Laurence O. Michalak and Jeswald W. Salacuse, eds. Berkeley, 1986, pp17–60.

Carré, Olivier. *Mystique et politique: Lecture révolutionairre du Coran par Sayyid Qutb, frère musulman radical*. Paris, 1984.

Carré, Olivier, and Gerard Michaud. *Les frères musulmans (1928–1932)*. Paris, 1983.

Enayat, Hamid. *Modern Islamic Political Thought*. Austin, Texas, 1982.

Haddad, Yvonne Y. "Sayyid Qutb: Ideologue of Islamic Revival." In *Voices of Resurgent Islam*. Edited by John L. Esposito. Oxford, 1983, pp. 67–98.

Kepel, Gilles. *Muslim Extremism in Egypt: The Prophet and the Pharaoh*. Berkeley, 1985.

Mitchell, Richard P. *The Society of Muslim Brothers*. Oxford, 1969.

Moussali, Ahmad S. *Radical Islamic Fundamentalism: The Ideological and Political Discourses of Sayyid Qutb*. Beirut, 1992.

Nayed, Aref Ali. "The Radical Qur'anic Hermeneutics of Sayyid Qutb." *Islamic Studies* (Islamabad) 31, no. 3 (Autumn 1413/1992), pp. 355–363.

Shepherd, William. "The Development of the Thought of Sayyid Qutb as Reflected in Earlier and Later Editions of *Social Justice in Islam*." *Die Welt des Islams* 32 (1992), PP. 196–236.

Sivan, Emmanuel. *Radical Islam: Medieval Theology and Modern Politics*. New Haven, 1985.

INDEX

MIZAN PUBLICATIONS
available from
ISLAMIC PUBLICATIONS INTERNATIONAL

On the Sociology of Islam Lectures by Ali Shari'ati tr. by Hamid Algar
Paperback   # 0-933782-00-4 $ 9.95   Hardback   # 0-933782-06-3 $ 19.95

Marxism and Other Western Fallacies: An Islamic Critique by Ali Shari'ati
tr. Robert Campbell
Paperback   # 0-933782-06-3 $ 9.95   Hardback   # 0-933782-05-5 $ 19.95

Constitution of the Islamic Republic of Iran tr. Hamid Algar
Paperback   # 0-933782-07-1 $ 4.95   Hardback   # 0-933782-02-0 $ 14.95

Islam and Revolution: Writings and Declaration of Imam Khomeini
tr. Hamid Algar
Paperback   # 0-933782-03-9 $ 19.95   Hardback   # 0-933782-04-7 $ 29.95

Society and Economics in Islam by Ayatullah Sayyid Mahmud Taleghani
tr. Robert Campbell
Hardback   # 0-933782-08-X $ 17.95

The Islamic Struggle in Syria by Umar F. Abd-Allah
Hardback   # 0-933782-10-1 $ 29.95

Occidentosis: A Plague from the West by Jalal Al-i Ahmad tr. Robert Campbell
Paperback   # 0-933782-13-6 $ 9.95   Hardback   # 0-933782-12-8 $ 19.95

The Contemporary Muslim Movement in the Philippines by Cesar Adib Majul
Paperback   # 0-933782-17-9 $ 9.95   Hardback   # 0-933782-16-9 $ 19.95

Fundamental of Islamic Thought: God, Man and the Universe
by Ayatullah Murtaza Mutahhari tr. Robert Campbell
Paperback   # 0-933782-15-2 $ 9.95   Hardback   # 0-933782-14-4 $ 19.95

Social and Historical Change: An Islamic Perspective
by Ayatullah Murtaza Mutahhari tr. by Robert Campbell
Paperback   # 0-933782-19-5 $ 9.95   Hardback   #0-933782-18-7 $ 19.95

Principles of Sufism by Al-Qushayri tr. B. R. Von Schlegell
Paperback   # 0-933782-21-7 $ 19.95   Hardback   # 0-933782-20-9 $ 29.95

Sales Tax: Please add 7% for books shipped to New York address.
Shipping: $4.00 for the first book and $ 1.00 for additional publication